Planning Derry

Planning is often misunderstood. Some believe it to be a kind of strait-jacket, which fixes and restricts. On the contrary, the purpose of planning is to create a framework within which the city can develop freely, a framework that should provide for the development of each city area without restricting other areas, that should facilitate any desired extension, while maintaining throughout the proper relation of the city's different parts.
Ludwig Hilberseimer

We must now conceive the city, accordingly, not primarily as a place of business or government, but as an essential organ for expressing and actualizing the new human personality—that of 'one world man'. The old separation of man and nature, of townsman and countryman, of Greek and barbarian, of citizen and foreigner, can no longer be maintained: for communication, the entire planet is becoming a village; and as a result, the smallest neighborhood or precinct must be planned as a working model of the larger world.
Lewis Mumford, 1961

Ancient and modern: Princess Macha, legendary founder of the first Irish hospital, with Altnagelvin Hospital, Derry, in the background

GERALD McSHEFFREY

Planning Derry

*Planning and Politics
in Northern Ireland*

LIVERPOOL UNIVERSITY PRESS

First published 2000 by
LIVERPOOL UNIVERSITY PRESS
Liverpool L69 7ZU

© 2000 Gerald McSheffrey

The right of Gerald McSheffrey
to be identified as the author of this work
has been asserted by him in accordance with
the Copyright, Design and Patents Act, 1988

All rights reserved.
No part of this volume may be reproduced,
stored in a retrieval system or transmitted,
in any form or by any means,
electronic, mechanical, photocopying, recording or otherwise
without prior written permission of the publishers.

British Library Cataloguing-in-Publication Data
A British Library CIP record is available

ISBN 0–85323–714–X (hardback)
0–85323–724–7 (paperback)
Typeset in 11/13 Stempel Garamond by
Wilmaset Ltd, Birkenhead, Wirral
Printed by Alden Press, Oxford

FOR NORMA,
LAURENCE, NIALL and AIDAN,
in recognition of their patience and love
for a frequently absent
husband, father and planner

Foreword

This book is devoted to planning Londonderry in Northern Ireland, written by a redoubtable person, formerly a vice-president and dean at Arizona State University, a dean at Illinois Institute of Technology, director of Architecture at Kansas University, and for years a practising architect/planner in Northern Ireland.

This book has relevance far beyond Ireland. There, it is a conflict between Protestant and Catholic; in the United States, the parallel is with race, black and white. There is no innocence here. The motivating theme has been retribution. Ireland shares the sorry distinction of contentiousness with Bosnia and Israel. The significance of the book lies in the use of the plan for Derry as an instrument for reconciliation and resolution. It became an important vehicle for remedying injustices. McSheffrey brings a balanced view to this beleaguered place. Born a Protestant, his paternal great-grandfather, a Catholic, married a Protestant but chose to be buried in a Catholic cemetery.

The plan was a landmark for advocating the preservation of the surrounding hills, a salmon river, and establishing the urban perimeter, but its distinction lies in the very strong public participation in its implementation. The act of planning became an important instrument for correcting injustices and developing co-operation.

The plan owes much to that Scottish patriarch, Sir Patrick Geddes, his commitment to surveys and informed participation. Happily, with the advent of Tony Blair as Prime Minister of the United Kingdom, there arrived a strong advocate for reconciliation. May he find a *modus vivendi* to which the plan for Derry aspired and contributed.

IAN L. McHARG
Department of Landscape Architecture and Regional Planning
University of Pennsylvania
January 1998

Contents

	Foreword	*page*	vii
	List of Illustrations		xi
	Acknowledgements		xv
	Introduction		1
1	Prelude		7
2	The Steering Committee		17
3	The Planning Team		24
4	Place, Folk and Work		30
5	The Housing Crisis		42
6	Breaking the Stalemate		51
7	The Bridge		66
8	Selling the Plan		85
9	Interlude		91
10	The Development Commission		98
11	Community Resolve		109
12	Retrospect and Prospect		115
	Appendix: Northern Ireland Regional Plans		128
	Bibliography		130
	Index		133

List of Illustrations

	Ancient and modern: Princess Macha with Altnagelvin Hospital, Derry, in Background	*frontispiece*
1.	Northern Ireland and its relationship to the British Isles and Europe	5
2.	Londonderry County Borough and Rural District (1966) in the context of Northern Ireland	16
3.	Craigavon Bridge prior to 1966	31
4.	Views of the city centre from Waterside	33
5.	Historical growth, from the Londonderry area plan	34
6.	Historical Derry: Walls, Court-house, Deanery, and Cathedral	36
7.	1863 Carlisle Bridge	37
8.	1933 Craigavon Bridge	38
9.	Petrochemical Industries at Maydown	38
10.	Village Newbuildings	39
11.	Proposed village expansion	40
12.	(a) Unfit housing in Derry: nineteenth century. (b) Early twentieth-century housing: Bogside Housing Trust redevelopment. (c) Deck access flats, Sheffield. (d) Rossville St. flats under construction, 1966 (e) Deck access flats, Derry. (f) Demolition of Rossville St. flats, 1996.	43
13.	Infill housing sites from unpublished Report No 1	46
14.	Infill housing sites from Interim Report No 1	52
15.	Population: rates of natural increase	53
16.	Population (a) Comparative household sizes 1961 (b) Projected population increase	55
17.	Hinterland zones	57
18.	Shopping sphere of influence	58
19.	Crescent of development	60
20.	Proposed advance factories at Springtown	61

21.	Location of industry	62
22.	Black Brae area—proposed harbour site	62
23.	Physical factors affecting development	69
24.	Options for development 1 & 2	70
25.	Options for development 3 & 4	71
26.	Ballyarnett/Shantallow, looking South with the Springfield industrial estate and city in background	72
27.	Proposed and actual development, Ballyarnett/Shantallow	73 & 74
28.	Derry: a sense of place	75
29.	Opportunities for change	76
30.	Riverside route	77
31.	Options for the second bridge	78
32.	Parking locations	79
33.	Landscape recreational opportunities	80
34.	City walls, a tourist attraction	81
35.	St Columb's Park	82
36.	City Park	82
37.	Farmland	82
38.	Area plan	86
39.	Richmond Centre under construction, and section of high-level bridge being floated downstream behind Guildhall	104
40.	Chris Patten and David White	104
41.	(a) Richmond Centre, entry from Shipquay Street. (b) Shipquay Street looking East towards Guildhall	105
42.	Housing: Derry Housing Association, Father Mulvey Park	105
43.	High-level bridge at the Narrows	105
44.	Fruit of the Loom	106
45.	Seagate	106
46.	Guildhall Square from Shipquay Street	106
47.	Guildhall Square looking south	107

LIST OF ILLUSTRATIONS   xiii

48.	Guildhall Square looking north	107
49.	New City of Derry Airport	110
50.	Museum and Craft Village	112
51.	Craft village dancers	112
52.	Ballyarnett/Shantallow showing bridge	115
53.	*Beauty of the River* from bridge to bridge	117
54.	Houses, William Street	118
55.	Houses, Caw, Derry	118
56.	Riverside housing west bank	118
57.	Creggan Street redevelopment	119
58.	Clooney Hostel for Homeless	119
59.	Housing, Brigade, Derry	119
60.	New bridge and access to Donegal from New Port at Lisahally	121
61.	New Foyle Street shopping centre from Waterside	121
62.	Walls exposed and talus landscaped	122
63.	Presence of the river	123

The author gratefully acknowledges the permission to publish photographs and drawings from the following individuals and public bodies:

Photographs for Illustrations Nos 8 and 12a, from the Londonderry collection of Mr David Bigger and Mr Terry McDonald.

Photographs for Illustration Nos 4, 26, 27, 28, 40, 41, 43, 44, 45, 48, 49, 50, 51, 52, 53, 60, 62 and 63 from the Department of Environment Northern Ireland Graphics Design Unit with permission of the Department.

Photographs for Illustration Nos 12(b), (c), (d) and (f), 54, 55, 56, 57, 58 and 59 courtesy of the Northern Ireland Housing Executive.

Photograph for Illustration No 7 courtesy of the National Library of Ireland.

Illustration Nos 5(a) and (b) with the 1622 and 1688 plans for Londonderry and other historical plans, are taken from maps from Thomas Colby's *Ordnance Survey of the County of Londonderry, 1837*. Courtesy of Department of Environment Northern Ireland.

Other illustrations and photographs are reproduced from the 1968 James Munce Partnership Londonderry Area Plan with perspective drawings by A. D. (Sandy) Bell and photographs by John B. McCrory. Diagrams from the Plan Report were based upon Ordnance Survey Maps of the time with the sanction of HM Stationery Office. Crown Copyright Reserved.

Acknowledgements

In addition to my wife Norma, to whom I owe everything, I want to thank my friends Professor Jack Morley and John J. Sullivan Jr of Kansas City, Missouri, for bringing me to the United States. Their lives symbolise for me all that is good about this country, and they have given me moral support and advice in all my endeavours.

It is more than three years since my colleagues at Arizona State University—John Biln, Beverly Brandt, Dick Eribes, Tim McGinty, Frederick (Fritz) Steiner, and Marcus Whiffen—encouraged me to write this book after seeing a brief outline. At that time I was not aware that all the files, illustrations, and drawings relating to the 1968 Londonderry Area Plan had been discarded by 'Consarc', the successors of the James Munce Partnership, the original planners. Fortunately my friend Peter Daniel, a consultant for the plan, had retained a file containing, among other notes, minutes of the meetings of the Londonderry Area Steering Committee, the body statutorily responsible for the plan. I had also in my personal library a copy of the plan and several interim reports. These documents were very useful in helping me recall events as they occurred.

Making the plan made such an impression on me that I carried the memories of the experience around with me for almost thirty years. The tale of how the plan was made could not have been told without the help of members of the original planning team, including Alan Bradshaw, Stanley Cochrane, Peter Daniel, Jim Foster, Michael Murray, and Jack Smyth. This book was begun as a tribute to the planning team, so it was with great regret that I learnt of the death of Mike Murray just months after I interviewed him in Belfast.

A number of people in Derry connected directly and indirectly with the making and implementation of the plan were also of enormous help. They assisted me in filling the gap in history of the development of the city from the seventies to the present. Barely touched on here, this latter period is an important story that others are more qualified to tell. For additional information on this and earlier events I am indebted to Jim Cavalleros, Joe Cowan, Eamonn Deane, James Doherty, Paddy Doherty, Frank Guckian, Gerry Henry, John Hume, Steven McGonagle, and David White. Dr Fritz Steiner was both helpful and encouraging in reading and advising on the early drafts of the book. I am also grateful to Dean John Meunier for making available the resources of the College's Herberger Center for Design Excellence and its enthusiastic Director, Associate Dean Mary Kihl, and Bill Kasson who were responsible for monitoring and organising the distribution of the prospectus. Elizabeth Shaw and Gregory McNamee of Tucson provided editorial services through the Center for the first draft and prospectus. They also provided the necessary encouragement and expertise in helping me find a publisher. Dr Ian McHarg of the University of Pennsylvania was kind enough to risk his international reputation as a landscape architect and planner by writing a foreword to the book. Jocelyn Ross was responsible for organising the illustrations and photographs, Donna Geary for secretarial assistance and Julie Russ of the Herberger Center earns my special thanks for final editing. My thanks also to publisher Robin Bloxsidge of Liverpool University Press for recognising the planning content of the book despite its hybrid character.

Finally I wish to disassociate everyone I consulted with for the perceptions and opinions expressed in this book. For these and for the accuracy or otherwise of the account, and for any indiscretions or lapse of memory, I take full responsibility.

GERALD McSHEFFREY
Arizona State University
January 1998

Introduction

This is a book about a city and regional plan for the Londonderry area that was published in 1968. The plan itself was not without its critics, as is any plan, but in time it was generally accepted by the local population and has largely been implemented, although some important aspects await the resolution of the current peace process and the continuation of investment in the city centre. The plan was the work of a few dedicated people from the James Munce Partnership, a Belfast firm of architects and engineers. Four members of the planning team have passed on; other members are still in Northern Ireland, some are retired, some are working in local government bodies concerned with public housing and planning, and others in teaching. As the only associate partner in the firm with city planning credentials I was given the task of co-ordinating the effort, although I was not privy to all the political dealings of the senior partners. Under the circumstances I had reason to be grateful that I was not, since it enabled me and the rest of the planning team to deal with the work at hand unhampered by pernicious and subversive political forces.

This story about the making of the plan is not an academic treatise on the art of plan making, rather it is an attempt to explain some of the major strategies involved based on personal recollection of the events as they occurred. More important it is a story of the dedication of people who believed, rightly or wrongly, that their planning efforts could make a difference and that they could provide better living conditions and choices for the people of the area. We were young and ambitious planners during that wonderful period when some of the more sterile solutions of modern physical planning were being questioned and when communities were beginning to demand an involvement in planning decisions affecting their lives.

Since these are personal recollections and involve value judgements concerning people and political and religious views in Northern Ireland at the time, I believe it is important for the reader to know something of the background of the storyteller. There is a tendency for Americans to look at the situation in Ireland in the light of their own War of Independence—as an Anglo-Irish war that has been going on for centuries, or more simplistically, as an internecine struggle between Protestants and Catholics. There is some truth in both views, but they form only part of an exceedingly complex picture. I cherish the faint hope that my own views and attitudes on the subject are objective, enlightened, and are certainly offered without bias. While they are not offered intentionally to promote any particular political viewpoint, or for that matter to change any minds, I can give no guarantee that my personal psyche has not been permanently damaged by my Northern Irish upbringing.

In 1983 I became a US citizen. For me it was a natural and rational decision since I could never quite come to terms with being Irish and British at the same time. Moreover my adopted country had offered me the kind of career opportunities beyond those ever dreamed of by a child of working-class Belfast. Yet as most immigrants realise, whatever their legal obligations and loyalties, deeply ingrained in their hearts, characters and souls is a tie that can never be broken. It is anomalous that in the great melting pot that should constitute America, these ties result in the ethnic loyalties and neighbourhoods one finds from New York to Chicago, Boston to Milwaukee, and from Miami to Los Angeles. In these and other cities people get together from time to time to celebrate their roots, raise funds for causes and bathe in the sweet nostalgia for a country that never was. These Disneylands of their childhood myths and memories are Utopias to which no one will permanently return other than in the guise of an American retiree. Apart from sending cards on St Patrick's Day and, along with most other Americans, wearing the token green clothing item, I have never personally felt the need to belong to any Irish or for that matter British organisations in the United States. While I owe much to the people and country of my adoption, the debt to my family, friends, and many people in Northern Ireland can never be forgotten.

Most people are now familiar with what is euphemistically referred to as 'the troubles' in Northern Ireland. While there are comparisons world wide with issues regarding human rights, nationalism, freedom fighters, terrorists, religious fundamentalism, bigotry—a whole glossary of terms associated with unrest from Europe to the Middle East to the Far East—nowhere apart from Lebanon and the Balkans have these issues been more prevalent and insidious than in Northern Ireland. While the media heighten our awareness of such events, for the long-suffering people of Ireland, north and south, living with violence, death, and destruction is just another page in the legacy and tragedy of being Irish. It is a tragedy that many try to rise above in their art, poetry, song and love of learning. For others there are no such aspirations and, like the deprived of all nations, they must face the hardship and brutality of everyday existence in a bureaucratised post-industrial society they can scarcely comprehend beyond the weekly pay-packet or benefit payment.

In retrospect my early understanding of Ireland and its history was much like that of Voltaire's Candide before he was forcefully ejected from the castle to learn of the world. As I write this I fear that many of my former friends in Ireland, if not others, will conclude that I have still not left the castle. I owe this understanding to four events in my life. First being born a 'prod' (Protestant) in a fiercely partisan area of north Belfast where I learnt that the 'micks' or 'fenians' (Catholics) were the bad guys. This puzzled me at times because my favourite playmate at the age of seven was a Catholic boy named Patsy Brackney, the son of a police sergeant in the Royal Ulster Constabulary. Moreover my mother always talked fondly of her Catholic friends in the small County Derry town of Limavady. I also discovered that my American cousins were Catholic, since my aunt Anne was married to one and lived in Seattle. Our family had only been rescued from a similar fate when my paternal great-grandmother, upon marrying a Catholic, insisted that all of her sons be brought up Protestant. My great-grandfather, lover that he was, acquiesced but was buried in the Catholic churchyard at his own request by the seven stalwart Protestant sons.

All of this liberal talk was not enough to enlighten a child who saw everything in the light of good-uns and bad-uns, and especially when there was an Orange Lodge meeting hall at the top of the street. On the twelfth of July the sight of neatly dressed men in bowler hats, wearing orange sashes with orange lilies pinned to their lapels or hats, marching in military style to the tune of a bagpipe, accordion, or flute band, was enough to stir the heart of any child:

> We'll fight and no surrender,
> And come when duty calls,
> With heart and hand,
> And sword and shield,
> We'll guard old Derry's walls.

As a child, I sang this with gusto together with my childhood friends as we gathered around bonfires on the eleventh night. The tune was the same as the English anthem to the Prince of Wales. I had never been to Derry nor could I have known that one day it would play a very important role in my life. Nor was this child aware that, a few miles west in the same city one month later, men wearing green sashes and carrying green banners emblazoned with the portraits of Irish heroes and martyrs to the cause, would be stirring the heart of some Catholic child as they marched to different, but equally stirring and more authentically Irish, tunes.

The second event to influence my understanding of Ireland came from a love of reading and history passed on to me by my mother and an older brother, John, and led to my enrolment at age thirteen as a day boy at Methodist College Belfast (MCB) where I received the basis of a liberal education. Only a handful of children in my neighbourhood could attend such schools, and these did so with the help of city scholarships. In my case, as the youngest of eleven children, I attended through the generosity of parents willing to sacrifice much to pay the annual school fees. Although I had courses in history every year for a period of five years, only six months were devoted entirely to Irish history though in our studies of British, European, and American history events relative to Ireland could scarcely be ignored. In Robert Dickson, Hayden Drennan, Randall Clarke, and Joseph Kingsley, I had wonderful teachers who made history a reality as they recounted the events and portrayed the lives of the great participants. From their accounts of these great men and women I had many heroes, but my greatest hero of all was Charles Stewart Parnell, the Southern-Irish Protestant who with Gladstone's help could have achieved the dream of a free and united Ireland. The great respect I held for the views of my housemaster, the Reverend Eric Gallagher, influenced my growing liberalism. He was later to become head of the Methodist Church in Ireland and an articulate advocate for non-violence and religious tolerance throughout his career.

My studies had opened my eyes to the injustices on every side and particularly to those perpetrated on the Catholic-Irish by Oliver Cromwell and English landlords both before and after the potato famine. Yet I had little contact with Catholics of my own age since Catholics attended church schools in their early years, and Catholic grammar schools similar to MCB were administered by religious orders. Also the Catholic grammar schools in Northern Ireland played only Gaelic games associated with Irish nationalism while other schools played the foreign games of rugby football or cricket. So ironically, my only contact with Catholics was when I played rugby in Dublin in the Irish Republic. There Catholic schools had developed more liberal attitudes to sport, and, there again, all was really quite friendly and had it not been for the ferocity of the sport itself, even civilised.

Although I was still too much of a Candide to recognise it, my first encounter of what many Catholics complained of as discrimination came at age nineteen when I applied to a prominent Belfast firm of architects for a position as an apprentice. The principal of the firm noted that I had a peculiar name and I thought nothing unusual about his remark as people often had difficulty spelling my surname. Even when he followed up by offering me the job and remarking that my Methodist College education was an important factor, I was still not aware that my religious credentials were being scrutinised. It had not occurred to me that it was odd to have an Irish name or that in some people's rather narrow view of life, only Catholics possessed such names. Later I discovered that just as there were Catholic and Protestant schools there were Catholic and Protestant architectural firms. Fortunately these barriers were beginning to break down, at least in architecture in the fifties and early sixties, as new firms with young principals began to spring up. As an apprentice I met my first Catholic architect friends at Belfast College of Technology where we attended night school together and where a common dedication to the art of architecture easily overcame our interest in either religion or the rather nasty brands of politics associated with it.

After completing my five-year apprenticeship I worked in a number of firms. It was while I was with Munce and Kennedy, a firm incidentally that employed architects without scrutinising their religious credentials, that I had the good fortune to receive a state grant to complete my architectural education at University College London. This was to become the third event to influence my understanding of Irish life and politics. For the first time in my life I had a glimpse of Northern Ireland from the outside, and I was suitably appalled by the revelation. It was when travelling on the London Underground reading a copy of H.G. Wells's *A Short History of the World* that I came to the conclusion that Christianity ended with the crusades. In the light of my experiences growing up in Northern Ireland, I could only conclude that I had arrived at a great truth.

The fourth event to complete my education and understanding of the Irish Question was my experience in planning Londonderry. It was during this period that I was able for the first time to put all the pieces together, and for the first time I was forced to become personally involved and to take a stand. About five years earlier I had become a member of the Northern Ireland Labour Party along with some like-minded architect friends. This non-sectarian political party with its roots in British trade-unionism was of little consequence in a province where Protestant Unionism and Catholic Nationalism prevailed. Both the Nationalist and Unionist parties accepted and even callously exploited the seventeenth-century religious divisions of the province for their own ends—Nationalists in their struggle peacefully to achieve the goal of a United Ireland, and Unionists to maintain the link with Great Britain at all costs. It was an uneven contest. The religious composition of the exploited population was bound to result in the perpetuation of Unionist rule since the Protestant population represented two-thirds of the population of Northern Ireland. Moreover, a majority of the Catholic population living in the border counties of Londonderry, Fermanagh, Armagh, and Tyrone, and gerrymandering was used in these areas. The city of Londonderry, for example, had a majority Catholic population in 1966 but a Protestant-Unionist mayor and majority Unionist city council.

Although I was generally aware of the situation in Londonderry—my sister Harriet and her family lived in the suburbs—I was not prepared for the obstacles we encountered in our planning studies. That the plan was eventually accepted and implemented was due in part to propitious timing, the assistance of many local people, particularly Councillor James Doherty, and a highly motivated, idealistic, and energetic planning team. This book is a tribute to all those people of vision involved including James Munce, Bob Simpson, Stanley Cochrane, Peter Daniel, Alan Bradshaw, Jim Foster, Mike Murray, Jack Smyth, and many others. The plan was implemented through the commitment of James Doherty, Jim Foster, and Alan Bradshaw who stayed with it from its completion in 1968 to this day. While James Doherty provided the political driving force from the beginning, Alan Bradshaw and Jim Foster continue to give important professional support and advice. Both Alan and Jim worked for the Londonderry Development Commission from its inception in 1986. Alan has more recently retired from his position as regional director for the Northern Ireland Housing Executive, while Jim is development officer with the Northern Ireland Department of the Environment (DOE). After 1968, the member of Parliament John Hume and Paddy Doherty, who had been sceptical about the plan during its preparation, were most important figures in promoting development. David White, a former official with the Londonderry County Borough Council, his successor in the DOE, Joe Cowan, and Stephen McGonagle of the Londonderry Development Commission also played major roles. Sadly, since then many subsequent events in Northern Ireland might suggest that liberal attitudes and social commitment have been abandoned in the widespread atmosphere of violence and bloodshed that prevailed until recently. Apart from violent men and their supporters, there are many on both sides of the political divide who continue the work of building a better future for the people of Northern Ireland.

Time will hopefully erase the bitter memories engendered by past struggles and the current situation. Perhaps the people of Derry, as they continue to develop and rebuild their city, can become a symbol of liberation from the past and expectations of a peaceful future for the Irish people. At the time of writing this, after more than a quarter century of violence, a new peace initiative has emerged, promoted by both British and Irish governments and led by a politician and man of peace from Derry, John Hume. At his urging Sinn Fein leader Gerry Adams took

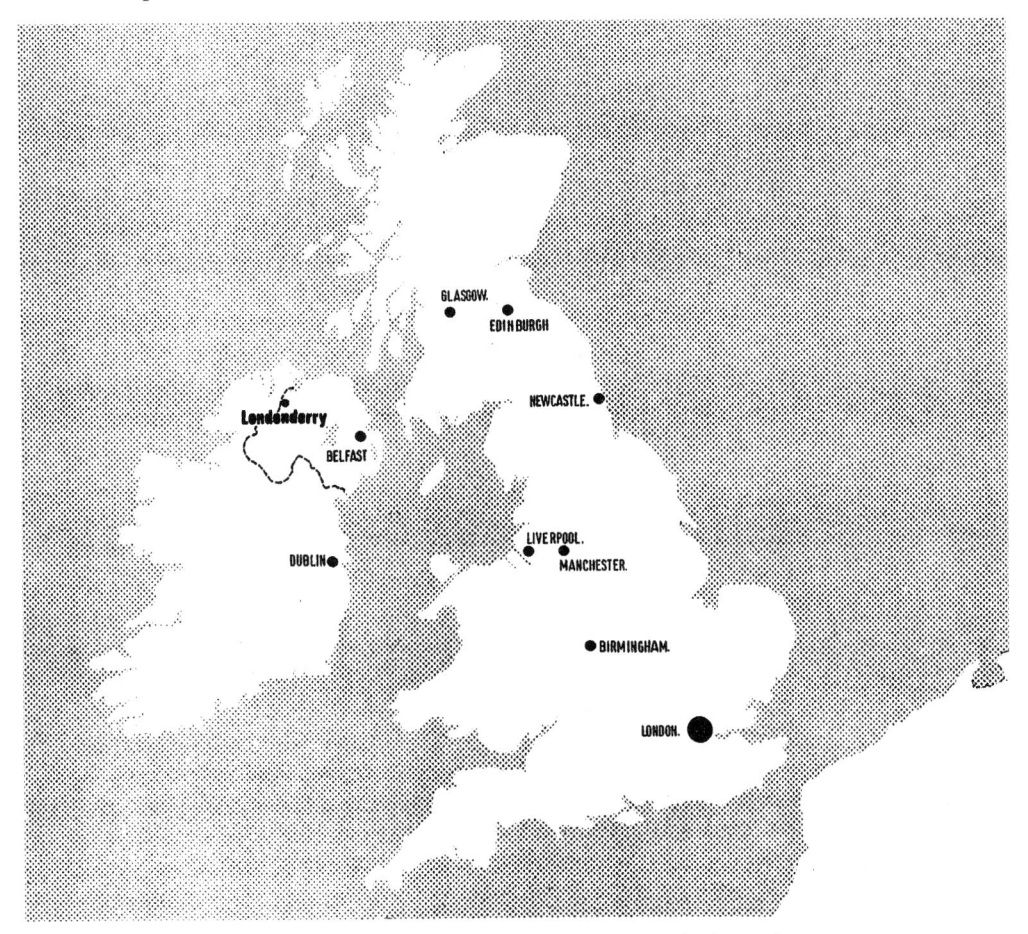

1. Northern Ireland and its relationship to the British Isles and Europe

steps to persuade the Provisional IRA to halt their campaign of violence. It is fair to say that no one has pursued the course of peace with more perseverance against all odds than John Hume. While Protestant paramilitary groups have also agreed to the peace initiative, the question of the future of Northern Ireland and its place in the whole of Ireland remains as enigmatic as it was when the controversial border, separating Irish from Irish, was first drawn.

1 Prelude

Little did we know in 1966 that as we planned for a new tomorrow, events would soon occur that would change the face of Northern Ireland and plunge the province into almost thirty years of civil unrest and violence and back into its dark past. To understand why this should occur the reader may need some background knowledge of Irish history. Many excellent books have been written on the subject, yet my introduction to the history of Ireland was from a small book by Randall Clarke, a history teacher at Methodist College Belfast which I attended from 1944 to 1949.[1] It was an excellent little book for a fifteen-year-old. First of all, unlike my books on European and American history it was not too lengthy, and second, the chronology of events was recorded in a way that made remembering them easy. To have these facts brought to life by no less than the author himself left a deep imprint on me.

For readers not familiar with the history of Ireland the following brief sketch is barely adequate, but I hope it will shed some light on the political and religious circumstances prevalent throughout the making of the plan for Londonderry. It is difficult for visitors to Ireland to understand the schism between those Irish who regard Northern Ireland as an integral part of the UK and those who regard it as a natural part of the Republic of Ireland. That they have been primarily identified as Protestant and Catholic, orange and green, without taking into account the various shades, may only serve to confuse that understanding further. While seemingly obvious from a historical viewpoint, the problems of modern Ireland are much more deeply ingrained and complex. They are also greatly exacerbated by social and economic inequities affecting both Protestant and Catholic working-class populations—although it must be stated that in Northern Ireland Catholic working-class people as a whole have been worse off than most of their Protestant counterparts. Conversely, at the bottom of the economic ladder the difference in living standards was hardly enough to be obvious in the post-Second World War welfare state. This was especially so in the case of housing for the lower working classes and the poor. Even today the remnants of a society organised by class are still prevalent in the UK and Ireland despite some advances made in this century.

In Belfast in the sixties, for example, one had only to look at the small nineteenth-century terrace houses that both Protestant and Catholic populations occupied in their respective self-imposed ghettoes. Both as a child and later as a planner with the Belfast City Planning Department I was familiar with this type of housing and the families who occupied them. Sanitary facilities consisted of a water closet in a shed-like space provided within a narrow walled backyard that one entered from the kitchen of the house. Each backyard was about ten to eleven feet wide, with similar dimensions from the rear of the barely two-storey house to the seven-foot-high rear wall. At the centre of the wall was a latched wooden door opening on to a narrow alleyway five or six feet wide. In the kitchen of the house was a large sink, or jawbox as it was referred to by the occupants, located under the single window that provided only dim light. In order to increase the available light the backyard was whitewashed annually with lime by proud and industrious families. Normally there was just a cold water supply and bathing (once weekly at least for children) took place in a metal tub in front of the coal fire in the living room. The water in the tub was warmed by hot water boiled on the kitchen gas stove. Adult inhabitants generally preferred to use the public baths to maintain a modicum of cleanliness whenever they could afford the modest charge. As dwellings deteriorated, the alleys between the rows of housing became insanitary and foul-smelling. Overcrowding occurred mainly, though not exclusively, in Catholic areas because of the larger families occupying the two-bedroom dwellings.

Moving up the social scale a notch meant moving further out from the city centre where turn-of-the-century three-storey terrace housing with internal bathrooms was available. In Belfast these were mainly occupied by Protestant families such as my own, and better off Catholics were accepted as neighbours as long as they did not threaten to arrive in great numbers. Generally though, for Catholic families, the site of the church and church/school was the deciding factor in where to locate. In the poorer areas the only way to distinguish a Protestant district from a Catholic district was by the sometimes beautifully executed gable wall paintings that served as a reminder of Ireland's troubled history. In Protestant areas the most common mural showed William III on a white horse as he was about to cross the River Boyne in 1690 to defeat the French and Irish armies of James II. Catholic wall gables generally displayed paintings of the current pope or martyrs of the 1916 Easter Rebellion. Either the Union flag or Tricolour of the Republic would be an integral part of the paintings.

The beauty and peace of the Irish countryside has seldom been free from human conflict since the time when the first Vikings raided Lambay Island near Dublin in 795. They occupied many of the coastal areas, and battles between Irish nobles and the Vikings continued into the eleventh century. Finally the Irish united under a king (Brian Boru) and defeated the Vikings at the battle of Clontarf in 1014, but once again the Irish had to give way when the Vikings were replaced in the twelfth century by Norman invaders and Ireland fell under the power of the English king Henry II in 1172. However the Irish nobles maintained their power through treaties and various other arrangements with the English until the seventeenth century. The tragic departure from Ireland in 1607 of O'Neill, O'Donnell, and the last great Irish nobles (an event known as the Flight of the Earls), began the change that was to make Ireland a subordinated country completely at the mercy of the British. Once the powerful northern nobles and their families fled to exile on the Continent, the last vestige of organised opposition to British rule went with them. Elizabeth I and James I's plans to colonise Ulster with Scottish and English settlers proved successful and finally gave Britain a stronger foothold in that most rebellious part of the country.

Britain's wars with Spain and France had always left her vulnerable to attacks through Ireland. For her protagonists it appeared as an open, inviting, rear entrance and as history records, British fears were not simply a case of paranoia. While in every instance the back door was firmly shut, the price paid in blood and suffering by the Irish people continued to mount. Cromwell's barbaric treatment of the Irish rebels at Drogheda and Wexford in 1650, the imposition of penal laws against Catholics and later Dissenters from 1536 to 1757, and the suppression of the 1798 rebellion led by Wolfe Tone and enjoined by Catholics and Presbyterians alike, are events that live on in the minds of today's Irish. After each of these events Britain's chances of maintaining the Union on other than a coercive basis dwindled.

It was in the eighteenth century also that Protestant and Catholic Irish sectarian groups began their violent attacks on each other resulting in evictions, home burnings and murder. These events took place in small towns and in the countryside, and involved disputes over land ownership and tenancies. R. B. McDowell records that

> In County Armagh ... protestants and catholics were numerically fairly equally balanced; and the protestant 'Peep o' Day Boys' and the catholic Defenders quarreled at fairs and cock-fights. In 1795, in the north of the county, the protestants ... drove some thousands of catholics from their homes. ... In September 1795 a serious affray between militant protestants and the Defenders occurred at a crossroads near Loughgall, in north Armagh—'the battle of the Diamond.' After this the protestants set up an Orange Society, and began to organise themselves in Orange lodges, some of which were headed by country gentlemen eager to rally the country people in defence of church and state.[2]

Although rejected by radical Presbyterians of the period who supported Wolfe Tone, the Orange Order today is the symbol of Protestant loyalty to the British Crown. Throughout its history Ireland has also been the breeding ground of militant organisations that threaten even Mother England should she seek to rid herself of her unruly stepchild.

During the 1960s, Unionist politicians in the Northern Ireland government at Stormont, Belfast, from Prime Minister to local representative, were as bound to the Order as the eighteenth-century country gentlemen of Armagh who preceded them. In the post-Second World War period, Prime Minister Sir Basil Brooke (later Lord Brookeborough) and Terence O'Neill (later Lord O'Neill of the Maine) took their place alongside the Protestant working-class marchers who filled the ranks of the movement ensuring that in Northern Ireland there would be a 'Protestant parliament for a Protestant people'.[3] For me, it was ironic in the 1960s to see newspaper photographs of a supposedly liberal Prime Minister such as O'Neill, take his place with other Orangemen for the annual parades in July and August. Brought up in London and educated at Eton before joining the Irish Guards, he must have had little in common with his fellow marchers, except for his respected war service. Liberal and well-intentioned by Unionist standards, deep down he may well have recognised his Irishness as he tried to improve relations between the two communities and the two Irelands. In his autobiography he is certainly proud of his historic links to the O'Neills, 'the oldest traceable family in Europe', and even goes on to complain that 'It is not generally realised what an appalling responsibility for the state of affairs rested, and still rests, on the shoulders of Queen Victoria. She loved Scotland, she loved Balmoral, she may even have loved John Brown. But she hated the Irish'.[4]

While Protestant supremacy and militancy in the North had always found its centre in the Orange Order, the rise of militancy in the rest of Ireland was more complex. The Catholic Defenders movement was later linked in the 1798 rebellion with the United Irishmen, but it was not until after the Potato Famine of 1845 that two new secret societies, the Irish Republican Brotherhood (IRB) and the Fenian Brotherhood became advocates for rebellion and the use of force to obtain Ireland's independence.[5] By 1865 the latter organisation was also well established in the United States where it could operate openly, its membership replete with Irish veterans from the American Civil War. In Ireland though, apart from maintaining the idea of achieving nationhood by force of arms, the Brotherhoods were unsuccessful in their endeavours to gain support for widespread revolt. Betrayed by informers from inside the organisations and foiled in their attempts to land arms in Ireland, they are remembered mostly for their patriotism and for a handful made martyrs by British executioners.[6]

In 1912, Protestants in the North of Ireland had successfully delayed the introduction of a Home Rule Bill by the Liberal government in Britain that would have allowed for the setting up of an independent parliament in Ireland responsible for all domestic affairs. Using large numbers of men from the Orange Order, a large paramilitary force of around 50,000, known as the Ulster Volunteers, had been formed in the same year. By April 1914, a large supply of arms had been smuggled into County Antrim from Germany and an Ulster Provisional government had even been formed. The Ulster Unionists were confident of their strength having enlisted the public support of British Conservatives under the leadership of Bonar Law. Moreover, a large number of officers in the British army headquarters at the Curragh, including high ranking officers, refused to take part in any operation to disarm the Ulster rebels. The Ulster Provisional government, led by Sir Edward Carson, the famous barrister, and James Craig, made demands for the exclusion of six, or at least four, counties from the Home Rule Bill. The Irish Republican Brotherhood in the South, taking note of the effectiveness of the threat of force, immediately formed their own paramilitary force known as the Irish Volunteers to defend the Home Rule Bill. Following the example set by the northerners, rifles, also smuggled from Germany, were landed near Dublin in July 1914. With Britain being drawn into what was to become the First World War in August 1914, the British government suspended the Home Rule Bill for a year or until hostilities with Germany ended. Leaving their politics behind, a quarter of a million Irishmen, including volunteers from both paramilitary groups, went off to France in Irish regiments of the British army. Thousands would never return.[7]

With the Easter Rising of 1916 in Dublin, a new and bloody chapter opened up in the history of Irish and British relations. Initially, without the knowledge of its leader, Eoin MacNeill, a secret IRB group within the Irish Volunteers had been planning an uprising. The group was led by Patrick Pearse, Joseph Plunkett, and Thomas MacDonagh and included James Connolly, a trade union leader who had merged the small 'Citizen Army' he had raised to protect striking workers from police and military intervention with the Irish Volunteers. Neither Pearse nor Connolly were enamoured by what they considered to be the meagre prospect and promise of Home Rule. They wanted a Republic free of any attachment to a nation that in their view had destroyed Ireland and its people both culturally and economically. To ensure the success of the uprising the conspirators were depending on a shipment of arms that was to be transported from Germany by submarine and landed in County Kerry. The arms were to be distributed throughout the South following the start of the rebellion in Dublin to support an anticipated widespread revolt of sympathisers. In this way the British forces, focusing on Dublin, would be unable to contain the rebellion. Sir Roger Casement, a British diplomat and an Irishman sympathetic to the Irish cause, and in charge of smuggling the arms from Germany, was to accompany the shipment on the voyage to Ireland by submarine. Unfortunately for the leaders of the rebellion, as in the past, British Intelligence had been apprised of the whole plan by informers. The key to the plan was that the arms shipment was to be transferred to an Irish trawler off the coast of County Kerry, but circumstances delayed the operation, and the submarine had to be scuttled as British naval vessels closed in. Casement escaped with some others in a dinghy only to be arrested by British forces as he lay exhausted and half-drowned on a Kerry beach. He was later tried and hanged as a traitor.

The British naturally thought that with the failure of the Germans to deliver arms the uprising would not take place, but Pearse and the others were determined. So while the population, including British armed forces, were enjoying the Bank Holiday, the Easter Rebellion became the event that was to change Irish history forever. As W.B. Yeats was to write:

> MacDonagh and MacBride
> And Connoly and Pearse
> Now and in time to be,
> Wherever green is worn,
> Are changed, changed utterly:
> A terrible beauty is born.[8]

The events of the uprising, and those that followed, have been thoroughly documented as quintessential moments in Irish history.[9] The uprising was not popular at first but as soon as the British executed the main conspirators as traitors, all Ireland was up in arms—that is to say all Ireland excepting those who supported the Union.

Under the charismatic leadership of Michael Collins (1890–1922) and Eamon De Valera (1882–1975), the Irish Republican Army (IRA), an amalgam of the IRB and Volunteers, fought a bloody guerrilla war with British occupying forces. In 1921, public opinion in England and elsewhere forced Lloyd George, the British Prime Minister to propose a treaty whereby the Irish Free State (later to become Eire and the Republic of Ireland) was created from twenty-six of Ireland's thirty-two counties. With the signing of the 1921 Anglo-Irish Treaty, Ireland had ostensibly shaken off her bondage, but six of the original nine Ulster counties had been excluded from the rest of Ireland by the terms of the Treaty at the request of the strong Unionist majority in the north. Winston Churchill, who was at the time Chancellor of the Exchequer, and was involved in the negotiations, displayed his uncanny grasp of history yet again and noted, 'The whole map of Europe has been changed. The position of countries has been violently altered. But as the deluge subsides and the waters fall we see the dreary steeples of Fermanagh and Tyrone emerging once again. The integrity of their quarrel is one of the few institutions that have been unaltered in the cataclysm that has swept the world.'[10] Collins reasoned that in signing the Treaty, 'We would save Tyrone and Fermanagh, parts of Derry, Armagh and Down by the Boundary Commission; the North would be forced economically to come in.'[11] At the same time Collins recognised the risk he was taking, and had a premonition that he had signed his death warrant by accepting the terms of the Treaty. On a lonely road in County Cork in August 1922 the great Irish patriot was ambushed and murdered by Republican opponents of partition. There were even rumours that De Valera was in some way involved in organising the ambush, but nothing was ever proved.

After the treaty there was a period of civil war with 'irregulars' from the IRA opposing the Treaty, the new government associated with it, and its new national army and police force. It was during the early years of the Irish Free State government from 1921 to 1924 that as many as seventy-seven irregulars were executed because of their roles in murder and mayhem that threatened the very existence of the new government. Among those executed were many important Republicans. The estimate of the number of executions was as much as three times greater than those executed by the British during the Easter Rebellion and the events that followed it.[12] De Valera, now leader of a the non-militant wing of the IRA and still opposed to both the Treaty and the exclusion of the six counties, was imprisoned without trial from 1923 to 1924, but he was patient as he waited for the opportunity to seize the power he instinctively knew was his. After resigning from the leadership of Sinn Fein, his new party Fianna Fail first took their seats as a minority party in the Dail (the Irish Parliament) in 1927, but it was not until 1932 that he finally came to power as leader of the majority party.

In the meantime, in 1924 a boundary commission had been set up under the terms of the Treaty to determine the precise boundary of northern counties claiming exclusion from the Free State. From the South's viewpoint this was an unmitigated disaster. The hope that the findings would result in a much smaller population and a more confined and ungovernable area were dashed when the report sustained the existing six-county boundary. This left the Northern Ireland Parliament with its substantial Unionist majority in place. The Nationalists, the main minority party representing the Catholics in the North, refused to take their seats until 1925. However, the pattern of Nationalists abstaining in protest against actions by the Unionists continued over the decades that followed, and there was to be no official Nationalist opposition party until 1965.

Although the Irish Free State at first accepted the findings of the 1924 Boundary Commission, during De Valera's long reign in office as Prime Minister (Taoiseach) of the Irish Parliament (Dail Eireann), the break with Great Britain widened with the establishment of Eire (Ireland) in 1937 to replace the Free State. Finally the withdrawal from the British Commonwealth and the establishment of the Irish Republic in 1949 severed all remaining bonds, as the government in the North became even more ensconced. De Valera consistently reiterated the right of the Irish people to rule all of Ireland. Legislation was also passed in the Dail so that anyone born in the North after 1921 could claim Irish citizenship. His government's acknowledgment of the special position of the Roman Catholic Church in the Constitution gave extreme Protestants all the ammunition needed to exploit the historic fears of Protestants—that they might become a minority in a Catholic State—a State where birth control methods were restricted, divorce was forbidden, and even books and newspapers were banned if they did not meet the approval of Catholic bishops. It was not until 1970, for example, that the bishops lifted their ban on Trinity College Dublin, and Catholics were permitted to attend the prestigious institution whose famous alumni included such names as Edmund Burke, Oliver Goldsmith, and Jonathan Swift.

Economic considerations were even more important for any Protestants who remained unconvinced of the dangers of living in a united Ireland. Northern Ireland was dependent on the generous subsidies of the British Crown. In 1938 Lord Craigavon, the Northern Ireland Prime Minister, received guarantees from the British that they would make up any difference in revenues resulting from a shortfall in revenue. This financial dependence on the rest of the UK would become even stronger following the Second World War, with the generous health and social security benefits enjoyed as part of the British welfare state. These benefits, enacted by the post-war Labour government in 1948, included a National Health Service, the brainchild of then Minister of Health Aneurin Bevan. Other benefits enacted by the Labour government included more generous unemployment benefits, child allowances, and subsidised housing and rents. It was economically impossible for Eire at that time in the post-war period to provide anything like the same safety net of welfare benefits for its population, many of whom were unemployed. Post-war emigration from the South to the United Kingdom, including Northern Ireland, relieved some of the pressure. Traditional emigration from all of Ireland continued with Northern Protestants favouring Canada and to a lesser extent other countries such as

Australia and South Africa. On the other hand the mainly Catholic Southern Irish preferred to follow the traditional pattern of emigration to England, Scotland, and the United States.[13]

Eire had remained neutral during the Second World War. In strict accordance with Irish neutrality De Valera denied the British the use of Irish ports to counteract the attacks on Allied shipping by German U-boats. This was to alienate further Protestants in Northern Ireland who, upon visiting Dublin, would observe the German swastika flying from its mast on the German embassy. De Valera's visit to the same embassy at the end of the war, to offer condolences to the ambassador on the death of Adolf Hitler, did not help relations between the two Irelands. The Germans carried out two horrific air raids on Belfast in the spring of 1941.

It must be acknowledged that on the whole Eire's neutrality became more biased in favour of the Allies once the US entered the war and the first US troops landed in Belfast. On the two occasions that the Luftwaffe bombed Belfast, fire-brigades from as far south as Dublin rushed north to offer their support. Moreover, a good number of southern and northern Catholics served with distinction in British forces during the war. It was equally noticeable that not all Protestant Orangemen rushed to enlist, unlike their predecessors in 1914, preferring instead to take refuge in De Valera's objections to the conscription of Irish in both the North or South. Northern Ireland's traditional industries, diverted to the war effort, provided many jobs as production rose in the shipyards, aircraft industries, and munitions factories, while Ulster's farms produced much of Britain's scarce food supply. Winston Churchill, who in the early part of the century had supported the Home Rule cause, changed his views after the war. He praised Northern Ireland's war effort in a victory speech and criticised De Valera for his policy of neutrality during the war. Certainly De Valera's position was not an enviable one, although historians may well attempt to vindicate his actions during this period. He was certainly an astute politician and a great leader of an old yet paradoxically fledgeling nation, but like Sir James Craig, De Valera's conservative and exclusive policies only served further to divide Irish Catholics and Protestants.

During De Valera's premiership (1932–48), the IRA remained active although both its character and focus of operations was to change. It played a defensive role during the 1935 riots in Belfast when Protestant mobs attacked Catholic areas. In 1936 De Valera declared the IRA an illegal organisation following three vicious murders of civilians, and by the 1940s members of the organisation both in the North and in the South could be interned without trial.[14] From 1939 and throughout the war the IRA's campaign focused on sporadic bomb attacks on border posts and murders of members of the Royal Ulster Constabulary. England's buildings and even public letter-boxes became targets in an ineffectual war-time campaign. The IRA's Chief of Staff Sean Russell was reported to have died of a heart attack in a German submarine off the Irish coast, while yet another leader, Frank Ryan, remained in Germany where he also died of natural causes as the war drew to a close. With many of its members imprisoned during the war it was not until 1949 that the IRA began to emerge again as a force. There were the usual statements in the press about liberating the North and in the early fifties a number of arms raids on military barracks took place. The campaign also followed a historic pattern of attacks on police stations and the bombing of obscure roads, bridges, and railway tracks. The murders of policemen and needless destruction of property alienated the IRA from support in many of the Catholic areas, and the campaign failed to disturb the Protestant hegemony in Ulster. Rather the links between Northern Ireland and the rest of the UK had been strengthened and consolidated as a result of its support of the war effort.

Militant Protestant counter organisations were dormant during this period since the Royal Ulster Special Constabulary (B Specials) provided an outlet for those who felt a compelling need to protect the province by force. Undoubtedly this auxiliary—armed Protestant force that could legally keep its weapons at home—was some deterrent to larger-scale operations by the IRA at the time. The vast majority of the Catholic population, on the other hand, probably viewed this paramilitary police force as a kind of Gestapo. By the sixties, during Sir Basil Brooke's premiership, Northern Ireland had become complacent about its future in the UK. His able, albeit ultra-conservative, Minister of Commerce Brian Faulkner, had begun, with some success, attracting industrialists to the province to replace the ailing shipbuilding and linen industries. From the fifties on, international firms such as Du Pont, Hoechst, Courtaulds, ICI, British Enkalon, and Monsanto had established large plants in Northern Ireland making it at one time the largest centre for petrochemical industries in Europe.

While even some Catholics at this time had begun to accept the *status quo*, they were at best tolerated or ignored by the Protestant majority and at the same time belligerently and noisily reminded of their minority status by the annual marches of Orangemen and Apprentice Boys. The latter organisation in particular was regarded as an affront to the Catholic majority population of Derry as they gathered from across the province and paraded around the walls of the historic city. By now the majority of Irish, both north and south, had become more absorbed with improving their living standards than removing the border that divided them.

Following the resignation of Sir Basil Brooke in 1963, Terence O'Neill became Prime Minister of the Northern Ireland government. One year earlier the IRA had called off its border campaign. Although never rejecting military action as a means to achieve its goal, the membership had shifted to the left as the organisation became more political in its aims. While O'Neill had a historic connection with Northern Ireland he had not grown up with the beleaguered 'fortress Ulster' mentality of the majority of his Unionist colleagues or the former Prime Minister. He was, as Robert Kee points out, 'a man of intelligence and some sensibility who saw the need to adjust Northern Ireland to the world of the 1960s'.[15] O'Neill, in his autobiography, describes his initiative in arranging the unprecedented 1965 meeting with Sean Lemass, the Republic's Taoiseach, and (in 1966) with his successor Jack Lynch.[16] He also made efforts to reach out to the Catholic population noting that his predecessor had 'never crossed the border, never visited a catholic school and was never received or sought a civic reception from a catholic town'.[17] These efforts bore some results in that by February 1965, the Nationalist Party, under the leadership of Eddie McAteer from Derry, accepted the role of the official opposition party for the first time since the debacle of the 1924 boundary commission.[18]

Friendly words or signs would prove insufficient in the face of the Unionist party's gerrymandering of Derry and other border towns to maintain virtually absolute political power. The franchise in local elections was limited to owners or tenants of a house. In addition property owners could have more than one vote depending on the amount of property they owned. So the Protestant Unionists could maintain control of a majority Catholic city like Derry by manipulating the electoral boundaries and by depending upon the majority Protestant property owners to vote Unionist. By the time O'Neill got around to dealing with the voting issues and introducing reform, we would have completed our plan for Derry and the retribution for past injustices would exact a heavy price. R.F. Foster, in contrast to Kee, writes that

O'Neill was an unconvincing liberal, as well as an inept tactician who refused to prepare the ground with his resentful colleagues. Subsequent events have created the illusion that he stood for introducing civil rights reform, for which there is no evidence; his 'New Ulster' still excluded Catholics from the Housing Trust, The Lockwood Committee to oversee university expansion, and many other public boards. O'Neill's visits to Catholic Schools did little to counter this; his jeers at 'jargon words … like community relations' are more representative as are his appallingly condescending memoirs.[19]

Yet in 1965 when we began our planning efforts, we were hopeful that the prevailing new spirit would continue and that the extremists on both sides would lose their credibility. From the 1950s, the basic policy objectives of the Irish economies north and south of the border were similar.[20] Each was committed to industrial growth by creating incentives for incoming industrialists through capital grants, loans, training programmes, and tax incentives. Both governments were also attracted to policies for establishing growth centres similar to those adopted by European countries at the time such as France, Holland, and Italy. During the early 1960s both physical and economic planning would become the accepted means of assuring a better future.

NOTES

1] Randall Clarke, *A Short History of Ireland* (London, University Tutorial Press Ltd, 1941). For a more comprehensive view, readers are referred to J.C. Beckett, *A Short History of Ireland from Earlier Times to the Present Day* (London and New York, Hutchinson, 1952).
2] R.B. McDowell, 'Ireland in 1800' in *A New History of Ireland.*, eds T.W. Moody and W.E. Vaughan (New York: Oxford University Press, 1986), p. 347.
3] In 1934 Prime Minister Sir James Craig told an approving Northern Ireland House of Commons that he prized the office of Grand Master of the Orange Institution of County Down 'far more than I do being Prime Minister. … I have always said I am an Orangeman first and a member of this parliament afterwards … all I boast is that we are a protestant Parliament and a protestant State.' Quoted in Robert Kee, *Ireland a History* (Boston, Little, Brown and Co., 1980), p. 228.
4] Terence O'Neill, *The Autobiography of Terence O'Neill* (London, Rupert Hart-Davis Ltd, 1972), p. 3.
5] In Irish mythology the Fenian cycle told of the exploits of Finn MacCumhail and his warriors known as the 'Fianna'. These events are traditionally believed to have occurred in the third century A.D.
6] William Philip Allen, Michael Larkin, and Michael O'Brien were executed in 1867, accused of killing a policeman while part of a group successfully releasing two prominent Fenian prisoners from a van taking them to prison. They became known as the Manchester Martyrs, and their martyrdom is remembered annually by Irish Republicans.
7] Robert Kee, *Ireland: A History* (Boston, Little, Brown and Co., 1980), Chapter 8, pp. 137–51, contains an excellent account of events here briefly described.
8] W.B. Yeats, *Easter 1916* (New York, Macmillan Company, 1924; renewed 1952 by Bertha Georgie Yeats).
9] The author wishes to acknowledge in particular Kee, *Ireland*, pp. 153–222; and Keith Jeffery, 'Orange and Green' in *The Divided Province* (London, Orbis Publishing, 1985), pp. 12–33. Also note T.W. Moody and C.J. Woods, *Ireland under the Union 1801–1921*, vol. VI of *A New History of Ireland* and T.W. Moody, J.G. Simms, and C.J. Woods, *Ireland 1921–76*, vol. VII (Oxford, Clarendon Press, 1986).
10] Winston S. Churchill, *The world crisis: the aftermath* (London, Thornton Butterworth, 1929), p. 319.
11] In a memorandum quoted by H. Montgomery Hyde in an article in the *Belfast Telegraph*, 6 December, 1960.
12] Peter and Fiona Somerset Fry, *A History of Ireland* (New York, Barnes and Noble Books, 1988), p. 318.
13] R.F. Foster, *Modern Ireland 1600–1972* (London, Allen Lane/The Penguin Press, 1988), p. 578; '… emigration provided a painful reminder that more drastic remedies were needed. In the decade from 1951 to 1961 more than 400,000 left—many to Britain—bringing the population down to 2,800,000 by 1961.'

14] Kee, *Ireland,* p. 215.
15] Ibid., p. 232.
16] O'Neill, *Autobiography,* pp. 68–76.
17] Ibid., p. 47.
18] This and other dates have been verified from T.W. Moody, F.X. Martin, and F.J. Byrne, *A Chronology of Irish History to 1976,* vol. VIII of *A New History of Ireland* (Oxford, Clarendon Press, 1986).
19] Foster, *Modern Ireland,* p. 585.
20] W. Black and J.V. Simpson, 'Growth Centres in Ireland', *The Irish Banking Review* (Sept 1968): pp. 19–29.

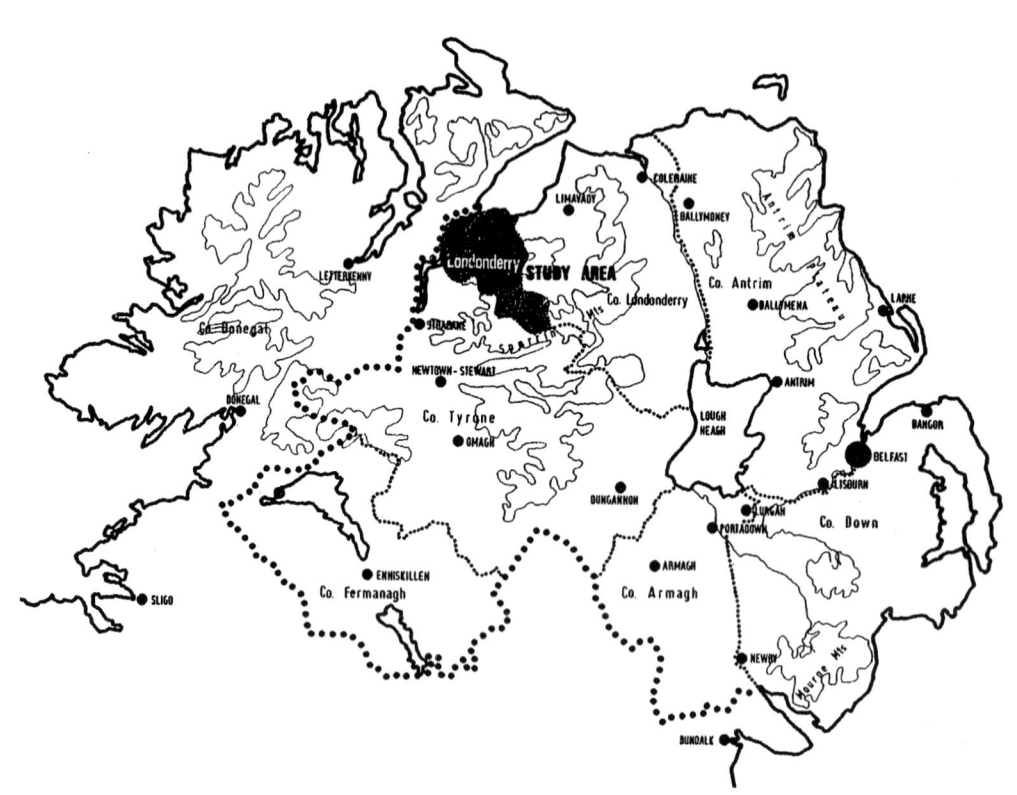

2. *Londonderry County Borough and Rural District (1966) in the context of Northern Ireland*

2 The Steering Committee

I was enjoying my first visit to the United States and my first full-time stint as a teacher in the School of Architecture at the University of Kansas when one morning in early February 1966, I got the long distance phone call. It was Jimmy Munce calling from the Belfast office of James Munce Partnership. His husky military-style accent with its slight English overtones sounded a trifle more excited than usual. 'We're going to be interviewed for a planning job in Londonderry,' he said. 'Can you fly back for a few days?' I felt myself suddenly caught up in Jimmy's excitement as I had been so many times previously in the seven or eight years I had known him. 'I'll arrange it,' I replied. 'When do I need to be there?'

Ten days later I found myself on my way back to Belfast thinking of the busy few days that lay ahead and wondering if Jimmy's optimism about getting the commission was justified. There had been some disappointments in the past and before my departure to the United States the firm's application to prepare a plan for Belfast had been rejected, even though the Munce Partnership (then Munce and Kennedy) had entered into association with the prominent Scottish planners Sir Robert Matthew and Percy Johnson-Marshall. James Frederick Munce was not a man to be deterred by a few temporary setbacks. He had returned from the Second World War a major and a toughened veteran of the Burma campaign, to inherit his father's small but successful civil engineering practice. Jimmy, at this time in his late forties, was an architect by training but an entrepreneur by nature. He had expanded the practice to include architecture, quantity surveying, and recently city planning as major components to form what was fashionably called at that time a multi-disciplinary practice. With a staff of some seventy or eighty in the Belfast office and branch offices in London and Glasgow, Jimmy had already some major industrial projects and a number of rural housing projects occupying his attention.

He had also been busy overseas and had followed up his success of completing a sports complex for the Pan-Arabic games in Amman, Jordan, with his similar current multi-million dollar project in Tripoli, Libya. Much to his chagrin none of this success bore much fruit in his native province. The professional jealousy of his competitors combined with their provincial attitudes denied him, as he saw it, the just reward for his labours and his daring, the latter being a skill, which in his hands, they deplored. For one thing, in a culture where modesty was still regarded as a virtue, modesty was not one of James Munce's strongest suits. His penchant for keeping local newspapers and magazines apprised of his prowess, however small, was perceived by his competitors as advertising. On reflection he probably was a man before his time. Certainly many of the methods he used in procuring business were at that time regarded by my contemporaries as being on the margin of ethical professional behaviour; yet today the marketing of his practice would be accepted as the norm. He made many of his more conservative partners and associates, including myself, uncomfortable with his style. In addition to his fierce ambition and energy Jimmy had given many young professionals opportunities that the best architects reserved for themselves: he sought fame as an architect, but aware that his own design talents were limited, he gave young architects opportunities far beyond their expectations and was rewarded with their industry and eventually their gratitude and affection.

Jimmy and his partner Bob Simpson were waiting for me at the airport as I stepped off the morning plane sleepy-eyed but excited. Bob was a genial Ulster-Scot with whom I had worked in another architectural firm before he joined the Munce office. In the early fifties, before returning to Northern Ireland, he had worked in the Scottish New Town of East Kilbride just outside Glasgow. During my years away from the Munce offices in Liverpool and Edinburgh, he had become a partner. He was a good counterfoil to Jimmy, reliable, loyal, and an excellent administrator who seemed to carry alone among all the partners, the burden of the firm's often precarious financial position. While his earlier experience in accountancy before becoming an architect did not fit well with Jimmy's cavalier expansionist style, Jimmy knew he needed Bob and valued both his loyalty and prudence. While I had expected to be met by Bob I was pleasantly surprised to find that Jimmy accompanied him, and as we walked to collect my baggage, both of them briefed me on the upcoming meeting with the Londonderry Area Plan Steering Committee, which was to take place the following afternoon. Bob dropped me off at my family's small council house in north Belfast where I spent most of the day catching up on family news.

Stanley Cochrane, a senior engineer and associate partner in the firm was to complete our team at the meeting. During the coming months I would get to know Stan better as he was to share in the management of the planning team inasmuch as all civil engineering aspects were concerned. We had some things in common; although a few years older than me, he also grew up in Belfast, attending a rival school and playing rugby. Stan had graduated with honours in civil engineering from Queen's University Belfast and had also completed a master's degree, making him the most qualified engineer in the Munce firm. His sharp mind and also his manner of speaking quickly, seriously, and rationally, was tempered by an equally warm sense of humour and generosity. Although occasionally quick-tempered, he was above all a person of integrity, completely reliable, and honest. It was reassuring to note that he would be attending the interview with Jimmy, Bob, and myself.

On our two-hour journey to Derry we discussed the interview, which Jimmy assured us would be more of a confirmation meeting since no other large firm was involved at this stage. He believed that we had been recommended for Derry because of our rejection as potential planners for the Belfast Area Plan despite our efforts to combine forces with Matthew and Johnson-Marshall. He was convinced that we had lost that opportunity because of his criticism of the city surveyor and his refusal to accept an elevated ring road as a starting point for the plan. Like the ubiquitous high-rise public housing blocks replacing older (slum) housing in Britain's city centres, elevated roads were becoming the preferred engineering solution for easing traffic in these centres, much to the dismay of many inner-city residents. Now at long last, Jimmy felt, the opportunity to become involved in city planning had arrived, and he had reason to feel some hope with his former public school friend William Craig now minister for development in the Stormont government. One, however, could never be quite sure of Jimmy's relationships in this regard. He often attacked the Establishment and had seldom anything complimentary to say about the Unionist Party. Seemingly his only social connections on the political side were related to acquiring commissions. He was probably as apolitical a person as one could find in those days, at least in business circles in Northern Ireland.

The strategy that Jimmy outlined for the meeting was not unusual. He and Bob had considerable experience working with rural district and city councils, so he would introduce the firm and members of the planning team, mentioning the major works of the firm both in Northern Ireland and abroad. Bob would also talk about the resources available within the firm and consultants we might require. Stan would deal with all questions pertaining to engineering matters, while I would field all questions related to the actual planning process itself. We could naturally step in to support each other should that be necessary at any point. Discussions on the likely nature of questions continued during the journey and through lunch after we arrived in the city.

I'm sure the difficulties of the political situation in Derry were also discussed, especially since in just the previous year the proposed new University of Ulster had been located near the largely Protestant city of Coleraine forty miles east of Londonderry. For the people of Derry this must have been seen as yet another blatant affront from the Unionist government and one even more difficult to endure in the worsening economic climate. Moreover rumour had it that a group of Derry Unionists, reputedly led by a former mayor of Londonderry, had been responsible for steering the development away from the city. The Unionists' portrayal of their own citizens as lazy Catholic troublemakers bred on welfare and their denigration of the city itself appalled many Derry Protestants as well as Catholics. Certainly there was a housing shortage made worse by the manœuvring of Unionist politicians, but this could have easily been remedied. Another former Unionist mayor, Sir Basil McFarlane, described this group as 'the nameless, faceless men who stopped the new university being located in the city'. It would have certainly been obvious to any objective person that as Northern Ireland's second largest city, and one of the oldest, Londonderry was a prime location for the new university. If the politics of this situation were indeed discussed among us before our meeting it would only have been in the general sense related to the task at hand. None of us at this time knew the details of the situation I have just described.

I now wonder how Jimmy Munce, with his unquenchable optimism, had concluded that, as a Northern Ireland firm and given the political situation, we would probably be more acceptable than an English firm to both Unionists and Nationalists on the committee. Northern Ireland is a small place and in the sixties had a population of just under one-and-a-half million, so it was not surprising that Jimmy, Bob, and Stan had on some previous occasion met some of the officials. I, on the other hand, knew no one on the committee but was hoping that the others' connections in the province might prove helpful during the presentation and interview.

As noted earlier, from 1921 until 1972 (when direct rule was imposed from Westminster) this small region had its own parliament and from the early thirties, its own parliament buildings at Stormont. It also had its own Prime Minister. Developing networks in the circumstances came easily to most people. Traditionally lagging behind the UK with most of its legislation, particularly in housing and planning since the Second World War, the 1963 Matthew Plan for the Belfast Region had provided new impetus in these fields and legislation based on the British model followed. It then became the task of officials and planners in the Ministry of Development to begin implementing the Matthew Plan.[1] This plan for the Belfast Region by Sir Robert Matthew proposed limiting the growth of Belfast, the establishment of two new towns, and the designation of a number of growth areas elsewhere in the province. It was adopted in 1963, and an economic report by Professor Thomas Wilson in 1964 endorsed the physical planning proposals for growth centres.[2] Specifically, Matthew's advice had been to restrict the growth of Belfast by a stop-line around the city and its suburbs. Growth was to be accommodated in a new town named Craigavon, linking the existing nearby towns of Lurgan and Portadown to the west. It had a target population of 100,000 thereby relegating Northern Ireland's second city of Londonderry to third place. A second new town, Antrim-Ballymena, just north of Belfast, based on and having the same name as the existing towns, was also designated. Development powers for these new towns were the responsibility of a government-appointed Development Commission similar to British New Towns. Later the city of Londonderry in the north-west and the town of Newry in the south-east were designated as growth centres. A third growth centre was established in the north-east around the towns of Coleraine, Portrush, and Portstewart (known as the Coleraine Triangle). The planning of these growth centres was to be the responsibility of steering committees made up of representatives from the towns and rural district councils involved.

The steering committee for the Londonderry area had just recently been established by the Minister of Development, and was comprised of three councillors from each of the three authorities that would be impacted by the planning proposals—Londonderry County Borough Council, Londonderry County Council, and Londonderry Rural District Council. In addition to the elected representatives the city (county borough) and county each had three officials as non-voting members while the rural district had two. The Ministry of Development had two officials in attendance while the Ministry of Commerce had one.

Steering committee meetings were to be held at the Rural District Council offices at Altnagelvin across the River Foyle, a few miles from the city centre and south of the city boundary but physically part of the suburbs. We were greeted by the chairman of the committee—the Unionist Mayor of Derry, Commander A.W. Anderson. (Unlike the United States, it was customary in the UK to use one's military title even after retirement from the military.) Among other members of the committee, seated on the dias with him, were Councillor Mackey, chairman of the Rural District Council and Councillor Lamberton, of the County Council.

Commander Anderson's voice welcomed us in the deep rich anglicized tones that I had come to associate with Ulstermen who believed they had reached the zenith of both rank and privilege. I had also observed that those involved in politics retained the faint veneer of an Ulster accent, presumably to make it digestible to the local populace. Although powerful and commanding of the listener's attention, his voice had a ponderous air that appeared to reflect the mind of the speaker. He introduced the other members of the committee seated at tables around the periphery of the room, arranged so that they faced ours and, representing the city of Derry, Councillor James Doherty,[3] a Nationalist who would have been in the mayor's seat but for the gerrymandered Unionist dominated council. Unlike Mayor Anderson, whose position in society was based on the remnants of Protestant ascendancy and military service, he was a very successful businessman. Among other endeavours he operated the largest and most successful butcher's shop and meat processing plant in the city. Educated as an economist, James was dedicated to serving the needs of his constituents and the city as a whole. Although stockily built and now into his forties, his body movements exuded the energy of a younger man while his ruddy complexion gave one the impression that he spent a considerable part of his working life outdoors. His slightly greying hair and spectacles on the other hand lent him a bookish appearance. He spoke clearly but deferentially with a soft Derry accent, and there was just a hint of suspicion in intelligent light blue eyes as he expressed his hope that housing and industrial development would not be delayed by the necessary planning endeavours.

Although Anderson and Doherty seemed to be the most significant political figures on the committee, the other rural district and county councillors participated in the discussions and enquiries about the firm and our previous experience.

The officials present were not part of the selection process and were principally involved in relaying information about developments that were in the pipeline, but they were to be the key personnel in providing access to local authority resources during the planning process. Representing the Ministry of Development was Gilbert Camblin, a well-known surveyor and city planner and author of *The Town in Ulster,* an excellent and beautifully illustrated historical record of the development of the Ulster town and village.[4] Along with Gilbert another civil servant, George Clarke, was responsible for recording the minutes of the meetings. Both were to become essential participants in ensuring that a plan would be published, although civil service diplomacy at the time required their overt neutrality at meetings. Camblin would prove to be an ally by often intervening at critical junctures to explain a point to the Committee or to elucidate on some of our findings. Clarke would keep excellent (though discreet) minutes of the meetings and was to be helpful to me personally when difficulties with committee members arose.

Officials representing the city were Roy Henderson, the town clerk; Colonel James MacKinder, the city surveyor; and David White, the city accountant. Henderson cut an imposing figure. Tall and just prosperously overweight with sleeked backed hair, he looked and behaved as if he were the most senior official of a major metropolis. MacKinder, a Yorkshireman, obviously regarded both our presence and the whole matter of a plan as an unconscionable intrusion into his own plans for the city. Ruddy complexioned and tweedy he was the epitome of the retired British colonel, complete with bluster and quick temper. White, on the other hand, an active, probably evangelical, Christian in his late thirties or early forties, neatly dressed and bespectacled, had the efficient look of someone whose main concern in life had to do with numbers. Soft spoken and, as I later found, completely ethical, he looked somewhat out of place and too normal alongside his colleagues. Although I was not to know it then, in later years he would play a prominent role in implementing the plan that we would later produce.

Major Harold Scott, the county surveyor and James Jackson, the county planning officer, were to prove helpful also, but both generally played a passive role in the early meetings. Scott had a military bearing but quite unlike that of MacKinder. Slim, elegant, and silver-haired, he was an Ulsterman and acknowledged as one of the best civil engineers in the province. Stan Cochrane held him in high esteem and was to establish a good working relationship with his office. Jackson, also a local, was in his late thirties and as a planner realized the importance and timeliness of a plan for the area. To be fair unlike the city and rural district there was not a great deal at stake for the county whose functions would probably remain unaffected by any reorganisation that might take place as a result of the plan.

Arthur McCahon, the rural district clerk, cut a more casual and provincial figure than Roy Henderson his city counterpart. A Derry man, McCahon appeared to be the most relaxed and reasonable of all the officials on the committee. In his early fifties, he was wiry and energetic and his deeply lined weathered face with its ever ready smile was difficult to read, betraying neither anger nor pleasure. Only when his eyes narrowed behind the smoke of his cigarette was one aware that something that one said had earned his displeasure. McCahon's antipathy towards both the plan and planners was to become evident early in the process, but at this first meeting he appeared to welcome us with open arms. His colleague William McKee the rural district engineer was in his late thirties and according to Stan Cochrane, had already acquired an excellent reputation for his expertise on water and sewage. He had the appearance of a clean cut farmer in his Sunday best. His pleasant, intelligent face seemed to reinforce professional opinions delivered in a firm no-nonsense tone.

At that first meeting we were received politely by all, and questions were asked in a friendly and gracious manner. It was only towards the end of the meeting that a most discouraging incident took place. I had been asked only a few questions when I was suddenly aware that Commander Anderson was addressing me directly. 'How would you go about making this plan?' I thought momentarily about how I should answer his question and, with an encouraging nod from Jimmy, launched into an academic explanation of the planning process and the need for first carefully surveying the existing situation. After speaking for five or six minutes and fearing that I might lose the committee's attention I concluded with what I thought was the most important aspect: 'People are at the heart of everything we do. The people of Derry must become participants in the planning process. We need to keep them informed, and we need their input and their ideas, but most of all we must understand their needs. This will mean numerous meetings with individuals, groups, and organisations of all kinds. In the end the people of Derry must feel that this plan is their plan.' I felt that I had answered the question completely and looked towards the chairman expecting to be greeted with either a word of encouragement or nod of comprehension. Instead I received the stony reply: 'Mr McSheffrey, as far as you are concerned, WE are the people.'

I cannot recall Jimmy's efforts to rescue the situation as he attempted to defend my answer and mollify the chairman. But both my carefully disguised embarrassment and anger at an authoritarian tone I had not encountered since school days, remained with me after the interview ended and during the journey home I had to put up with some unmerciful ribaldry at my expense from Stan and Bob. Jimmy was at first silent, but rescued me from an onset of depression by supporting what I had said at the meeting. It was agreed then and there that there could be no wavering during the planning process and that we could not pander to the whims of local Unionist politicians. If the plan was not to end up on someone's shelf as just another public relations exercise, we would have to produce a document that was technically incontrovertible and that at the same time would both catch the imagination of the Derry populace and win their support. After our interview it was becoming clear that if we won the contract, this might have to be achieved in spite of the Steering Committee rather than with their acquiescence.

At dinner that night Jimmy felt that he might still have to do some work behind the scenes to ensure that we got the commission, but the evening ended on an optimistic note. Before returning to Kansas I was to meet with Bob the next day to determine what extra staff and consultants we would need for the project, while Stan was to determine his engineering staff needs. Though the firm had more than fifty architects and engineers in the Belfast office, the small group working on planning and housing layouts consisted of one young architect, Alan Bradshaw, a young architect-planner, Mike Murray, both in their mid-twenties, and myself.

The next day back in Belfast Jimmy, Bob, Stan and I met in the conference room in the University Street offices. I suggested that we would need someone experienced in survey work, preferably a geographer, and a highly experienced economist with expertise on shopping centres, probably as a consultant. I also recommended the appointment of my friend and mentor Peter Daniel as landscape consultant. In addition, we discussed using Dr Fred Boal, a Queen's University professor of geography with expertise in industrial location theory. Stan thought we would need someone with traffic engineering experience and mentioned that Jack Smyth, currently working on the Belfast urban motorway proposal, would be an excellent addition to the team. We would just have to wait and see whether or not we were successful after the somewhat foreboding encounter with the Steering Committee. But as I tried to sleep on the Atlantic leg of my long flight back to Kansas City I hoped the journey had not been in vain. Some of Jimmy's optimism seemed to engulf me, just as sleep eluded me, and I thought of the exciting prospect that a plan for Londonderry offered.

About the first week in March Bob telephoned me at my apartment in Kansas to let me know that we had been appointed as consultants and that he would be sending on details. I was concerned that I could not return to Belfast until near the end of the spring term in late April, but he assured me that as there were still negotiations to determine fees and the scope of the contract, it would probably be late March or even April before we could begin. Meanwhile he would proceed with recruiting the remaining team members. He was also going to open a small office in Londonderry, and Alan Bradshaw had already agreed to move there with his family to begin establishing contacts in the city. I could now scarcely wait to return but somehow managed to channel my energies once more to teaching my fifth-year design studio. It had been an exciting interlude, but the reality of the task at hand and the enthusiasm of the students now fully occupied my time.

NOTES

1] Sir Robert Matthew, *Belfast Regional Survey and Plan* (HMSO Cmd 451, 1963).
2] Thomas Wilson, *Economic Development, Northern Ireland* (HMSO Cmd 479, 1965).
3] Note: Doherty is a commonly found historic surname in the Derry/Donegal area. James Doherty is not related to Paddy Doherty mentioned later in the book.
4] Gilbert Camblin, *The Town in Ulster* (Belfast, Wm Mullan & Son, 1951).

3 The Planning Team

Numerous theories exist today on teamwork and team building. From a distance of thirty years, it seems to me that more than chance brought our small planning team together. Each one of us—and each of our consultants as well—turned out to be vital for the making of the Londonderry plan. The contribution of consultants proved to be essential in the successful outcome of the plan and the absence of even one of the participants, whether staff or consultant, would have greatly diminished the end result. Interestingly as it turned out, the backgrounds and philosophical outlook of everyone involved were so intertwined that we could almost anticipate each others thoughts. Not that there wasn't argument and even dissension at times, but the infrequent nature and substance of the arguments and the goodwill and humour of the participants, combined with incredible dedication and hard work, enabled us to accomplish much within a very short time.

While at least half the team had known each other for many years in the Munce office and had established good working relationships, there were other factors influencing the strong philosophical direction that evolved during the making of the plan. Paramount was the influence of the pioneering, turn-of-the-century planner, Patrick Geddes. The attitude of Geddes to industrialised countries was succinctly explained by Percy Johnson-Marshall who wrote that:

> As far back as 1911, Patrick Geddes explained that two kinds of vision were necessary in countries such as Britain, which includes numerous urban agglomerations: one, a vision of economic activity and broad land use distribution, was regional in scale; the other, essentially visual, was a three-dimensional exploitation of the imaginative possibilities inherent in all technological inventions which had, by their misuse, tended to destroy the existing environment rather than help create a new one.[1]

Also important to the team was the emphasis Geddes placed on survey, and we were always mindful of his paradigm of Place, Folk and Work. I suspect also that with the exception of the engineers on the team we were all in some way Utopians, although I personally liked to think of myself as a pragmatist—a term then in vogue and frequently overused by British Prime Minister Harold Wilson, a Socialist. Peter Daniel, Mike Murray, and I all had strong Edinburgh connections where the ideas of Geddes and his 'Outlook Tower' had been kept alive by Johnson-Marshall. Moreover the writings of Lewis Mumford were ample testimony to the worldwide relevance of Geddes to the contemporary scene. For us Mumford's ideas about the size of cities, adopting those of Peter Kropotkin and Ebenezer Howard, seemed a natural fit with the character of Londonderry and its environs.[2]

Mike Murray, a native of Belfast, and I had worked together in the Belfast office for a number of years. He was at least ten years younger than I and a more promising designer by far. He sported a copious but trimmed black beard and thick black raven hair. His round quizzical brown eyes were ever ready to wrinkle and close with laughter at the least pretext. After leaving the Munce Office to complete his architectural education in Birmingham, he had obtained a post-graduate diploma in civic design at Edinburgh University as I had some years earlier. The unique programme at Edinburgh was the brainchild of Percy Johnson-Marshall and was located, together with the Architecture School under Professor Sir Robert Matthew, in the Faculty of Social Sciences. This arrangement reflected the thinking of Matthew and Johnson-Marshall that while architecture was undoubtedly the 'mistress art', it had also an important social purpose in the fields of housing and city planning. It was also in line with modernist thinking still prevalent from the thirties and promulgated by the various manifestos of the Congrès Internationeaux de l'Architecture Moderne (CIAM). Both Percy and Sir Robert had played leading roles in the London County Council after the Second World War in the rebuilding of London.

Mike was responsible for most of the map-making and diagrams required for the reports and final document. A small group worked with him in the Belfast office and assisted the Derry office with numerous surveys. The group included two former students of mine from when I had taught part-time at the Belfast College of Art in 1961. The first of these John McCrory, who in addition to his architectural drafting skills, was an excellent photographer, and his superb photographs of the Derry area greatly enhanced the reports and final document. The other former student, Mervyn Hegan, had excellent graphic skills and assisted Mike in preparing the plans and diagrams. Two other members of the group providing support were Eamon Fitzpatrick, a young engineering assistant from Dublin, and Sue Wolfe, a recent graduate in geography from Queen's University Belfast. This small group, as well as participating in surveys, prepared large coloured overlay maps and diagrams of outstanding quality with a precision approaching those generated by present-day computer systems.

All work carried out under Mike's supervision included the printing and binding of reports and the final plan. In this he was assisted by Jack Wilson, the technician responsible for dye-line printing for both architects and engineers. A budding author, Jack had just published his first novel *Adam Grey* and was working on his second. To support the planning effort Jimmy Munce had invested in an offset printing machine for the office, and Jack and Mike soon became experts in a process that they were able to control from first sketch to finished print. For plates and larger drawings Belfast photographer Robert Anderson and the printing firm of Sigma Services were involved. Mike also worked with Sandy Bell, our consultant/perspectivist in Edinburgh who translated maps and diagrams into pictures of a possible future. Sandy was a former chief designer in the Munce Office and was also responsible for assisting Mike with getting the larger scale final plan printed by the Edinburgh firm of James Deas & Sons Ltd.

Alan Bradshaw, who was in charge of the office, had also grown up in Belfast and completed his architectural education at the Architectural Association in London. He had worked with Mike Murray and myself in the Belfast office. As the first small planning team we were involved in Jimmy Munce's abortive attempt to be appointed the planning consultant for Belfast, with Matthew and Johnson-Marshall. The contract instead was awarded to Building Design Partnership, a large English firm of architect-planners. Alan was thin and artistic looking, with light brown long hair and a wispy beard. His pale eyes somehow looked weak behind strong horn rimmed spectacles, but his ready smile and soft-spoken firm voice concealed a mischievous trait and dry sense of humour. The new office in Derry was located in the Northern Bank Building, from the north windows one could glimpse Guildhall Square, and get a clear view of Magazine Gate then a derelict corner of the city walls.[3]

Alan's main task was to establish contacts in the local community and to ease communication between Belfast and Derry. He had also to attend and take notes at numerous meetings involving other members of the team, and in particular, meetings involving Jimmy Munce and Bob Simpson. His busy life included the local organisation of surveys and assisting consultants, yet he still found time to make major contributions to many other aspects of plan making. With only a young assistant, Bernard Donaghy, whom he hired upon arrival in Derry and a young secretary, Maureen Dunn, Alan immediately started collecting information. Within a very short time he had his finger on the pulse of the community, and his participation in the decision-making process was often critical when it came to dealing with the needs of various community organisations.

Alan worked closely with Jim Foster who spent time in both the Derry and Belfast offices as he organised surveys and analysed the mountains of data that would become the basis for our recommendations regarding future growth. The whole of the study area was surveyed in minute detail using staff from both offices and student help. Peter Daniel even organised a group of students from Heriot-Watt University in Edinburgh who came to record and measure some of the historic buildings.

Jim Foster, a geographer, joined the team in June upon returning home from Nottingham, where he had been employed as a researcher by the Ministry of Housing and Local Government. Like Mike and Alan he was in his mid-twenties and had graduated with a degree in geography from Queen's University Belfast. Following this he travelled to Canada where he completed his master's degree at McMaster University in Hamilton, Ontario. The position in England had been his first permanent job after graduating, but he had gained considerable research experience in the position. In appearance Jim was just under six feet tall, straight backed, clean cut, and always neatly and conservatively dressed. While there was just a hint of shyness in his demeanour he was articulate and when necessary firm in his opinions. He had a good sense of humour and like Bob Simpson, he had the advantage of being born and raised in the area, a fact which seemed to endow him with an innate ability to focus on information that was most critical in making planning decisions.

Jim was responsible for organising most of the surveys, except those related to the traffic and landscape studies, but even in these instances his assistance with population projections was critical. In addition to providing all the in-house expertise he was our liaison with Gerald Eve & Co., our economic consultants, and with Fred Boal, our consultant on industrial location. It was his work on survey and analysis that formed the basis for five of the seven preliminary reports presented to the Steering Committee, and his influence was evident in the remaining reports.[4] Jim also worked with me on the final document, which was in essence a summary of the more technical reports but omitting most of the planning jargon. He brought with him, as did all the team, the strong desire to conserve all that was worthwhile and good about the city and its environs. It was his understanding of the historic city and its morphology that enabled the rest of us to absorb quickly background information that would otherwise have taken many months. After the plan was completed in 1968 he would later play a leading role in the 1972 review of the plan, the 1981–96 review and the current *Derry Area Plan 2011–Preliminary Proposals*.

Stanley Cochrane was the associate engineering partner responsible for all the communications aspects of the plan and for all infrastructure decisions on water, sewage, electrics and telecommunications. As a member of the planning team he was involved in all major decisions, but, as was the case with Jimmy and Bob, the Londonderry Plan was not his only responsibility. Stan delegated the day-to-day responsibility for engineering aspects of the plan to another experienced civil engineer, Jack Smyth, who he had recruited from the Belfast City Surveyor's office where he had been working on the proposed ring road. In his late thirties or early forties, one of the oldest members of the planning team, he was born in the County Antrim town of Ballymena, just twenty-five miles or so north of Belfast. Either naturally diffident or politically astute, I was never quite sure which, he blended naturally into the team and had the difficult job of serving two masters, Stan and me. The team could not have had a better engineer. Apart from his tact and ability to work amicably and constructively with other members of the team, he had a genuine interest in planning and was studying for the external examinations of what is now the Royal Town Planning Institute. His participation was needed in almost every decision made in preparing the plan.

Both Stan and Jack had the difficult task of liaison with the city, rural district, and county surveyors. At the same time they had to be aware of the views of senior engineers, Jackson McCormick and Bailie Russell attached to the Northern Ireland Roads Service, a branch of the Northern Ireland Civil Service. Both McCormick and Russell proved to be well informed and cooperative. The same could be said for William McKee, the rural district surveyor who earned the respect of both Stan and Jack. Major Harold Scott, the county surveyor, was also very supportive and provided valuable information for the plan. Unfortunately the City Surveyor, James MacKinder was less supportive: he seemed to see us as a temporary impediment to what we considered to be his self-aggrandising plans for the city. A particularly difficult proposal for the team to accept was MacKinder's plan for a high-level bypass dual carriageway road (the Lecky Road flyover) that would have effectively severed the Catholic Bogside population from the city centre. One, of course, might have argued that the historic city walls had already done that, but this was such a major proposal affecting a residential area that we had no choice but to review it.

Although not as influenced as the rest of the team by the ideas of Geddes, Stan and Jack shared other important conceptual ideas that were to influence and guide our planning decisions. As was the case with many British and Irish planners of that period, sporadic development, the wasteful use of land, and the destruction of natural resources were anathema to us. Also we all believed that the approach outlined by Professor Colin Buchanan in his book, *Traffic in Towns*, describing his theory of environmental areas, contained some of the most civilised and advanced thinking on handling traffic problems of the modern city.[5] We were able to obtain a copy of his then recent plan for Bath, a better known historic city than Londonderry, where he again demonstrated the efficacy of his concept of subdividing cities into environmental areas.[6] His assertion that traffic should be a function of land use, and not vice versa as most other traffic engineers averred, had a major impact on our team's thinking. The ready acceptance of these ideas by the engineers on our team proved critical to the quality of the plan we eventually produced. In keeping with our ideas on conservation, the prohibition of building on good quality agricultural land would become a key factor in our decisions concerning the location of new development—all of this, notwithstanding the additional costs to the developer implicit with building on poor quality land.

Peter Daniel's appreciation of the natural setting of the city, which he consistently conveyed to us all, and the projected needs for tourism and recreational use were also major factors influencing our ideas on future growth, particularly as it pertained to industry and housing. He was a well-known English architect, planner, and landscape architect for whom I had worked when he was chief architect planner at Livingston New Town in Scotland. Before that appointment he had been deputy chief at Peterlee New Town in North-East England where he and Frank Dixon had received wide acclaim in the architectural press for their innovative ideas on housing and landscape. I had met Peter while I was still a graduate student (albeit a mature one) at Edinburgh and had been much taken with his approach to design and his achievements. His black flowing beard and long hair, his clear open manner of speaking, his obvious enthusiasm for new towns and the natural landscape, his affiliation with the ideas of Geddes (in appearance he even looked like a modern version) drew me, as well as other students, to his guest lectures and seminars. Always casually dressed in black sweater and pants in an age of collar and tie, he was the epitome of all we hoped we would become.

Our views on Peter, however, were not shared by the Establishment, especially when he opposed their efforts to circumvent the principles of sound planning. When he resigned from Livingston New Town in 1964 following a difference of opinion with the general manager, a number of us left with him. He then set up in private practice as a planning and landscape consultant about the time I returned to Munce and Kennedy's office as it was then known. When the Derry team was being assembled, just one meeting with Peter was enough to convince both Jimmy Munce and Bob Simpson that he would add considerable strength and experience to our young team.

Peter's insight and ideas about conserving the landscape and natural setting of the city permeated all the team's concerns about future development, including vehicular traffic. His method of working as a consultant consisted mainly of sitting down with various members of the team at their drawing boards or desks and discussing their various tasks informally, making suggestions where appropriate. In retrospect he noted that our attempts to create country parks from what might now be considered as a very crude landscape assessment, played no small part in the success of preserving areas such as the Faughan River and Lough Enagh. The decision we made early on to advise against permitting any development above the five-hundred-foot contour line was also important in preserving the natural setting of the city. Even more important was the fact that the folly of trying to establish isolated communities on exposed hilltops was avoided.

Although not part of the team, Louis Adair Roche, the design partner in the firm, was also peripherally involved in the plan. Adair, then in his early forties and whom I also regarded as a mentor, was the most flamboyant and dynamic of the partners. At that time within the narrow confines of Belfast, his design ideas would have been considered avant-garde and his political leanings socialist and republican. The latter was not surprising since he was raised in the South and, apart from his architectural education at University College London, had worked many years in Dublin before joining Munce and Kennedy in the late 1950s. After a few years he became a partner, and in the sixties he was responsible for the design of most of the major projects. He was supervising several design projects at the time including a multi-million pound project for Belfast City Hospital, but he would often take time off to join in our discussions on the Derry plan. His support and confirmation of our efforts was important to the team, and he was an excellent resource when it came to urban design issues. He also let it be known, albeit jocularly, that he was keeping a watchful eye on Jimmy and Bob in case they wilted under Unionist pressure. Also peripherally involved was Gordon MacKinnon, then an associate partner and quantity surveyor in the firm, and now senior partner of Consarc, the successors to James Munce Partnership. Gordon advised on cost aspects of the plan and produced a final report on the cost of implementing the plan over a fifteen-year period.

This was the team that set about the task of preparing the Londonderry Area Plan in April and May of 1966. The Terms of Reference set out by the Ministry of Development for discussion in early March first mentioned the recommendations of Sir Robert Matthew and Professor Thomas Wilson regarding centres for industry outside the Belfast Region.[7] It was estimated that by 1981 the population of the urban area of Londonderry (60,000 in 1961) would likely be 80,000, rising to possibly 100,000 by the end of the century. We were required to 'take into account Londonderry as a port, an industrial, commercial, cultural and tourist centre, and to suggest means of stimulating its development'. The area of study was defined as the county borough and rural district of Londonderry but it was to be looked at 'in the context of adjoining areas and the province as a whole'. The terms of reference were extraordinarily well-written and one could certainly see the skilled hand of a planner like Camblin in framing the document. Moreover the terms as set out were definitive yet not constraining and provided good guidelines for us and helped establish priorities.[8]

However, the timetable for completing the plan caused us some concern given the experience of our first meeting with the Steering Committee. A Draft Report and Plan was to be prepared and ready for approval by the Steering Committee in the short period of eighteen months. It was to be a 'broad brush' plan—that is, avoiding specific land use proposals on delimited boundaries, and generally in accord with the aims suggested in the report of the Planning Advisory Group.[9] At first this seemed an impossible task, nevertheless despite our early misgivings, a draft of the final plan would be in the hands of the committee by January 1968, and the final plan would be released to the press on 4 March 1968. Before this would happen the team would experience numerous pitfalls along the way, and a slow and uncertain start would jeopardise the whole project. The underlying political situation would prove to be much worse than even we could have expected, so before we get to that part of the story, let us turn to the physical and social characteristics of the city of Londonderry and its environs.

NOTES
1] Percy Johnson-Marshall, *Rebuilding Cities* (Edinburgh, Edinburgh University Press, 1966), p. 110.
2] Lewis Mumford, *The City in History* (London, Secker and Warburg, 1961), p. 514.
3] Within this derelict corner of the city walls was the site of the ancient O'Donnell tower house or castle. Today on this site stands the new Tower Museum, an attraction for many tourists.
4] While Jim Foster and Fred Boal were both familiar with the work of Geddes, their mentor—and that of most Ulster geographers—was Professor E. Estyn Evans. Evans, who taught at Queen's University Belfast, was trained in geography, archaeology and anthropology. His understanding of Ireland's ancient history and its influence and repercussions on modern Ireland was unique. Naturally, like Geddes, he understood the critical importance of survey.
5] Colin Buchanan, *Traffic in Towns,* London, HMSO.
6] Colin Buchanan, *Bath Report*.
7] Sir Robert Matthew, *Belfast Regional Survey and Plan* (HMSO Cmd 451, 1963). Thomas Wilson, *Economic development in Northern Ireland* (HMSO Cmd 479, 1965).
8] For the full text of the 'Terms of Reference' see Appendix 1.
9] Planning Advisory Group, *The Future of Development Plans* (HMSO, 1965).

4 Place, Folk and Work

The city of Derry, or Londonderry as it was known at the time of the plan, is situated on the River Foyle at the neck of the Inishowen Peninsula, five miles south of the river's confluence with the large sea inlet of Lough Foyle. While no precise records exist, it is known that people have settled in the area at least since the Bronze Age. In 1965 it had a population of around 56,000. By contrast the larger rural district had a population of about 25,000 and extended south-eastwards from the city in an isosceles triangular-like form for a distance of some twenty miles towards the Sperrin Mountains. Its northern boundary ran along the border with County Donegal and the Irish Republic while its western boundary followed that of County Tyrone. The eastern boundary aligned with that of Limavady Rural District and the remainder of County Londonderry. The total area of the county borough and rural district combined is about 134 square miles, and the rural district is bisected by the smaller River Faughan, which terminates in the Foyle Estuary.[1] The Foyle itself flows majestically in a north-easterly direction, then embraced by its lough, reaches out to meet the broad expanse of the Atlantic Ocean.

Dominating the valley of the Foyle lie the foothills of the Sperrin Mountains to the east and the Donegal Hills to the west. From these mountains and hills flow the River Faughan and the smaller tributaries of the Foyle, first racing through the narrow upland glens and then slowing as they wend their way towards the rich, flat floodplain near the Foyle Estuary. About one half of the area lies at heights of 400 feet or more to as high as 1,500 feet in the mountains. The valley of the Foyle is overlooked by high, rounded hills in the vicinity of the city itself and especially to the south where the valley slopes rise steeply from the tidal river. The topography around Derry and the River Foyle contrasts sharply with the flat reclaimed mudflats ('slobland') on the east shore of Lough Foyle protected by sea dykes.

Ian Nairn, referring to the high unemployment figures in Derry in the early sixties, suggested that: 'For forty years it has been the victim of real topographical tragedy, something that it cannot help', and 'inevitably as the industrial goods of Derry have to go largely to the mainland ... it is as remote as Inverness'.[2] Nairn, one must remember, is writing as a visiting Englishman, captivated by the charm of the city and its surroundings, comparing it with Scottish cities isolated from the central belt of Scotland and industrial England by the Highlands. To an American it must seem odd to describe a port city on an island as small as Ireland as being 'remote'. As planners we would carefully refer to Derry's 'apparent remoteness' to emphasise that with fast-improving transportation, what appears to be a geophysical reality could to some extent be overcome by investment in communications.

From the end of the nineteenth century, Belfast had become the major port and industrial centre of Northern Ireland. In the sixties with its population of three-quarters of a million it was the dominant city, absorbing most government investment, including the establishment of two new towns to curtail its growth and accommodate overspill. This, too, was seen as politically accommodating the needs of the Protestant majority in the east of the province at the expense of Catholics in the west and border areas, as Derry was a port also, moreover with a much longer history than Belfast. Notwithstanding Derry's apparent remoteness and the imposition of a political frontier on its doorstep, 'it was', as Jim Foster was quick to point out, 'a giant among pygmies in the local urban hierarchy'.

There were at least two routes by road from Belfast to Derry, the most direct and scenic being west along the shore of Lough Neagh to Randalstown, then through Maghera and the Sperrins via the Glenshane pass to Dungiven, and from there to the city bypassing the village of Claudy. This journey of seventy-three miles took between one-and-a-half and two hours depending on weather conditions. By the mid sixties a motorway had been built reaching as far as Randalstown, and the intention was to build another motorway north from Antrim to Ballymena. From Ballymena the motorway would continue north to Coleraine and head west for Derry across the River Bann and through Limavady. Approaching Derry from Donegal the roads from Letterkenny and the Inishowen Peninsula converged on the city with the roads from the east at the last bridge across the Foyle before the open sea. The nearest alternative bridge was some twelve miles south upstream at the town of Strabane. All of these roads 'were confined by the corridors formed by the Foyle valley, the Lough shore and the Swilly depression'.[3] At one time four railway lines served Derry and the lower level of the two-deck railway bridge originally served to link east and west. The one remaining link between Belfast and Derry now terminated on the east bank or Waterside area of Derry. With dredging the Foyle was navigable as far as the bridge, although in the sixties the Harbour Commission was already considering moving the harbour downstream to accommodate larger vessels.

3. Craigavon Bridge; the lower deck was originally used for rail, but before 1966 was converted for road traffic

With the exception of the polder-like area behind the sea dykes the agricultural landscape is similar to that found elsewhere in the province. The larger farms and fields are found in the valleys of the Foyle and the Faughan, while the smaller farms, more conducive to cattle raising are to be found in the uplands. Most of the land below 400 feet is medium quality agricultural land; above that level, one encounters the denuded landscape of rock and peat bog, gorse and heather that epitomises much of the Irish landscape. On a wet day these conditions, combined with the mist, tend to emphasise the barrier that the Sperrins represent to isolate the Derry area from the more populated eastern part of the province, but on a clear day the beauty of the journey through the sometimes snow-swept Glenshane pass only serves to whet the appetite for what lies ahead.[4]

As one approaches Derry from the steep escarpment on the south bank of the river one can still just perceive the outline of the seventeenth-century citadel, built on a hillock 119 feet high and marking the present central area. This hillock formed the apex of an oak-forested island before the river changed its course leaving a broad marshland area to the west. The centre, marked today by the spire of St Columba's Cathedral, sits amid a tapestry of later building to the north along the river and to the west up the steep Creggan heights, more than 400 feet to the skyline. The city's expansion south and east to the Waterside district is facilitated by the Craigavon Bridge, which spans the Foyle where it narrows to about 100 yards. In the far distance lies the dark blue outline of the Donegal Hills and the Inishowen Peninsula.

The city has a recorded history stretching back to at least 545 when St Colmcille (Columba 521–97) founded a monastery where the present city now stands. At that time there was already a fortification on the island then known as *Daire Calgach*. When the land was given to St Columba for his monastery an oak grove covered the site, giving the place its Irish name *daire*. Following its role as a fortified site and monastic settlement, subsequent centuries evidence development of the site for housing and commercial uses. Records also exist of a growing settlement around the twelfth century which declined by the fourteenth century.

During the Plantation (or colonisation) of Ulster by the British around 1613, Derry was built as a fortified new town to accommodate overspill population and proliferate the trading functions of London. This was part of a regional plan envisaged by representatives of the London Companies and a group of civil servants including Francis Bacon. In choosing new sites for these towns, 'The task of these planners ... must indeed have been an exciting one because provision was made for the building of twenty-three new towns in a country which had few towns at the time'.[5] It must be remembered that at this time London was becoming overcrowded and there was a concerted effort by both the government and city of London to stabilise the population. Apart from the obvious difficulties of controlling a large influx of population over a short timespan, the danger of plague in such circumstances had by now been recognised.[6] The site of Derry was chosen for one of these new towns because of its defensive potential and its location on a navigable river. Londonderry became the English name for the town since it was, '... simply the joining together of two place names to signify the close financial and other connections of the city of London with the ancient site of Derry'.[7]

The new town of Londonderry became one of the last bastides or fortress towns to be built in Western Europe and one of the last with a defensive wall to withstand artillery fire. It may also be truly regarded as the first new town of London preceding by some three centuries Welwyn, Letchworth, and the ring of post-Second World War new towns. A planned grid of streets, with

4. Two views of Derry city centre from Waterside

a central square where the two principal streets crossed, was laid out behind a defensive wall, which, conforming closely to the existing topography, was completed in 1618. At the centre of the square a building combining a market house, town hall, and guard house was planned. Also within the walls St Columba's Cathedral, now the oldest remaining building in use in the city, was completed in 1633.[8]

There is evidence that the plans for Londonderry and the neighbouring new town of Coleraine were well known to the builders of towns in the new American colonies. John Reps, the American planner, argues that James Oglethorpe, the planner of Savannah, Georgia, was aware of the London Companies' town building activities in Ulster. In a tract

34   PLANNING DERRY

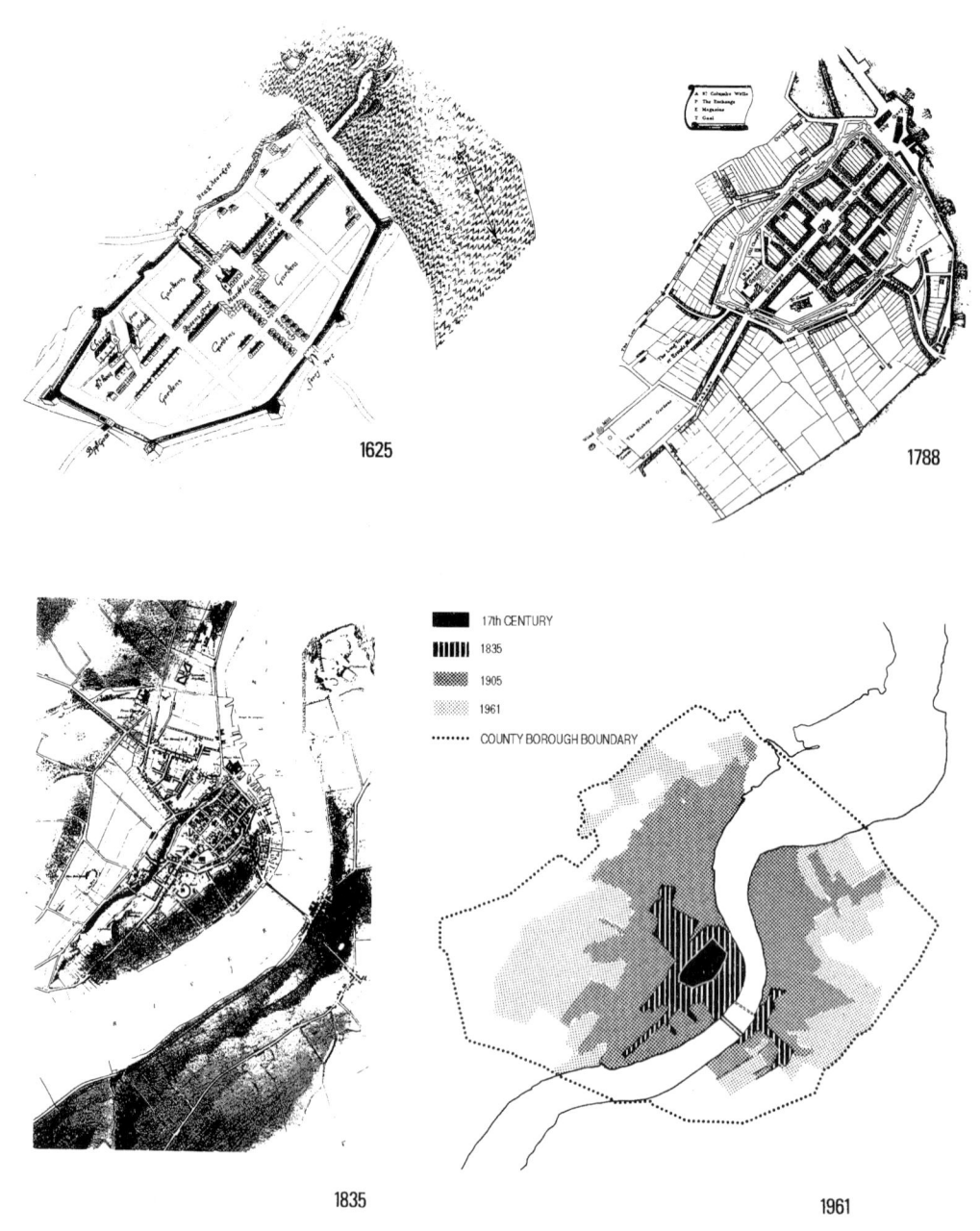

5. Historical growth, from the Londonderry area plan

referring to the Ulster towns attributed to Oglethorpe, he states that they were 'a precedent of our own for Planting Colonies, which perhaps in Part or in the Whole may be worthy of our Imitation'. The central square of Coleraine for example, 'is an almost exact duplicate in shape and its pattern of access streets to that of several open spaces in Savannah'.[9] Reps also notes that 'many of those involved in the Ulster plan were also active in the settlement of Virginia and New England, and it is only logical to assume that some of the experience gained in town building in Northern Ireland under English direction found application in the American Colonies'.[10]

Londonderry's role as a port and market centre expanded in the seventeenth century under the aegis of the Irish Society but remained essentially a fortress town. Other London Companies such as the Fishmongers, Goldsmiths, Skinners, Merchant Taylors, Haberdashers and Vintners were responsible for establishing British settlers in the remainder of the county with the exception of Coleraine, which was also the responsibility of the Irish Society.[11] Outside of the two cities it became difficult to attract British tenants, who were quite naturally concerned for their safety, and there was 'a reluctance to displace Irish natives ... on grounds of trouble and expense'.[12] A fort had been established at Culmore about three miles downstream from Londonderry to warn of approaching danger of attack from the sea. By 1640 the city had grown to, 'the largest in the six planted counties' and had become 'very similar in size to Boston, which in 1640 had a population of 1200'.[13] The defences however were to be needed by the settlers throughout the century, and the city had to withstand a number of sieges. The most famous was that of 1689 when an Irish-, Scots-, and French-Catholic army in support of James II's claim to the Engish throne attacked the city, but the city inhabitants of mostly Protestant colonists had already declared their support for William of Orange. A boom was placed across the river to prevent the garrison from being relieved, but this was broken by the British supply ships *Mountjoy* and *Phoenix* after a siege lasting more than a hundred days. The city, in addition to its own inhabitants, was overflowing with refugees who had fled from the advancing Jacobite forces, and large numbers died of starvation during the siege.[14] The whole fabric of the city also sustained considerable damage, and the task of rebuilding began in 1690 following a report on the extent of the damage by Captain Francis Neville.[15]

During the eighteenth century Londonderry slowly recovered as new residential and civic buildings arose within, and to a smaller extent, outside the walls. Its military role also waned in significance as it developed its new role as a commercial centre and port. Draconian laws imposed upon Irish Catholics ensured more peaceful conditions for those loyal to the crown, and another wave of immigration by British, and later French Huguenot, settlers increased the Ulster population. At the same time Derry's expansion as a port brought prosperity and increased trade with the American colonies. During the early part and indeed throughout the century, the port was to become the point of departure to the New World for many Scots-Irish Presbyterian emigrants also beginning to have their liberties impinged upon by the penal laws of the British church-state. Many of these new colonists and their descendants would later play leading roles in the American movement for independence. Huguenot settlers with their many skills had been encouraged by the British to establish roots in Ulster and to develop a linen industry, the climate being conducive to the growing of flax. By the end of the century Derry would become central as the market and main port for the export of Irish linen.

By the middle of the century the city had already begun to prosper and expand marginally outside the walls. In 1769 plans were being prepared for a new (the first) bridge over the River Foyle.[16] Fine Georgian façades lined the major streets within the walls, and Bishop's Gate was rebuilt to a new design. Finally the bridge, a prefabricated wooden structure, was completed in 1791 as designed by the Boston, Massachusetts, engineering firm of Lemuel Cox and Jonathan Thompson, experts on long-span structures. The great Scottish bridge builder, Thomas Telford would have been about thirty-four at this time and probably building his first canal structures as

36   PLANNING DERRY

6. Historic Derry: (a) City Walls 1614–18 (above left). (b) St Columb's Cathedral 1628–33 (above right). (c) The Courthouse 1813–17 (below left). (d) The Deanery 1833 (below right).

a prelude to his bridge-building feats. The fact that American engineers were employed for the Londonderry bridge serves to illustrate further the strength of the city's port and its links with America.

With the burgeoning linen industry and the growing use of the port for emigration, especially in the years following the Potato Famine of 1845, commerce in the city flourished. These factors and the concomitant growing trade with the western hemisphere saw the population of Derry rise from around 11,000 in 1800 to 40,000 by the end of the century, and the city experienced a belated industrial revolution.[17] Many fine public buildings were completed between 1800 and 1840 as the city began to expand. These included the Courthouse (1813–17), the Bishop's Palace (remodelled 1803), the Deanery (1833), Great James Street Presbyterian Church (1835), the Asylum (1814), and next to it Foyle College (1840). By 1863 a two-deck iron railway bridge was

7. 1863 Carlisle Bridge

built to replace the older eighteenth-century wood-frame structure and to accommodate the four rail links then serving the city. The industrial growth by then included the establishment of the shirt-based industry, shipbuilding, and distilling complementing the more established industries such as bacon curing. By 1911 Derry had become the fourth largest town in Ireland; yet following the First World War the city began to decline with the closing of the shipbuilding industry, the demise of its distilleries, and contraction of other industries, especially shirt manufacturing after the depression of the thirties.

The inability of Derry to compete with the more accessible larger centres of Belfast and Glasgow and the onset of the thirties depression are obvious factors in its decline, but Derry was also hard hit by the imposition of the political border in 1921. This action automatically relegated the city from that of a significant Irish port to the less prestigious status of a border town between the Republic of Ireland and the UK. While today the major part of Donegal is still dependent on Derry for many of its trade, social, and cultural functions, there can be no doubt that the border diminished Derry's potential influence. Both the Catholic and Protestant population of Derry had assumed that the city would automatically become part of the new Irish Free State in 1922, but this was not to be.

A new two-level bridge (the Craigavon Bridge) was built in 1933 to replace the 1863 bridge; the lower deck was built for rail, but significantly, the upper deck was built strong enough to withstand loads from tanks and armoured vehicles.

The economic stagnation that persisted through the thirties was to some extent alleviated by the onset of the Second World War when Derry's role as a port was once again perceived as strategically important. It became a major naval base first at the outbreak of war for British and later, in 1942, for American naval forces. In this role it was the centre of the Allied counter-offensive against German submarine attacks on shipping in the North Atlantic. Following the war the city's prosperity began once again to wane, although some new-found industrial developments

8. 1933 Bridge

began to appear. Most significant was the establishment of the complex of petrochemical industries at Maydown. Though by nature these industries did not require a large work force, they were an indication of the advantages that the area still held for industries requiring the open port facilities that had made Derry attractive through the ages.

In 1968 we reported in the Londonderry Area Plan (14) that for the area encompassed by about thirty miles from its centre, Derry remained, 'the principal regional centre for port facilities, some higher order shopping, collection and distributional activities, specialized medical services and a variety of educational, cultural and social facilities'.[18] This area included the towns of Moville, Buncrana, Letterkenny, and Stranorlar in County Donegal; Strabane in County Tyrone; and Dungiven and Limavady in County Londonderry.

9. Petro-chemical industries at Maydown

10. Village Newbuildings

The natural growth and spread of the city by 1966 had reached beyond the designated county borough limits into the rural district. Beyond the contiguous built-up areas along the principal traffic routes, it had spawned urban villages such as Prehen and Strathfoyle. Further out still were the older villages such as Claudy, Eglinton, Newbuildings, and Park.[19] Apart from villages, clusters of public housing built by the Rural District Council had sprung up along rural routes, some of them, such as Lettershendony, in rather isolated and inhospitable locations. According to Census figures, by 1966 the population of the city was more than 55,000 while the rural district and city combined to reach more than 81,000. As was the case elsewhere in Ireland, many people lived in dispersed dwellings and small farms. These patterned the countryside in a symbiotic relationship with the city and embracing work, commerce, and recreation activities. Unlike modern urban dispersal resulting from a high incidence of car ownership, this type of dispersal stems from a traditional native love of earth and nature and the reliance on garden allotments to provide food.[20] Therefore, although many people worked in Derry, they continued to live in the countryside.

The plan group's studies showed that 2 per cent of the work-force were involved in primary or extractive industries involving agriculture, commercial salmon fishing, and quarrying. Another 40 per cent worked in the manufacturing sector, which included shirt and pyjama manufacturing, engineering and electrical goods, chemical and allied industries, and food industries including the traditional bacon curing industry. The remaining 58 per cent were employed in the growing service sector resulting from Derry's regional influence and its function as a port and naval base.[21] The potential of a growing population in the area resulting from high natural growth rates was offset by an equally high outward migration rate stemming from the area's long history of chronic unemployment. Moreover in the clothing industries more than 90 per cent of the work-force was female, and of the total work-force involved in manufacturing, 5,300 females were employed as compared to 4,800 males.

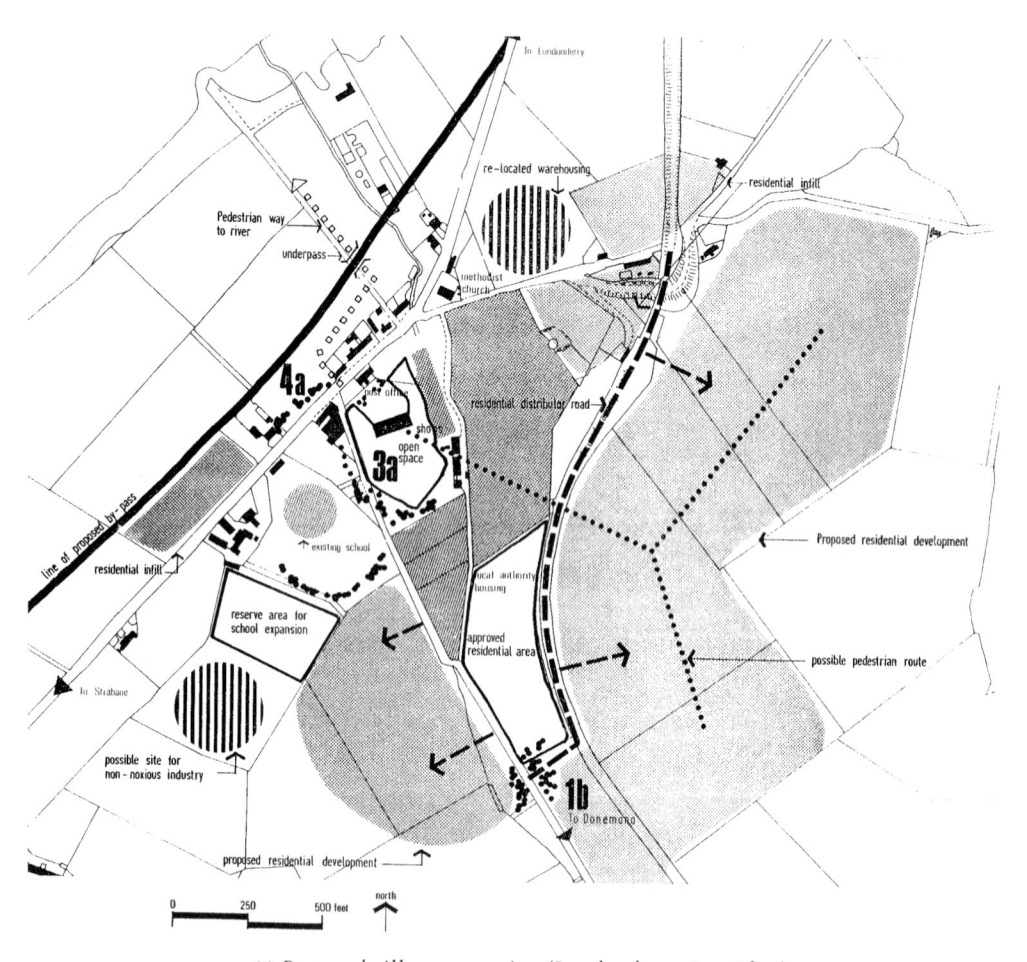

11. Proposed village expansion (Londonderry Area Plan)

Nairn attributed the area's high unemployment rate to the city's location and notes that:

> A less proud place would have had its spirit broken under its crippling topographical disadvantage. Derry needs help, and its pride is not the false variety that would scorn assistance. There is a famous inscription in the Cathedral, recording the original foundation:
> *If stones could speake then London's prayse would sounde*
> *Who built this church and cittie from the grounde.*
> It is time that the bulging money-bags of London began to merit Derry's praise again by looking after the welfare of its oldest, most distant, and most individual New Town.[22]

As planners we were determined to produce a plan that would attract both government and private sector investment in the area. We did not know of the difficulties that lay ahead and, given our mien, would probably not have been distracted from the task even if we had. We were soon to learn that the politics of planning involved more than the resolution of the conflicts of private interest with those of public good.

NOTES

1] James Munce Partnership, *Londonderry Area Plan* (Belfast, 1968), p. 4. Excerpts from the final plan and reports have been freely adapted for the present publication.
2] Ian Nairn, *Britain's Changing Towns* (London, British Broadcasting Corporation, 1967), p. 115.
3] *Londonderry Area Plan*, p. 5.
4] Ibid., p. 7.
5] Camblin, *Town,* p. 19.
6] A.E.J. Morris, *History of Urban Form,* 3rd ed. (Harlow, Longman Scientific & Technical, 1994), p. 249.
7] James Stevens Curl, Introduction, *The Londonderry Plantation 1609–1914* (Chichester, Phillimore & Co. Ltd, 1986), p. xxii.
8] *Londonderry Area Plan,* p. 10; Camblin, *Town,* p. 33.
9] John W. Reps, *Town Planning in Frontier America* (Princeton, Princeton University Press, 1965), p. 251.
10] John W. Reps, *The Making of Urban America* (Princeton, Princeton University Press, 1965), p. 12.
11] Curl, *Londonderry Plantation,* p. 74.
12] Ibid.
13] Brian Mitchell, *Derry A City Invincible* (Eglinton, Grocers' Hall Press, 1994), p. 40.
14] There are many detailed accounts of this early plantation period in Londonderry's history the most relevant here being that contained in Curl.
15] Curl, *Londonderry Plantation,* pp. 105–7.
16] Ibid., p. 109.
17] Brian Lacy, *Historic Derry* Irish Heritage Series: 61 (Dublin, Eason & Son Ltd, 1988), p. 42.
18] *Londonderry Area Plan,* p. 14.
19] Ibid., p. 8.
20] E. Estyn Evans, *Irish Heritage, the Landscape, The People and Their Work* (Dundalk, W. Tempest Dundalgan Press, 1942), p. 163: 'In essentials Ireland is and has been a peasant country, and it will be well to examine objectively some of the characteristics of peasant society. A permanent link with the soil on which man lives and works is the essence of peasantry: and in this work of the fields woman co-operates with man.'
21] Ibid., p. 25.
22] Nairn, *Britain's Changing Towns,* pp. 122–3.

5 The Housing Crisis

We had spent the time from our appointment in March to our next meeting with the Steering Committee in June beginning the surveys necessary to prepare the plan. We had yet to determine if and how the planning process should be adapted to take account of a number of developments in the pipeline. The June meeting opened with the Chairman, Commander Anderson, forcefully reminding us once more that it was the Steering Committee that had been established to produce a plan for the area. Our role, as he saw it, was to serve as technical advisers. I was relieved that Jimmy had now decided to present the report prepared by Stan and myself, and that we were only to field questions when necessary. This was obviously more acceptable to the Chairman and became the *modus operandi* for all our meetings. Jimmy knew that a number of road proposals were of immediate concern and mentioned the need to consider a second river crossing when establishing the future road pattern. He went on to assure the committee that road improvements and other developments in the pipeline, which would not prejudice the overall planning of the area, would not be unnecessarily delayed.

Councillor James Doherty succinctly explained that he saw the task of the committee as operating at two levels. First, there was the task of dealing with pressing situations requiring first aid and second, the preparation of a plan to accommodate future growth. He then raised the question of housing need in the area, explaining that within the city boundary, land had become restricted for new housing, and many needy families were living in deplorable conditions. Housing need had become critical, and he suggested that we prepare an interim report defining possible sites for executive and public housing as a matter of urgency.

We already knew there was a long waiting list for public housing (which in the UK and Northern Ireland was subsidised), and the city had been involved since the fifties in a number of developments carried out by a quasi-government organisation, or Statutory Authority, the Northern Ireland Housing Trust.[1] Recently the Trust had been involved in the urban renewal of the Bogside (the area immediately west of the walls), which had housed a large part of the Catholic population since early times. Although the Trust, with a reputation for quality housing, had done their best to rehouse the existing population, this could only be achieved by building at a higher population density.[2] To achieve this they built ten-storey deck-access blocks based on the ideas of the Swiss born architect, Le Corbusier, and the English interpretation of these ideas found at Roehampton in London and Park Hill in Sheffield.

Redevelopment (or urban renewal) is the process of rehousing people living in areas of unfit housing, demolishing the housing, and then rebuilding to a new pattern and scale. It should be noted that even when redeveloping areas using high-rise buildings (more than four storeys) it is impossible to rehouse all former residents of an area. From my experiences as a planner in Liverpool, I learnt first hand of the problems created when the life of existing communities is disrupted by large-scale renewal proposals preceded by slum clearance, and had come to prefer more gradual approaches involving rehabilitation wherever possible. In the early part of the century Patrick Geddes had already pointed out to the authorities in India that what they considered to be slums

12. Unfit housing in Derry (a) Nineteenth-century. Photo, courtesy David Bigger and Terry McDonald. (b) Early twentieth-century. Bogside—Housing Trust redevelopment area. (c) Deck access flats, Sheffield. (d) Rossville St flats under construction 1966. (e) New deck access flats, Derry. (f) Demolition of Rossville St flats 1996

were in fact living, viable communities that required only conservative surgery.[3] Michael Young and Peter Willmott in their 1953–5 study of Bethnal Green in East London had already described the importance of family and kinship relationships in working-class areas.[4]

The Housing Trust was attempting by careful phasing to rehouse as many of the existing Bogside community as they could, particularly those who wished to remain in the area. Actually they were also compelled to do so by virtue of the fact that the few sites left within the city boundary were unsuitable (according to the city), and there were problems with providing water and sewage to sites outside the boundary (according to rural district). However, as our subsequent studies were to show there was no scarcity of sites close to the city. Instead there was a politically motivated lack of will to deal with the problem, by both the city and the rural district.

Not only was the housing situation for the working class critical in Derry but it was becoming so in Belfast and many other parts of Northern Ireland. Even as late as 1973, the housing stock in Northern Ireland totalling 455,500 was comprised of 62,100 (13.3 per cent) dwellings built before 1870, 95,100 (20.9 per cent) before 1919, 75,250 (16.6 per cent) before 1944, and the remaining 223,050 (49 per cent) after 1944.[5] Of the total, almost half (46.6 per cent) or 212,140 dwellings were owner occupied. The high birthrate in Northern Ireland and the formation of new families combined with a fast-deteriorating pre-1930s existing stock of dwellings was sufficient in itself to indicate why demand for new housing far outstripped the supply. The county boroughs and rural district councils had dragged their feet concerning housing compared to their counterparts in the rest of the UK. Had it not been for the efforts of the Housing Trust, what was already a grave situation would have been immeasurably worse, but their efforts in Derry had been stalled, and in its 1966 annual report the Housing Trust noted that:

> As there is virtually no land left for housing within the city boundary it is essential that the Trust should acquire new sites in the Londonderry Rural District with a view to undertaking a substantial programme of house-building in the vicinity of the city.... The grave concern which is widely felt about the shortage of housing in Londonderry is reflected in the report on *Londonderry as a Location for New Industry* submitted to the government by the Economic Council early this year. This report states that 'the visiting industrialist ... is unlikely to feel confident of being able to establish a new undertaking successfully in a centre where there is an acute shortage of houses'. It states further that industrialists should be assured that houses for key workers would be available without difficulty or delay. The report recommends, therefore, that the Steering Committee should as a first priority approve areas for new housing. In the meantime, the Trust is unable to build to ease the acute housing shortage in Londonderry ... and to prevent the redevelopment scheme from coming to a standstill.[6]

I discovered later that James Doherty had strongly supported the efforts of the Trust, although this had made him unpopular with some of the local Catholic population who perceived redevelopment as a Unionist ruse to keep Catholics penned up in their traditional electoral districts, and the preservation of the *status quo* was the only means by which Unionists could retain control of city government. Years later Doherty explained to me that he was moved by the deplorable conditions in which families were living, and he felt that his own nationalistic goals and political advantage were secondary to their needs. He knew that although popular, to take a negative stand would have resulted in even greater misery and deprivation for his constituents; moreover it would have speeded up the impending violence lurking just below the surface. Although I was unaware of his position or role regarding housing in Derry at this June meeting, I felt that his impassioned enquiry about housing sites was something that could not await the outcome of the plan. Other members of the Steering Committee asked questions about the provision of sites for private development. The provision of executive housing was recognised as a means of attracting incoming industrialists. Since it appeared on the surface that the whole area of housing was of interest to the committee, we agreed to report back as soon as possible.

On the return journey to Belfast, Bob Simpson expressed his concern about the political implications of what we had been asked to do. He had discovered that the Rural District Council had not been amenable in the past to assisting the city with its housing needs. We were also beginning to understand that the Unionists in Derry and the rural district worked together to maintain the *status quo* in the city. This was the major factor affecting the lack of availability of sites. To make things even more complicated we had just begun to organise the various surveys needed to prepare a plan within a very short time-frame and now were immediately faced with a major distraction of identifying housing sites. We decided that this project should be operated from the Derry office with Alan Bradshaw taking the initiative. To avoid limiting our planning options we also decided to look for sites on the periphery of the city, away from major traffic routes. We assumed that if we could identify a number of sites that would round off or infill existing housing developments the accumulation of numbers of dwellings on these sites might ameliorate the housing shortage. The sporadic field-by-field housing developments in the rural district were a problem and had begun adversely to affect the attractiveness of the natural landscape. Peter Daniel's considerable experience in housing and landscape would be at Alan's disposal, and Stanley Cochrane undertook the task of providing an engineering appraisal of the sites to take account of soil conditions, drainage and sewage.

On 15 September 1966, we were able to produce our first report to the Steering Committee (Report No. 1—Interim Housing Report) making available six sites ranging in size from 13.6 acres to 56.4 acres and accommodating potentially 2,500 dwellings. This number would have provided sufficient public housing for those on the city's and rural district's waiting lists, and a number of the locations were also suitable for single-family executive-type dwellings. At the meeting James Doherty expressed satisfaction with the report and made a motion for its acceptance with two of the sites referred to the Housing Trust for its consideration. The committee voted against the motion. The chairman and others complained that they needed more time to consider the report. There were additional requests for more detail and for studies to be made regarding the availability of water and sewage to the sites. A more precise breakdown of sites available for private housing was also requested, and the chairman acknowledged the request that the Rural District Council would need time to study the report. A motion by James Doherty and Paddy Gormley to have the report sent to the rural district and county borough councils for information was denied. Unionist members were probably well aware that had the report been sent officially to the councils, the information would have been public knowledge in no time.

As if to add to the burden and distraction from our main task that we now faced over the Steering Committee's attitude to the housing crisis, yet another major problem emerged. Roy Henderson, the Derry town clerk, had written to the committee to raise the matter of the redevelopment of the Waterside District of the city. A scheme had been prepared by the prominent firm of English architects and planners, Covell Matthews for a large-scale modern shopping mall

46 PLANNING DERRY

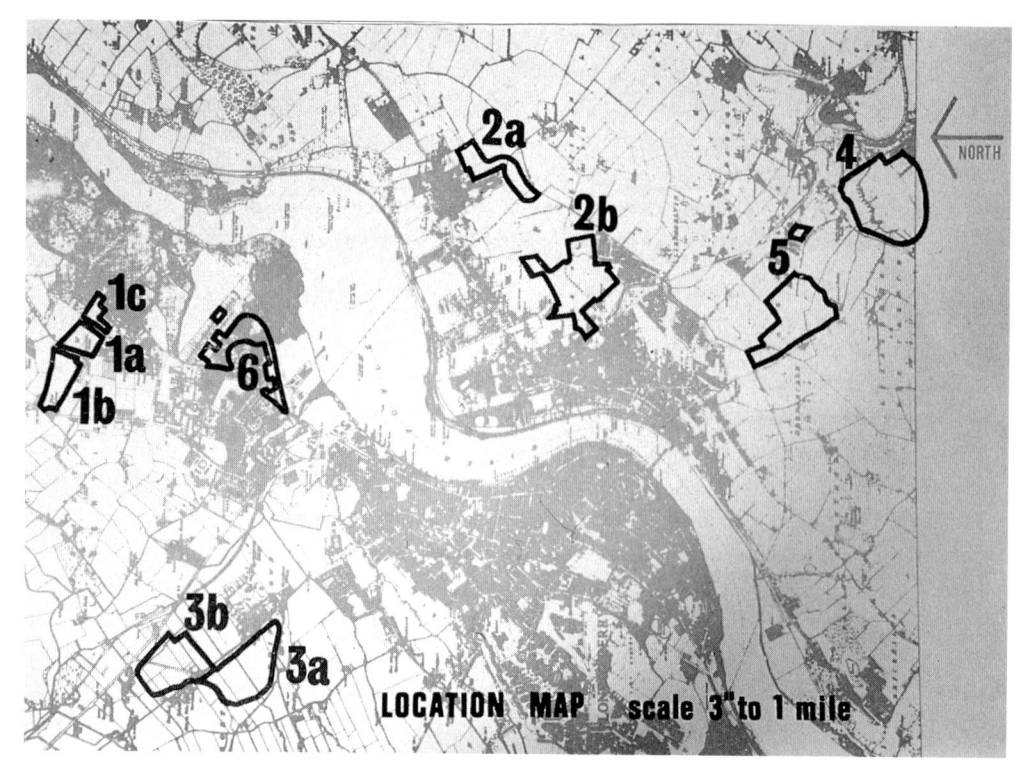

13. Infill housing sites from unpublished Report No 1

to include office development and apartments. As well as proposals for road improvements in the area, there was a proposal by the city to construct a new regional shopping centre as part of an urban renewal project in the Waterside area. The fact that this was located directly across the Foyle from the historic city centre made it a major planning issue. We had previously met with Brian Falk, the partner in charge of the project, and had received a copy of the proposal. The report showed the character of the new centre, and included an economic shopping appraisal that suggested the new centre would be complementary to the existing city centre and would have little effect on its continuing commercial viability.

Contrary to this view and after studying the report, we were concerned that a development of this magnitude would have a negative effect on the existing centre and any proposals we might suggest for its expansion. In addition we felt a new centre in this particular location on the Waterside would further restrict the little flexibility we had to provide solutions for the growing traffic problem including the location of a second bridge. Roy Henderson was nothing if not persistent in his demands that we deal with the issue of Waterside, and in anticipation of just this kind of difficulty we had taken the precaution of including Fred Boal and Geoff Powell of Gerald Eve & Co., on our team from the outset. Both were to prove invaluable, not just in dealing with this issue, but in our subsequent studies of commerce and industry in the area. At this meeting, therefore, we had enough information to convince the Steering Committee of the need to delay action on the Waterside proposal, but I sensed that Roy Henderson was somewhat peeved by the decision. Both he and James MacKinder were already beginning to play their roles as servants of civic

THE HOUSING CRISIS 47

progress subjected to the roadblocks and delays imposed by upstart planners and Stormont government bureaucrats. Yet, for our part, we had not completely closed the door on the proposal. Rather we had bought the time necessary to study its impact on the central area and on the capacity of the city region to absorb additional commercial development.

The October meeting of the Steering Committee began with Stan Cochrane commenting on the various road proposals planned by the city. This included road developments associated with the proposed Waterside centre. While the widening of Duke Street could proceed while our surveys were being carried out, Bob Simpson asked that other road proposals be delayed for a period of six months to enable us to complete our traffic study. In reply to a question from James Doherty, I confirmed that we wanted to strengthen the central area and that other major shopping centres, including that proposed for Waterside, should remain at the district level.

A discussion of our housing report took up the remainder of the meeting. Councillor Mackey from the Rural District led the discussion by pointing out that he thought the consultants had been 'pressed to prepare their report too hurriedly'. He commented on each of the sites and, with one or two exceptions where he thought executive-type housing might be suitable, found a reason to object to all of them. These objections ranged from lack of water or sewage, to time to investigate services, to the inappropriateness of the location. Finally he noted that while we had estimated the most urgent needs of the city at 550 dwellings and those of the rural district at 500, the Rural District already had 456 houses in the pipeline. Since most of these sites would accommodate mainly city dwellers, the Rural District Council would want to know where the money was coming from to finance the needed infrastructure. He then mentioned that before the establishment of the Steering Committee he had talked to former Minister of Development William Craig, who had suggested a modern satellite town well away from the existing city and equipped with modern amenities. This satellite town would be enough to meet the housing needs of the area. Other members of the committee raised objections over the suitability of the sites for public housing. Commander Anderson suggested that once the Lecky Road scheme was completed and a possible site at Foyle Street redeveloped, the city's immediate needs could be largely accommodated. James Doherty estimated that 4,000 houses would be needed to accommodate overspill population from the city, and a satellite town would not provide an immediate solution. The immediate need was for at least 500 houses. In the end, over the protestations of James Doherty and Paddy Gormley, we were asked to reconsider our report in the light of the committee's comments.

The meeting was then adjourned rather abruptly without any date being set for the next meeting. We felt that we had got off to a very bad start with the committee, and things looked worse than we could ever have expected. A perfectly good short-term solution to the housing crisis had been rejected, and we were uncertain as to what our next step would be. With the exception of James Doherty and Paddy Gormley we seemed to have alienated almost everyone on the committee. None of us on the planning team was aware that Jimmy and Bob were having less than fruitful meetings with various officials and committee members. Much later I was told that on one such occasion they were greeted by a Rural District official who remained seated as they entered, his feet on the desk, 'What the f— do you boys think you're doing here anyway? We'll see to it that you never produce a plan!' Bob Simpson also received a letter from the Clerk of the Council, dated 22 November 1966, suggesting that we consider approval of council housing at a remote site at Lettershendony and 'that the existing sewage disposal works and the water supply to the present site are capable of serving the proposed additional houses'. At one point there was even a suggestion of building a major settlement (Craig's suggested satellite town?) in the area to accommodate city overspill. Jim Foster was later to ironically describe the suggested site in a report as, 'an area of indeterminate drainage' or to put it succinctly, a bog!

Even without knowledge of the difficulties Jimmy and Bob were facing in their public relations efforts, it appeared that we were up against forces on the committee who wished to manipulate the planning process for their own purposes. To me James Doherty seemed to be the only one on the committee who understood what we were trying to do. He obviously had a knowledge of the area that could prove useful to us, and now that I was beginning to grasp what I saw as the injustice of the political situation in Derry, I felt drawn to him in some inexplicable way. Later while staying overnight in Derry at my sister's home I called him on the telephone, requested to see him, and was invited to his home that evening. Once there, I discussed the impasse we had reached in our work with the committee and my concerns about the political situation. He was disappointed that our housing report had been rejected, but had been working in the same climate for many years and knew of all the difficulties we would face. Patience and persistence were two qualities obviously not lacking in his character. I learnt of his background in economics and his genuine interest in the planning process. His expressions of enthusiasm for the city and its potential for sustained growth were inspiring, and he was convinced that if we could produce a realistic plan, it would be difficult for the Steering Committee to oppose it.

I shared with him the determination of the team to prepare a plan based on our analysis of the area's assets and on realistic projections for its future. He felt that we had proved our integrity by producing an unbiased report and hoped he could be helpful in getting it accepted. I knew I was taking a political risk by contacting James, and I know he was probably also taking a risk inviting me to his home. But it was a move I would never regret. We became firm friends, and as I was to continue discussing the progress of the plan with him at future meetings, I began to think of him in much the same way as our planning consultants. His advice and support were essential in confirming my own confidence in the import of what we were doing. When I discussed our meetings with him recently he modestly explained his unflagging support for the plan and his major role in its implementation as simply a case of being, 'always interested in broad brush strategic decisions'. For James Doherty at that time politics had to be 'the art of the possible'. He was not prepared 'to let the city go to rack and ruin' and he 'could see the coming of the Common Market and Derry becoming a backwater if matters were allowed to continue as in the past'.

There was little he could do in the fifties and early sixties other than accept under protest the reality of the gerrymander and the consequent housing of the population along ethnic lines. The North Ward of the city, for example, had only a 60 per cent Unionist majority, and it would have taken little more than a 10 per cent movement of the Nationalist population to shift the balance. While there was no great demand for new housing for the Protestant population, an urgent need existed for the Catholic population. It was for this reason alone that James Doherty had assisted the Housing Trust in their proposal to develop the Bogside with high-density housing, including the multi-storeyed deck-access blocks at Rossville Street. The rent equalisation policy of the Trust ensured that rents were affordable for even the most impoverished families. Yet forty years later, as a member of the Board of the Northern Ireland Housing Executive, Doherty was to take pleasure in voting to demolish these high-rise blocks once their usefulness was outlived and the Catholic population was no longer restricted by the boundaries of a Unionist-imposed ghetto.

Looking back it is fair to say that without James Doherty's support from the very beginning, our work would have been doomed to failure. He was only one member of the Steering Committee, but for me he became the one person I could trust politically and from whom I could expect both reasoned criticism or approval, and I availed myself of his wisdom and guidance on every possible occasion.

But on this, the occasion of my first visit, I knew nothing of the events touching the life of James Doherty that I have just described. I felt the inexplicable and irrational doubts and fears that one encounters for the first time when coming face to face with the romantic aura of intrigue surrounding Irish politics. James and I scarcely knew each other, yet here I was following my best instincts and revealing where my hitherto unexpressed sympathies had always lain. Many of my friends and some members of my family would have felt betrayed had they known that my theoretical support of the labour movement and Irish Nationalism was moving into the realm of the practical. Yet I could not bring myself to hate the British or dwell on the injustices of the past as Catholics did. I had never felt the pain nor suffered the oppression ever alive in their memories and passed on from generation to generation and still experienced in Catholic ghettos. A convinced modernist, educated in British schools, I agreed with Percy Johnson-Marshall, himself a Catholic, who after his experiences in the province told me 'the whole situation in Ireland is medieval!'

It was a while before I informed Jimmy and Bob that I had established a relationship with James Doherty on my own initiative and that I thought it was important to have his input as we prepared the plan. Jimmy liked the idea of involving him as he undertook the task of fending off the pressure from the commander and others. Alan Bradshaw was also given free rein to explore every avenue with every person who could help us prepare the plan. Although we now appeared to be in the doldrums as the weeks went by without any contact from the Steering Committee, the work of collecting and sifting through the mountains of information went on. Soon we would become familiar with every part of the area as we surveyed the first maps and diagrams looking for clues that would inform our decisions.

In some ways the absence of Steering Committee meetings allowed us to focus more clearly on the bigger picture and enabled us to explore various hypothetical scenarios on city expansion. Nevertheless the uncertainty of what was going on politically with majority Unionist members of the committee and the threat that the whole exercise might grind to a halt was ever present. We reasoned that it would be difficult for the Steering Committee to terminate our contract without exposing themselves publicly on the housing issue and their attempt to maintain the *status quo*. Jimmy Munce also reassured us that the endangered profitability of the project, incurred by the delay, was of secondary concern to the importance of the publication of the plan for professional acclaim and for establishing the firm in the planning field. He emphasised that he would be 'prepared to lose money to make a good plan'. Not unreasonably, he hoped that a successful outcome would lead to more profitable architectural work in housing and commercial development. Weeks were to turn into months before we again established contact with the Steering Committee, although we knew that Jimmy and Bob were doing their best to get things moving again. Yet I could not erase from my mind the memory of a cocktail reception several weeks earlier where Jimmy had introduced me to William Craig, then still minister of development and a right wing member of O'Neill's Cabinet. He introduced me as the person who would be responsible for the Derry Plan. 'Ah,' the Minister had remarked with what I might only have imagined to be an ominous smile and tone of voice, 'I know what I would do with Derry'.

My comparative political naïvety had by now been replaced by an almost unfettered imagination that suspected political intrigue around every corner. Although I had assumed the worst from his remark, Craig was considered to be an able and progressive minister of development (he was made an honorary member of the Town Planning Institute in 1966). His subsequent role as minister of home affairs, his right-wing opposition to the reforms of O'Neill, showed him in a different light.

NOTES

1] The Northern Ireland Housing Trust was established in 1945 to supplement the efforts of local authorities who retained the statutory responsibility for housing in their areas until their function was subsumed along with those of the local authorities by the Northern Ireland Housing Executive in 1972. The Trust had from its founding completed a total of 75,000 new dwellings. It also established a record for fairness in its policy for allocation on a points system based on need. Most local authorities on the other hand were discriminatory in their allocations, with preference given on the basis of religious/political affiliation. This was a major issue in the civil rights campaign of 1968.
2] Housing density, a term used by planners, is a measurement normally expressed in persons, dwellings, or habitable rooms per acre.
3] Jaqueline Tyrwhitt, ed., *Patrick Geddes in India* (London, Lund Humphries, 1947), pp. 40–59.
4] Michael Young and Peter Willmott, *Family and Kinship in East London* (Routledge and Kegan Paul, 1957; revised edition Baltimore, Pelican Books, 1962).
5] Northern Ireland Housing Executive. House Condition Survey 1974.
6] *Annual Report of the Northern Ireland Housing Trust* (1966), pp. 12–13.

6 Breaking the Stalemate

November and December passed and we entered 1967 with Bob and Jimmy still exploring ways of moving beyond the housing issue. Somehow we managed to keep our hopes and spirits alive as our knowledge of the area grew and the possibilities for future growth captured our imaginations. Perhaps, we reasoned, we had been too optimistic about our first report.

The location of new housing and the possible extension of the city boundary were controversial political issues for the Steering Committee, so why not present them with reports that were less so and leave the controversial issues to the end? I don't know who thought of it but it was a brilliant strategy. Looking back I like to think it was me, since I had just returned from the US inculcated with the incremental American approach to problem solving, but it could just as easily have been Jim Foster who had been drafting the first reports or perhaps Peter Daniel who was carrying around a copy of Machiavelli's *The Prince* about this time. For example, if we were to present reports on shopping, industry, population, and other incontrovertible issues we could ask for approval of these reports by the committee. Since decisions on these issues narrowed the options for housing location (they were spatially interrelated by journey-to-work patterns, shopping, etc.) the committee could arguably not refuse to consider housing options irrespective of their political connotations. Also these reports taken together would be the essence of the plan, and we would therefore be making measured progress towards our ultimate goal.

This meant that the small planning team would have to produce several finished planning documents over a short period of time instead of simply a draft interim plan and final plan, but finished and approved documents would make it difficult for the committee to go back on its own decisions and delay the plan. Altogether this would mean an incredible workload for everyone, especially for Jim Foster and Mike's publication team, but everyone embraced the idea. It also appealed to the more devious side of Jimmy Munce's character, and Bob Simpson, though worried about the expenditure involved, acquiesced. In November we came up with the idea of presenting a progress report that would become 'Report No. 1–Interim Report'. Since this would displace the original Report No 1, the Steering Committee were bound to accept such a document. By making it the first formal report we would be able to set aside the original controversial report on housing and include it under the broader heading of a report for information rather than one calling for immediate action. In a way this could be looked upon as a retreat but it could open the door to progress where previously it had been firmly closed. The Ministry of Development had requested that we produce a preliminary draft plan by March 1967 if possible and a draft report and plan by the following September. With our new strategy we would have to produce a report every four or five weeks on average. Despite the many difficulties and heavy workload for everyone involved, the stepped-up reporting would introduce an element of discipline into the process that was to pay dividends in the long run.

It was early March 1967 before the Interim Report could be presented to the committee. Jimmy and Bob had informed us that, if we were to move forward, we would have to omit two of the interim housing sites on the west bank at the request of the Rural District Council and two of the sites on the east bank would have to be reduced in size. The council claimed that these sites could not be serviced by water and sewage at a reasonable cost within a short time period. Although we now knew from our own findings and working with their officials that these excuses could only be political, we reasoned that there was still enough land available to meet the most urgent housing needs. This small concession would at least allow us to make progress with the plan. Compared to the first report we had made to the committee, there was a reduction in the number of dwellings that could be accommodated from 2,500 to 1,460, although we pointed out that with slightly higher densities these remaining sites could accommodate 1,720 new homes. Later the Rural District would dispute even the minimum figure and argue for more private and less public housing.

This had now become a progress report rather than a report solely addressing the housing issue, and it appeared to be more acceptable to the committee. It included our first estimates of land needed outside the city boundary for various uses to accommodate a projected population growth of 23,500 by 1980. The problem of land for industrial development was less acute, although expansion of some of the existing sites both inside and outside the city boundary would be required. The issue of preserving good-quality agricultural land and the natural amenities and character of the area was also addressed in this report. Despite our attempts to keep the report on a purely technical and non-controversial level it was to be April 1967 before it received the approval of the committee. Meanwhile we had prepared two additional reports on Population and Hinterland, and another on Industry was ready for submission.

If quantitative evidence was required to justify the need for a plan these first reports certainly provided it. Our population study revealed that the overall density within the city boundary was 25 persons per acre. This was a city density comparable to major industrial centres such as Liverpool and Glasgow. An overall town density of 10 persons per acre, found in cities such as Edinburgh and in the new towns, was thought to be desirable by most planners. A lower density allowed more space to be assigned for other uses including more parks and other amenities. It also curtailed the use of high-density, high-rise development solutions for housing since most housing could be provided at medium densities with adequate open space. The natural increase in the population of the area (births over deaths) at 2.3 per cent in the city and 2.7 per cent in the rural district was higher than elsewhere in Northern Ireland, which was already substantially greater than other parts of the UK. The age structure of the population was also substantially greater with 33 per cent of the population in the 0 to 14 age group com-

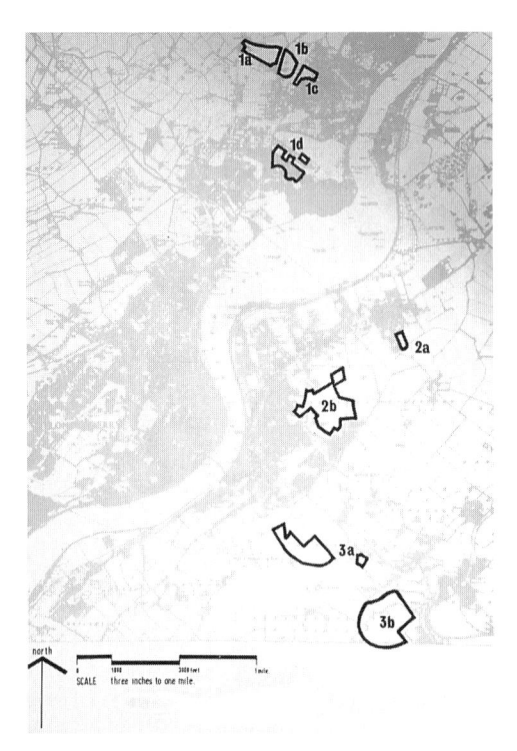

14. Infill housing sites from Interim Report No 1

BREAKING THE STALEMATE 53

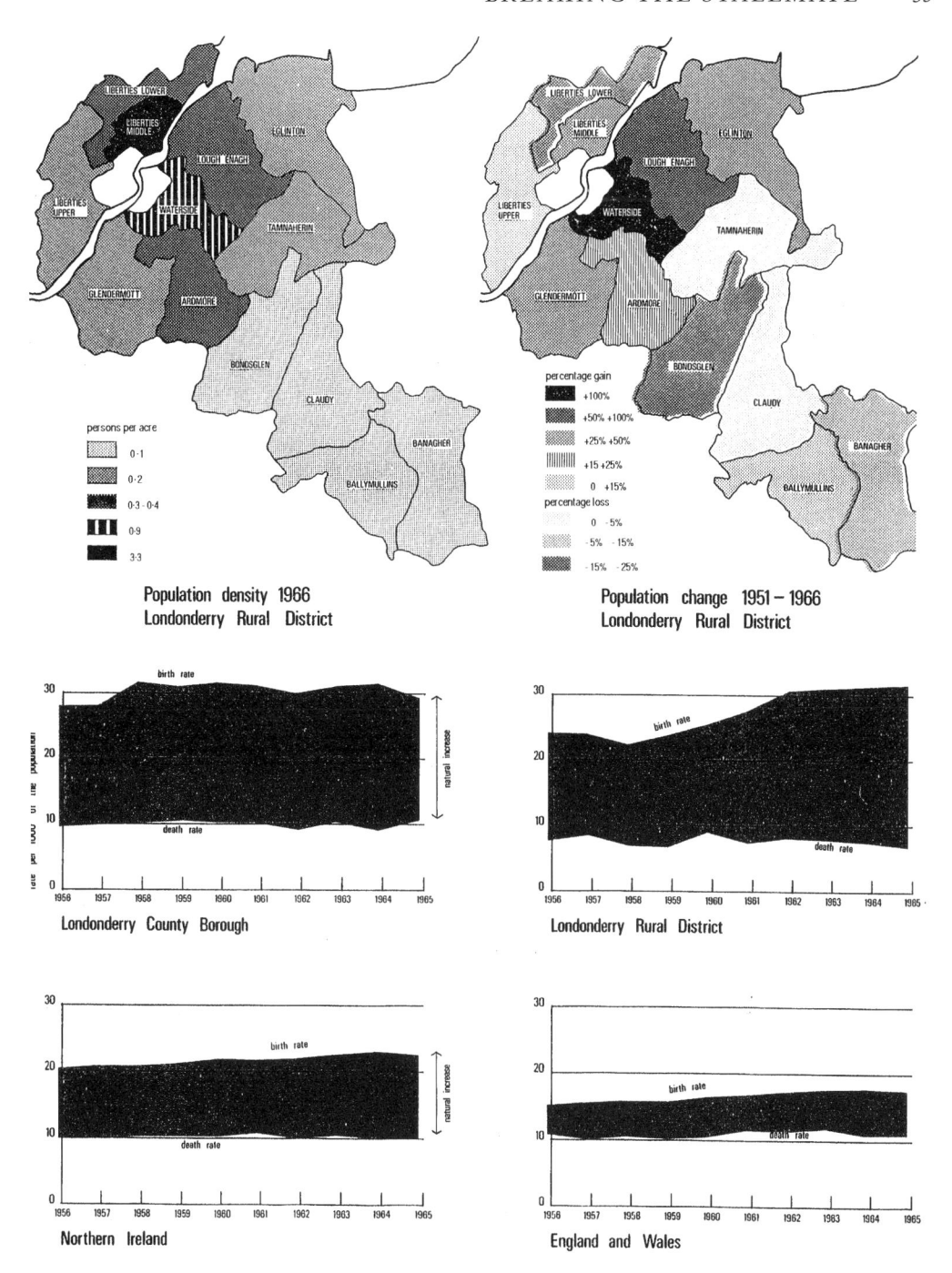

15. Population: rates of natural increase

pared with 29 per cent in Northern Ireland and 25 per cent in the rest of the UK. This natural growth rate and youthful population persisted despite the high rate of emigration in the 20 to 39 age groups, and the population structure was more comparable to that of a new town than to an older urban centre.[1]

The high rate of outward migration made accurate estimates of future population difficult, and since we were determined to produce a realistic plan, our projections were on the conservative side. On the other hand we knew that changes could be accommodated in flexible proposals for land use with functions being accommodated at a pace to meet the likely demand. For example, housing would have to proceed quickly to provide for the pent-up demand already existing. Therefore while it was possible to project a population in excess of 110,000 by 1981, excluding the migration factor, using past trends for natural change and migration, the population would more likely be around 94,500.[2] This was a conservative view because two other inter-related factors were ignored. First was the fact that Londonderry had been designated a growth centre by the Northern Ireland government, implying that population would be attracted to the area by the creation of new jobs. These jobs would have to be created by government-sponsored firms through direct and indirect subsidies and other economic incentives.

While Londonderry was the only major centre west of the River Bann (a dividing line of the province), east of the Bann the new towns of Antrim-Ballymena and Craigavon had also been targeted for industrial development. Speaking at a Town and Country Planning Summer School in Belfast on 7 September 1967, James Aitken, chief planner of the Ministry of Development, made it clear that the priorities of the government were primarily focused on the Belfast region. He thought that 'West of the Bann' was a rather emotive phrase and went on to point out that these towns feel 'that less money should be put into the easterly towns which, they think will attract industry anyway and instead that the investment should be used in building up the attractions of those in the West. It appears difficult to convince them that choice of location is the prerogative of the industrialist, that his desires are reasonably well known and that he is not particularly interested in the social welfare of any particular community until he has made his choice'.[3]

This was an enigmatic comment from a planner who was advocating growth centres on the one hand and on the other accepting the conservative doctrine of *laissez faire*. Certainly our assumptions in preparing the plan were that there would be an effort, if not an obligation, by the government to direct industry to Londonderry. As an area it had many of the advantages sought after by incoming industrialists, although incentives would be required to offset the advantages enjoyed by the Belfast area and Derry's apparent remoteness. The Ministry of Commerce had recently proposed a new industrial estate at Springtown, just north of the city boundary, that would create 3,000–4,000 new jobs. In terms of estimating population growth and given the past record of the Unionist-dominated government, it was difficult to allow for incoming industry as a growth factor that would positively influence migration rates. So although we thought it possible that a total population of 100,000 by 1981 was not out of the question, the figure of 94,500 and the creation of 4,400 newly formed households became the basis for our land use proposals. We also included the proviso that population change should be reviewed at regular intervals so that implementation of the plan could be related to the rate of growth.[4]

From a planning viewpoint the acceptance of the assumptions by the committee would be

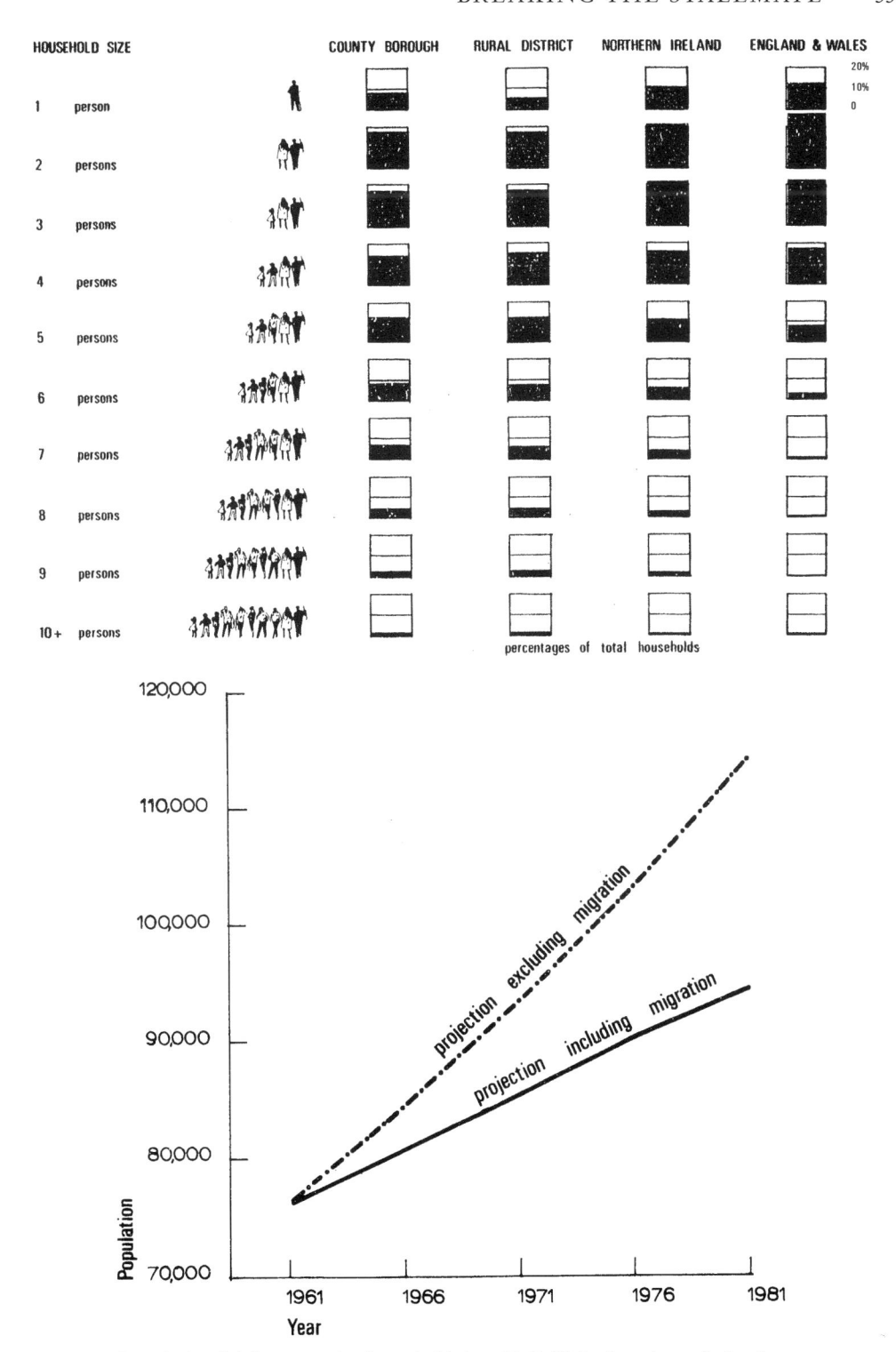

16. Population (a) Comparative household sizes 1961. (b) Projected population increase

crucial to the production of a plan for growth in the area. As all planners know it is a universal precept that one could always rely on organisations such as the Chamber of Commerce to promote the idea of growth even in situations where it may not be desirable. It was not surprising, therefore, that this report, with Jim Foster's statistical findings carefully set out and reinforced with pictorial illustrations prepared by Mike Murray's team, was acceptable to the political representatives on the Steering Committee who accepted our assumptions. We had similar success with our third report describing the Londonderry hinterland or 'sphere of influence' and the city's role as a centre for north-west Ulster. The measures we used, based on central place theory, may seem crude to today's regional economists.[5] Nevertheless we were able to measure its influence as an administrative centre; a centre for manufacturing, distribution, collection, shopping, and transport; and as a cultural, social, and educational centre. Because of its geographical isolation from the east of the province by the Sperrin Mountains we were able to survey the city as a freestanding centre serving an extensive natural hinterland.

As one moves further from the centre the city's influence is shown diminishing from its primary, and secondary zones to its tertiary zone. From the outset of our appointment we were determined to ignore the political border, and our surveys included towns in County Donegal as a matter of course. Years later Peter Daniel chuckled as he reminded me that, 'we even included the population of Buncrana in our considerations'. Peter and Alan had met informally from time to time with Michael Dower, an English planning consultant, who was engaged in a study of Donegal for the government of the Irish Republic. At these meetings they were able to discuss the development of the north-west region. Given the attraction that Donegal held for tourists and the size and importance of Londonderry in the region, it was no surprise to find that the political frontier had not created an absolute barrier between towns in the Republic and the city. Derry after all had been the market town and major port in the area for centuries, and although its influence had been somewhat reduced and its expansion westward restricted by the border, the eastern half of Donegal still depended on the city for a lot of its important services. Towns such as Moville, Buncrana, and Letterkenny lay within its secondary zone of influence; their counterparts, Dungiven and Limavady lay in Northern Ireland. A number of workers were drawn to the city from this zone for which it continued to provide port facilities; some higher order shopping, distribution and collection activities; specialised medical services; and a variety of social, cultural, and educational facilities. In the tertiary zone, extending as far as 45 miles from the city and even into County Fermanagh and North Sligo, these services were utilised while basic urban services were provided by local service centres.[6]

Following the non-controversial submission to the committee of our hinterland studies, we submitted our fourth report, an extensive and thorough study of industry in the area. This was well received by the committee as a whole since most members recognised the importance of attracting new industry to the area. James Doherty was an articulate spokesman on the subject, as was civil servant John Armstrong, who represented the Ministry of Commerce. He certainly gave the impression of being enthusiastic about promoting industrial growth and encouraged the committee to play its part in this endeavour. In an introduction to our report we quoted from an earlier report published by the Northern Ireland Economic Council pointing out that:

> Londonderry is located at the periphery of industrial Britain.... Londonderry from its position on the far outside has to pit its attractions against the counter attractions of

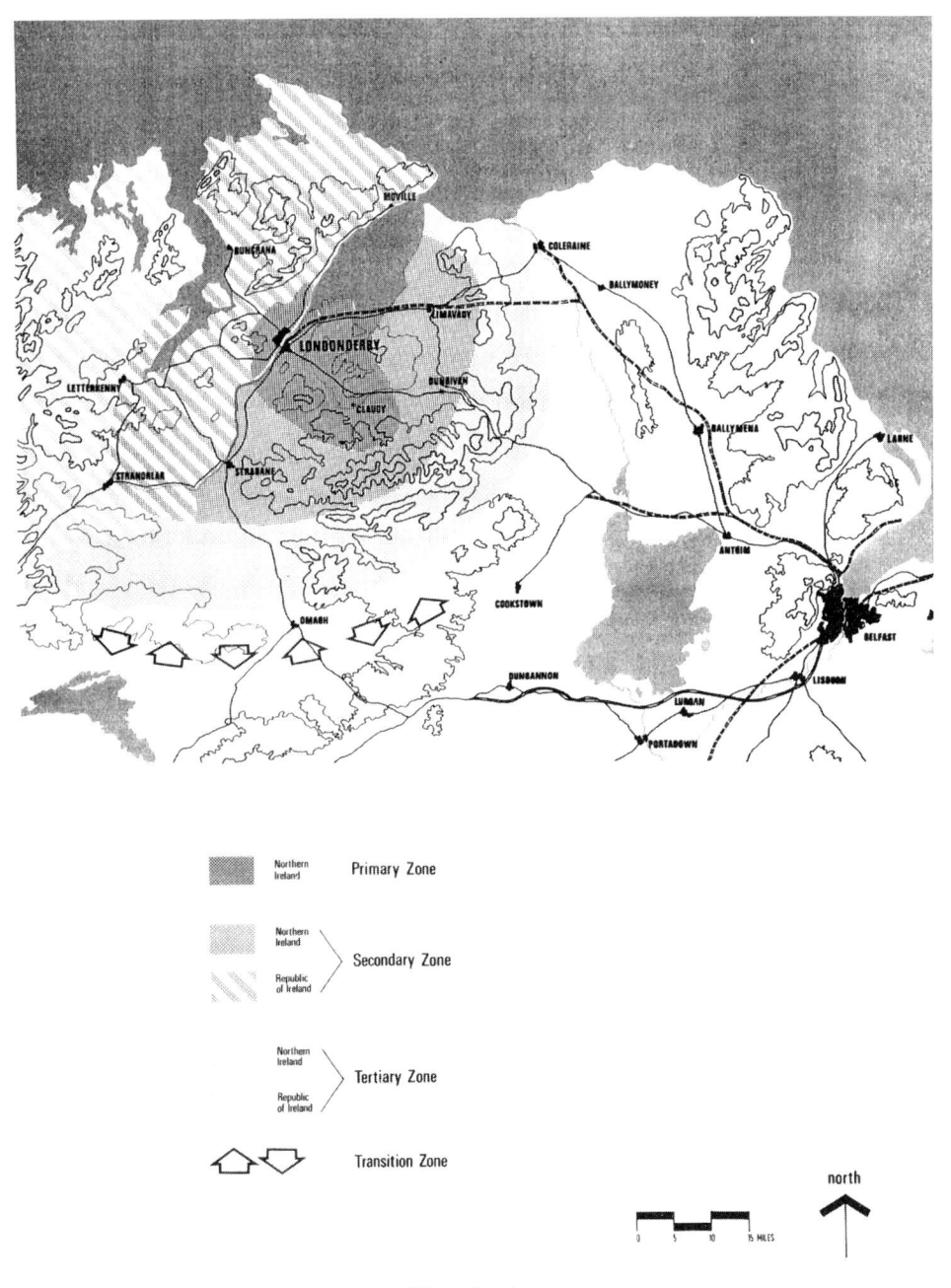

17. Hinterland zones

larger industrial areas closer to the centre. Londonderry's advantages should therefore be strong and certain. Weaknesses in its appeal, that might in a more central situation be dismissed as unimportant, matter greatly to Londonderry and will weigh heavily against it. The attractions which Londonderry has to offer must, as far as it is possible to make them, be second to none.[7]

58 PLANNING DERRY

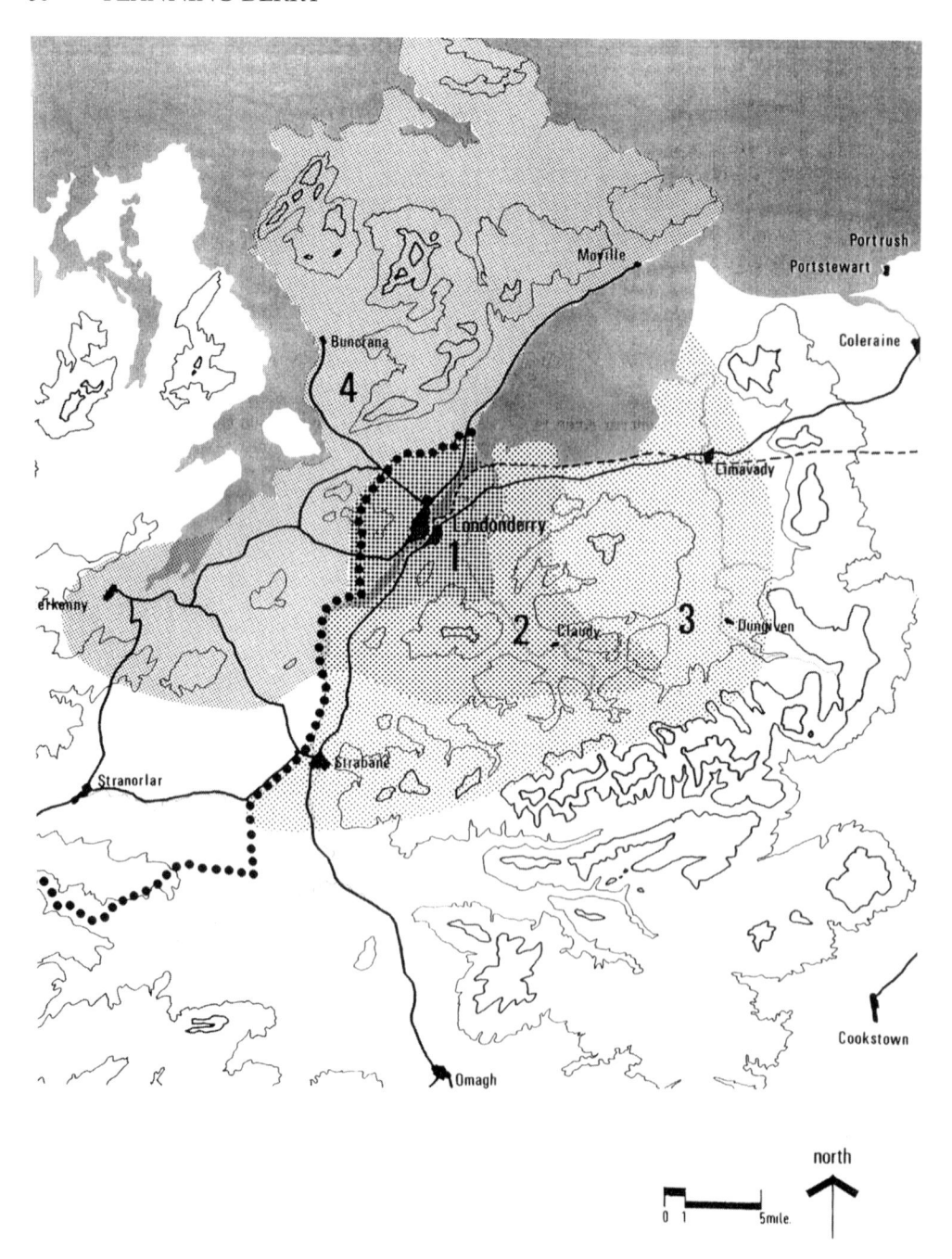

18. Shopping sphere of influence

Matthew's and Wilson's recommendations for growth centres outside the Belfast region had placed Londonderry top of the list of four centres in the north and west that included Coleraine, Omagh, and Dungannon. In the east of the province, within easy reach of Belfast, a number of small towns had also been selected for growth in addition to the new town of Craigavon and the proposed new town of Antrim-Ballymena.[8] This, in combination with the plan for the Belfast region, was an attempt to 'demagnetize the centre' as Matthew put it.[9] Obviously while this strategy helped to control growth and restrict the sprawl of Belfast, it provided no real impetus, apart from government incentives and restrictions, for industrialists to locate outside the Belfast region.

Unlike some of the towns in the Belfast region, Derry had a long-established industrial base, an excellent harbour, and a virtually unlimited supply of land and water to support industrial growth for a population of more than 100,000. In order to offset the disadvantage of its apparent remoteness and concomitant higher transportation costs, a more efficient communications network would be required at the local, regional, and national level. There was already a proposal to build a second motorway between Belfast and Derry. We reasoned that on a motorway the travel time between the two cities could be reduced to little more than an hour. From this and our study of potential industrial sites, we arrived at the idea of what we called a crescent of development. Starting at Strabane along the crescent of the Foyle Valley to Limavady and Coleraine, with Derry as the focus of an industrial subregion, this could become the impetus to building closer links between the two major cities. This was one of two more imaginative long-term proposals, the other being the creation of an industrial land bank preserving key sites in the area where future manufacturing industries could be located. Ever conscious of the need to address immediate concerns, we included more modest recommendations such as relocating industries from inappropriate central city and quayside sites and demolishing obsolete industrial structures that had become eyesores. Also included were proposals for the adaptive re-use of vacated industrial buildings and for the relocation of established shirt factories from 'cramped unsuitable premises'.[10]

In addition, we strongly endorsed implementation of the Ministry of Commerce's proposal to expand industry at Springtown and for the building of advance factories. This policy of providing new buildings on industrial estates for incoming industrialists was an innovation employed successfully in the Belfast area and elsewhere by the Northern Ireland government. The post-war downturn in the shipbuilding and linen industries created major unemployment problems for the province and these new factories, along with other incentives, attracted industrialists from the rest of the UK and abroad. There were two vacant factories at Drumahoe and Bligh's Lane, which we calculated could employ over 1,000 persons, and there was ample room for expansion of Du Pont and British Oxygen, the two major petrochemical industries in the area, although it was recognised that these were low labour-intensive industries, that is to say, the number of workers per acre is less than half the number that can be accommodated on smaller sites provided for manufacturing industries such as engineering. It is almost an axiom in urban and regional planning that like attracts like, and it is for good reasons that planners use zoning to accommodate the needs of specific types of use, so we proposed that this east shore area of the Foyle with its flat land and easy access to road, rail, and to the lough be reserved for expansion of petrochemical and related industries.

Despite the lack of concrete evidence to support it, Jimmy Munce proposed that the former Royal Naval Air Station at Eglinton be expanded and developed as a regional airport. History

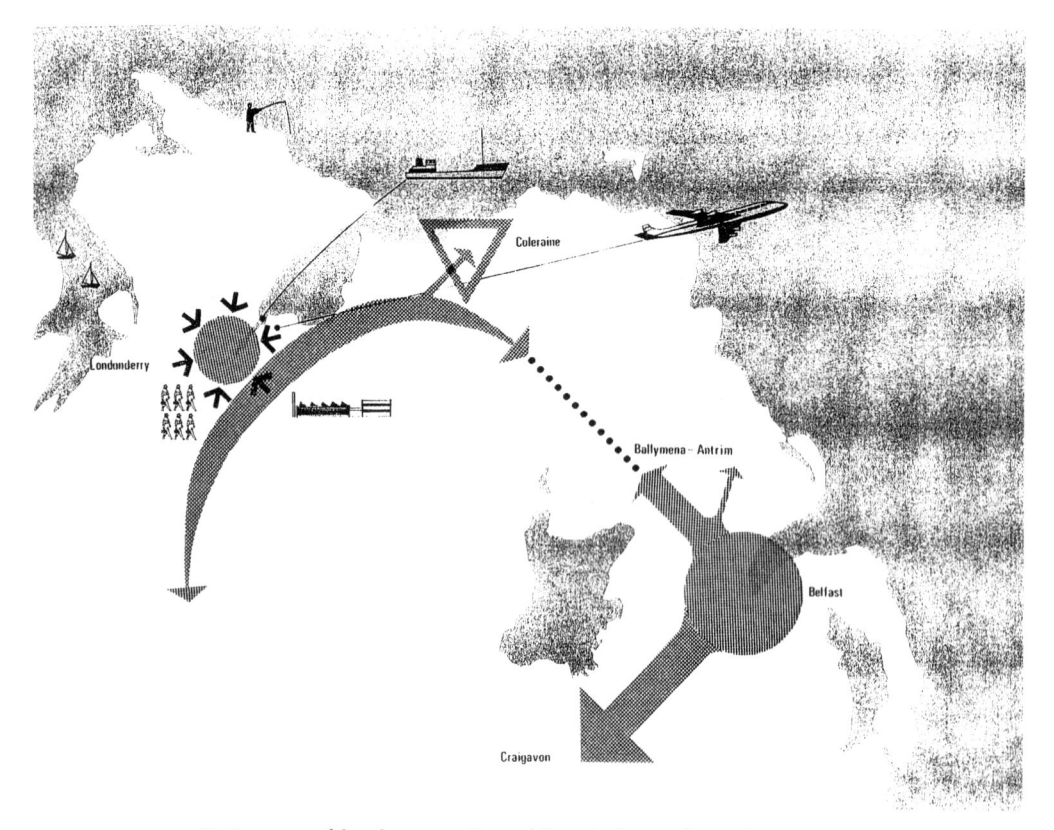

19. Crescent of development. Dotted lines indicate planned motorways

was to prove Jimmy's prescience, but it was one of the few proposals we made in the report that was not soundly based, and was considered by some to be in the realm of wishful thinking.[11] The idea was received with acclaim by the committee at the meeting in January 1968. All of the other proposals contained in the report were based on a detailed survey and analysis of existing industrial and commercial firms with the aim of determining likely employment levels over five-year periods to 1971, 1976, and 1981.

Yet another important recommendation in this Industrial Report was the possibility of a container service port terminal at the mouth of the estuary in the vicinity of Black Brae to provide direct shipping facilities for large, low labour-intensive industries.[12] With these sites and upgraded communications the area would be well placed to attract new industry and both the local governments, chambers of commerce, and organisations like the Industry for Derry Committee would have a diversity of sites to offer prospective industrialists. Immediate steps would be needed to improve the infrastructure, and here again we warned of the need to protect and enhance the existing landscape and natural amenities for both residents and tourists. We also took the opportunity to mention housing need once more, since this issue was often raised by industrialists. Their focus was not just on the need for executive-type housing, although the need was real, but as we had been able to observe ourselves, conditions in the city were de-

BREAKING THE STALEMATE 61

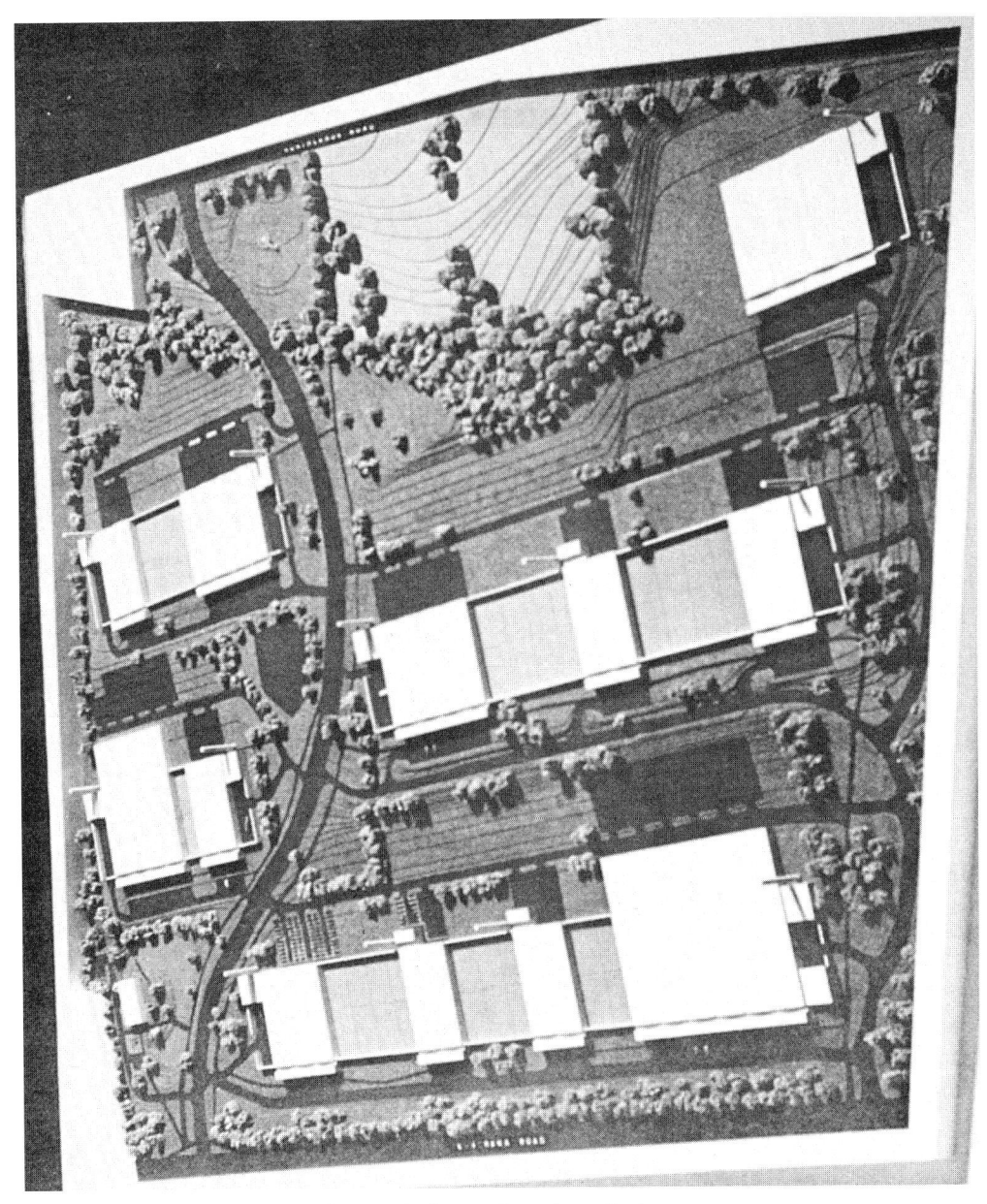

20. Proposed advance factories at Springtown

plorable and the scattered housing in the rural district and efforts of the Housing Trust were insufficient to alleviate the problem.

As far as I can recall, there were no major objections to this fourth major study report. We had naturally chosen industrial sites based on plans in the pipeline for expansion and their location near major residential areas and major lines of communication to reduce transportation time and costs. If members of the committee were not aware of the land use implications of these reports,

62   PLANNING DERRY

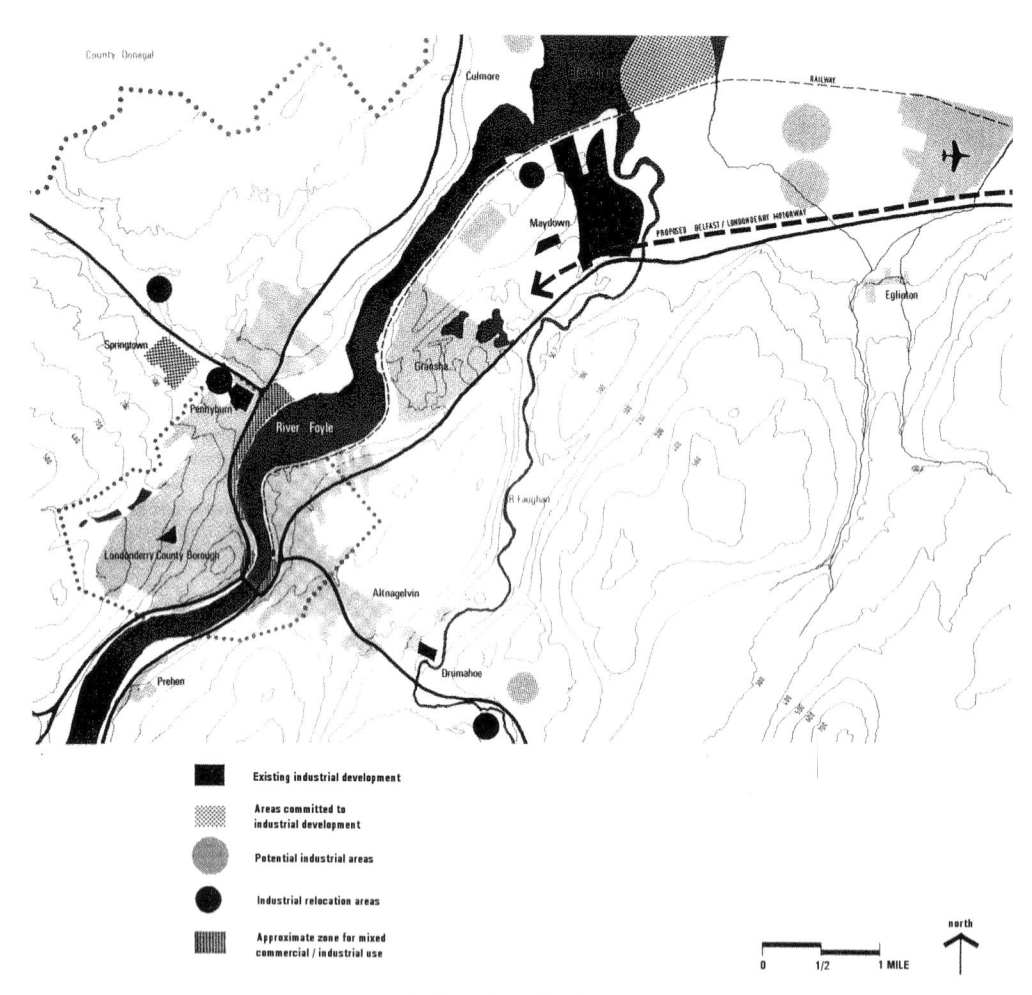

21. Location of industry

22. Black Brae area—proposed harbour site

we certainly were. Soon schematic plans began to emerge from team members, especially the architects, suggesting areas for residential expansion, locations for a new bridge, and expansion of the city centre. Peter Daniel and Alan Bradshaw were the instigators, and soon Mike Murray and I were drawn into their speculations as we gathered sometimes late into the night in the Derry office. Wisely, Jack Smith and Jim Foster, aware of the research still to be completed, held back from the fray, but this visual brainstorming would prove to be useful in the long run as we refined our options and as more information became available. It was clear to us all by now that despite possible vehicular access difficulties in the future, the existing city centre should first be consolidated and adjacent twilight areas designated for future development and parking. This factor, together with the strategy for industrial development, meant that while there was pressure from the Rural District Council to designate remote residential sites east of the Foyle it was clear that a major area near the city boundary would be required on the west bank. It also became obvious that in order to convince the committee of the indisputable logic of our final recommendations, we would have to examine several alternative plans and present our findings. Also if the plan was to be accepted by a sceptical Catholic majority population and a suspicious Protestant minority, they would also have to be convinced of the probity of our recommendations.

About this point in our deliberations nothing was to make us more aware of this need than an issue raised by the Derry Housing Association, whose chairman at the time was John Hume, later to become prominent in the civil rights movement and then in politics as a member of both the British and European Parliaments. I was first introduced to him by Alan Bradshaw. His interest in approaching Alan was to see if we, as planners, would support the development of a small site for housing in the Pennyburn area. Unfortunately this was a site that we considered inappropriate for housing because of its location in an area that we had recommended for industry and its close proximity to existing industry. The location also happened to be part of a larger area we were examining for a second bridge and for a major traffic route to the bridge. Our pleas to the Association to wait for another six months or so were interpreted by an already suspicious group as evidence of our collusion with the Unionists to preserve the *status quo*. John Hume could not accept our recommendation and, concealing whatever his true feelings might have been, politely indicated that he would have to appeal against our recommendation to the Planning Authority. I had carefully explained our situation to James Doherty and shown him some of our draft proposals. Understanding our predicament and the suspicions it would cause in the circumstances, he courageously undertook to support our position and try to explain it to members of the Association and other concerned citizens.

Both he and Alan Bradshaw were to experience the ire of another member of the Association, Father Anthony Mulvey, a dedicated man of God, with a fiery personality and a resolve to meet head on the social injustices experienced by his flock. He was less diplomatic than John Hume in his judgement of our motives. In the coming months Alan Bradshaw, James Doherty, and myself were all assailed for our lack of honesty and moral courage. James Doherty bore the brunt of this and felt the pain keenly, since he had been striving for the past decade to improve housing conditions, working where possible to support the Housing Trust in their endeavours. There can be no doubt however, considering the appalling housing conditions, that for many the plan seemed to be too little too late. Indeed that same 'too little too late' lack of generosity by the majority Unionist Party was to be the major impetus for the outbreak of violence that was later to engulf the province for more than a quarter of a century. The Unionists' grudging acceptance of equal rights and justice for the minority population and their reluctance to disavow the fascist-like views of extreme right-wing members primed the resurgence of violence led, though not initiated, by a Provisional wing of the Irish Republican Army with equally fascist-like views.

The Derry Housing Association approached the Rural District Council about purchasing some of the land we had recommended for housing in our interim report, and were turned away with the usual excuses about the lack of services or the need to preserve sites for private executive-type housing. No small wonder when at last they had the opportunity to purchase a site and found us in the way, they assumed it was more than fate that was dealing them a cruel blow. Of course we had not been privy to their experiences with the Rural District and it was only upon reading the Association's Evidence Report at the subsequent appeal hearing some months later that we knew of all the details.

At the appeal hearing in which I had to appear as an expert witness in opposition to the Association just before our plan was released, the expert witness for the Association was Brian Falk of Covell Matthews and Partners, whose proposal for a new commercial centre in the Waterside had been rejected on our recommendation. I immediately suspected that another enigmatic city official was involved in this somewhat devious arrangement although I could never prove it. It was for me and the rest of the team yet another distraction from preparing a plan we knew would release more than enough land for housing to accommodate the population for the next twenty years. Peter Daniel recently unearthed the Association's report prepared by John Hume, and it contained ample evidence of the horror of some of the housing conditions. The Association had carried out their own survey and had found for example 'that 336 families or 25 per cent of those surveyed lived in tenements, 160 families live completely in one room. Altogether about 1300 share toilet facilities … 181 families had to carry water from outside … In 140 cases the principal worry is rats … in a flat in Bishop Street, a mother discovered a rat in the cot feeding on the baby's bottle'.[13] It was difficult for us faced with such facts not to appear heartless and uncaring. Yet James Doherty had made us aware of the situation from day one, and we had seen much of the evidence ourselves in our own studies. We needed the evidence of surveys like this to support our planning proposals, but were prevented by the Steering Committee from releasing any of our findings regarding possible housing sites. In fact we were still embroiled in our own battle with the Steering Committee and the continuing attempts by members of the Rural District and others to thwart our efforts.

It seemed to us that only the Rural District Council and its officers, who had impeded even the efforts of the Housing Trust to build outside the city boundary, were the only winners in this situation. In the long run the Association, while refused permission in this instance, did get permission to build housing in other areas. Later in the seventies and eighties it was to play an important role in the development of Derry. [see Fig. 42] In concluding his report John Hume had noted that: 'the Pennyburn site is the only one which enables the Association to get on with the job immediately. In agreeing to allow us to develop the site we do not believe that the Minister will in any way upset the Area Plan. We accept the concept of, and the need for an Area Plan for Londonderry. Our proposals, as our expert witness will show, will in our opinion, achieve some of the objects of the plan'.[14] While thankful that the Association accepted the need for an area plan we were never convinced about the Pennyburn location or the possible outcome of their proposal. Although our proposal to reserve the area for industrial use was upheld, the Housing Association had forcefully made its point. The incident had been a trying experience for us all, and we could not help but see this as yet another impediment to the successful completion of the plan and its implementation.

While all this was going on, the team was involved in parallel studies—studies that were speedily turned into attractive reports for the Steering Committee by Mike Murray's team in Belfast working into the early morning hours and through weekends. We were trying to complete our other important reports including the Communications study, which had been in progress since April 1966, and here, Stan Cochrane and Jack Smyth were having their own difficulties with the City Surveyor.

NOTES
1] *Londonderry Area Plan*, pp. 18–20.
2] The actual figure in 1981 was estimated at around 90,000.
3] J.M. Aitken, *Regional Planning in Northern Ireland*. Report of the Town and Country Planning Summer School, Queen's University Belfast (1967), pp. 17–18.
4] *Londonderry Area Plan*, p. 23.
5] For readers unfamiliar with Central Place Theory see W. Christaller, *Central Spaces in Southern Germany* trans. C.W. Baskin (New York, Prentice Hall, 1966); and B.J.L Berry and W.L. Garrison, 'Recent development of central place theory', *Papers and Proceedings of the Regional Science Association*, vol. 4, pp. 107–21.
6] *Londonderry Area Plan*, p. 14.
7] Northern Ireland Economic Council, *Londonderry as a Location for New Industry* (HMSO 1966), p. 6; see also James Munce Partnership, *Report No 4 Industry*, 1967.
8] Wilson, *Economic Development in Northern Ireland.*
9] Matthew, *Belfast Regional Survey and Plan.*
10] *Londonderry Area Plan, Report No 4*, pp. 20–8.
11] This was not the first example of Jimmy's prescience. In the mid fifties he had produced a proposal (unsolicited) to convert the former Sydenham naval air station on the outskirts of Belfast into a civil airport. The idea, with its rapid transit link to the city centre was considered far fetched at the time. By the eighties Sydenham had become a civil airport and was renamed Belfast City Airport.
12] *Londonderry Area Plan, Report No 4*, p. 24.
13] John Hume, *Evidence Presented on Behalf of the Derry Housing Association Limited* (1968), p. 3.
14] Ibid., p. 13.

7 The Bridge

Creative people such as artists, inventors, engineers, and architects often become so absorbed in their work that it becomes a part of their persona. Any ridicule or even well-meant criticism of their work can be, for some, a personal affront, and their consequent defensive posturing often leads others to presume them arrogant—of course the same generalisation can be made about other professions, including doctors, lawyers, the rich, and persons in authority. In UK cities, up until the mid-seventies, the office of city surveyor carried with it considerable power in decision making, and even though the town clerk was the chief officer, unlike the city surveyor he did not have the advantage of a specialised professional background. I use the term 'advantage' because most mayors and city councillors became as dependent on the city surveyor's expertise as they did on their own lawyer, doctor, or dentist. Since water supply, sewage disposal, and well-paved roads have determined the success or failure of cities since Roman times, an expert city surveyor could do much to relieve councillors' minds of these practical concerns, so enabling them to pursue more ethereal occupations.

Colonel James MacKinder, surveyor for the city of Londonderry, was not oblivious of his power. He well understood the importance of his operation and protected his bailiwick with all the zest and vigour of a medieval baron. Certainly he seemed to be both pompous and arrogant and, despite his tweedy look, had never discarded his military rank upon returning to civilian life. He always addressed Jimmy as 'Major Munce', seeming to imply that he knew who was in command if Jimmy did not. After one or two meetings with MacKinder where others were present, I felt grateful that Stan Cochrane was in charge of this part of the operation. To be fair it would have been difficult for us to perceive MacKinder in any other light than that described since he saw us as usurpers from whom he had to defend his territory and treated us accordingly. But all that Stan and Jack were seeking from him was existing information on water supply and sewage disposal within the city boundary. They also needed information concerning road proposals he had submitted to the Ministry of Development (Roads Branch) including a major city centre bypass elevated road known as the Lecky Road Flyover. As he had carried out a traffic survey justifying this and other proposals, it would have been wasteful and unnecessary to replicate this given the time constraints. He knew he was obliged to give Stan and Jack the information, and reluctantly allowed Jack Smyth to liaise with his assistant Victor Watson. With Watson's help we collected most of the information we needed for our Traffic Report, but there were many skirmishes with MacKinder before it was finally completed. Part of the problem, of course, was that our remit included the rural district where the responsibility for roads lay with Major Harold Scott, the County Surveyor, and as noted previously there had been no difficulties in obtaining information from him or the Roads Branch of the Ministry of Development at Stormont.

In a memorandum in June 1966 Stan Cochrane had asked for a draft development plan for the traffic engineers. He requested six-inch scale maps showing proposals for redevelopment and preservation areas in the city, and a six-inch map of the whole area showing proposals for the location of industry, housing, and main shopping and business areas. He wrote:

> This 'Draft' development plan, or anticipated future land use plan will allow us to calculate approximate future traffic movements and to investigate various alternative road networks. In the light of this road network investigation, it may be possible to improve the proposed future land use arrangement. ... I would be glad if you could arrange to have Jim Foster spend a few days in the Belfast Office as soon as possible to advise on the growth factors used in MacKinder's Traffic Report, and to help us with a simplified zoning approach.[1]

In some ways this memo was a reminder to me and the others that we had agreed that 'traffic was a function of land use and not vice-versa', and that he and Jack could not make much progress in dealing with issues such as Lecky Road until he had this information. Given our mutual commitment to produce a plan based on Buchanan's concept of environmental areas, I understood the need even at that stage to have some kind of sketch plan that we could use before making commitments through formal reports.

All of us had known from the beginning that transportation would be a major factor in whatever form the plan took and that a second river crossing would be needed. Indeed, as early as 1834 when only the wooden bridge existed, the prominent English architect William Tite had proposed a bridge upstream in the area of Newbuildings.[2] One of the ideas we had developed, envisaging a northern expansion of the city on the west bank of the river, was for a bridge, high enough to allow shipping to enter the harbour, to link with a future extension of the M2 motorway in the area of Madams Bank with Buncrana Road. It would have least impact on the historic city, and would provide easy access for new industries on both sides of the river. Our proposal would also have placed the bridge within the county area and the county surveyor's jurisdiction, something that would definitely not have pleased Colonel MacKinder had he known. At this stage we were examining a number of other options and were trying hard to keep all of them open. As a result of these preliminary investigations we asked the town clerk to consider delaying the city's proposals for Lecky Road and asked that the city co-operate with us in investigating a Quayside route on the west bank and locations for a second crossing.

Colonel MacKinder was furious, both at us and the Stormont civil servants. In a four-page memorandum to members of the city's General Purposes Committee on 14 December 1966, he referred to letters Roy Henderson, the town clerk, had received from us and the secretary of the Steering Committee. In it he dismissed our suggestion that we should jointly investigate the possibility of a quayside route since he had already considered such a route (presumably at least partially outside his jurisdiction) and had submitted proposals to the Ministry of Development. He was appalled with our suggestion that the Lecky Road route should be reconsidered to reduce its adverse impact on the Bogside residential community. He had been considering this route since 1961 and noted:

> I do not consider these matters lightly, but give them prolonged and detailed thought, and I do not attempt to produce solutions in a matter of months, which would appear to be the case insofar as the Consultants to the Steering committee are concerned. The Secretary of the Steering Committee makes reference to a second River Crossing, which I first raised in 1964, and the Council has now at its meeting on 29th November, 1966, decided to appoint, subject to Ministry approval, Messrs. Mott, Hay & Anderson

to give a feasibility report in accordance with my recommendation.... I consider, as city Engineer and Surveyor of Londonderry, that I am quite capable of advising the Council on this matter.[3]

He went on to inform the committee that if the second crossing had to be explored on a 'wider basis' that he would advise them accordingly. He also advised the committee 'to continue with your present plans for Lecky Road and the Quay Route'. Now warmed to the task he continued, 'The Consultants state further that "they are considering the possible location of car parks, so that the future road pattern can be related". I would suggest that it would be more rational to decide the road pattern and then provide car parks in suitable places in relation to that pattern.' Moreover he continued we had, 'seen fit to criticize my Traffic Survey, which they state was carried out within very limited Terms of Reference.... on the contrary, the Traffic Survey was carried out on a very wide basis, and virtually embraced the area which is presently under consideration by the North-West Steering Committee'.[4]

Of course MacKinder had no jurisdiction beyond the city boundary and any surveys or test drillings would have to be carried out jointly with the county surveyor or at the very least with his knowledge and approval. Moreover the Ministry's Road branch and the county would have the final say in such matters since major roadworks could not be carried out without Stormont government funding. However, MacKinder was probably frustrated, as a man of action, to see what he had fought so hard to obtain begin to slip from his grasp. That his plans and actions might not have been in the best interests of the city seemed not to alter his views. But in the end he could not prevent Stan and Jack completing their task and a well-documented, technically sound report on Communications (No 8), would be in the hands of the Steering Committee by late autumn of 1967. This report following upon those on Land Use (No 5), Shopping (No 6), and Rural Settlements (No 7) began to establish the basis for a final plan. While opposition from the city and rural district officials did not diminish, it became less overt and more infrequent. The quality and attractiveness of the easy-to-understand reports presented to the committee seemed to encourage their participation and channel it into a constructive manner.

After the hostility we had experienced at the beginning of our task, Steering Committee members were now contributing information based on their local knowledge for inclusion in the drafts without changing the substance of the documents. We could sense that they had taken ownership of the process and that this was now becoming their plan for the area. The thought that it might be implemented probably never occurred to most of them. They had seen plans before and knew that time and appropriate pressure at the right level of government had a way of erasing both good intentions and memories of commitments, but others could not help but feel the excitement engendered when faced with the prospect of a better economic future—a hope that many people on both sides of the political divide in the area shared. As for us, we began to feel that we had succeeded in building a bridge of a different kind, between ourselves and the Steering Committee. We had now been working with them for a year, and we were emboldened in this seemingly more benign atmosphere to present them with a short report that would lay the groundwork for our broad brush land use proposals. This nine-page document (Report No 5) was submitted with our Shopping Report for their consideration, and for the first time enunciated the planning aims and principles we had adopted based on the original terms of reference and our now more detailed knowledge of the area.

THE BRIDGE   69

These were to consolidate the existing central area of the city and strengthen its role as a regional centre; to upgrade amenities and attract more industries; to provide land for residential development related to places of work, social activity, and amenity; to ensure provision of an adequate infrastructure of communications to accommodate growth proposals to 1981 and beyond; to conserve the inherent natural beauty of the area and its historic city and buildings; and finally, to make proposals that would encourage future tourism. We stressed the need for flexibility in the proposals to accommodate different rates of growth and the need to relate new residential growth to places of work in order to minimise traffic flows and to avoid unnecessary travel and expense. We had produced a sieve map for the committee showing physical factors that would affect future development. This excluded land for future development if it was above the 400-feet contour line, had slopes of more than 1 in 10, or had severe drainage problems. Water catchment areas, areas of high-quality agricultural land, and areas of natural beauty were also excluded from future development within the plan period. Naturally, areas already built on or committed to development were excluded, and the remaining land suitable for future develop-

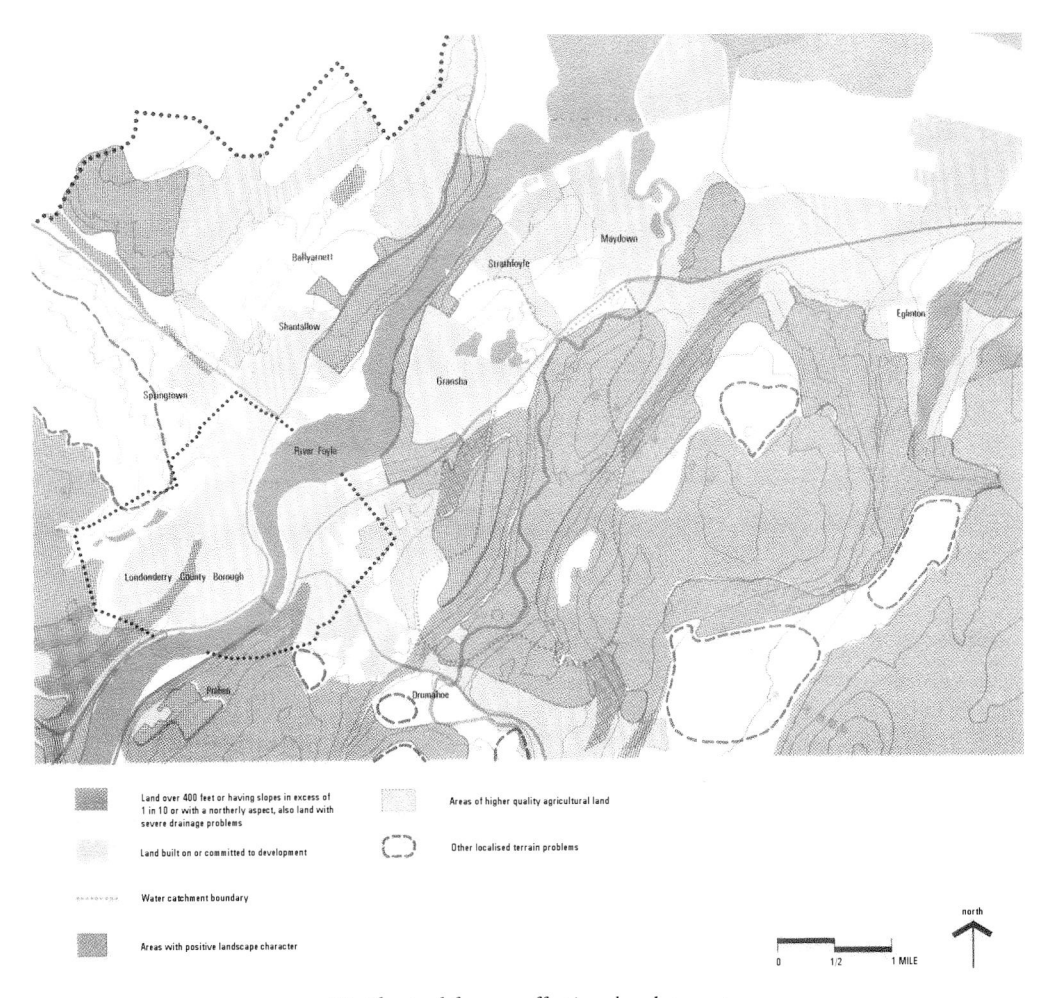

23. Physical factors affecting development

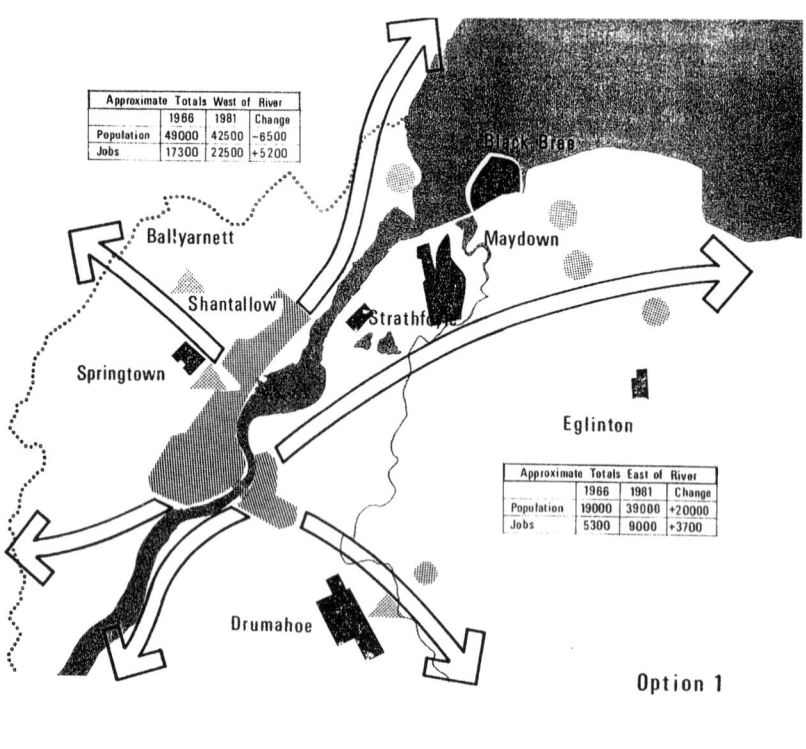

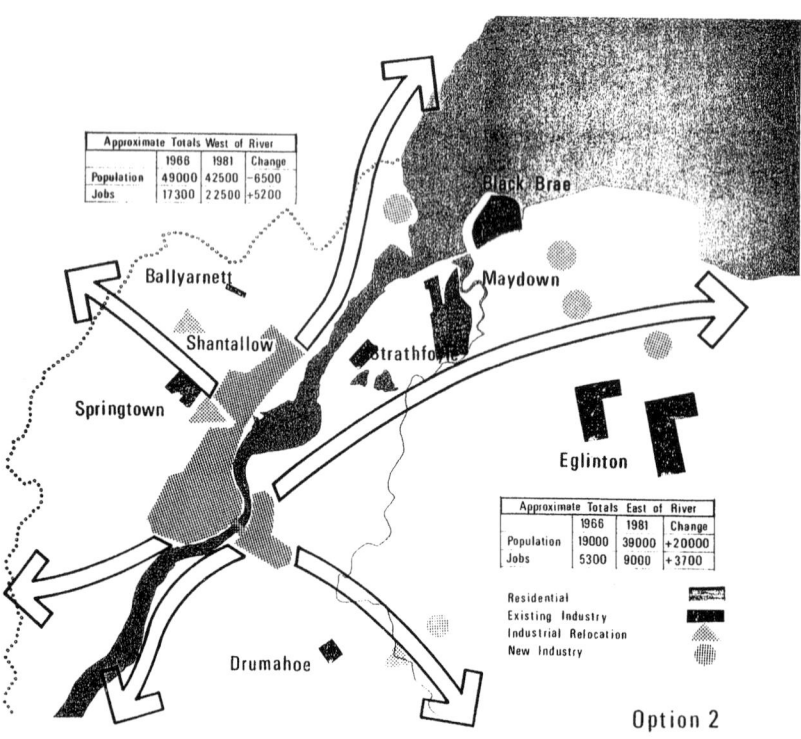

24. Options for development 1 & 2

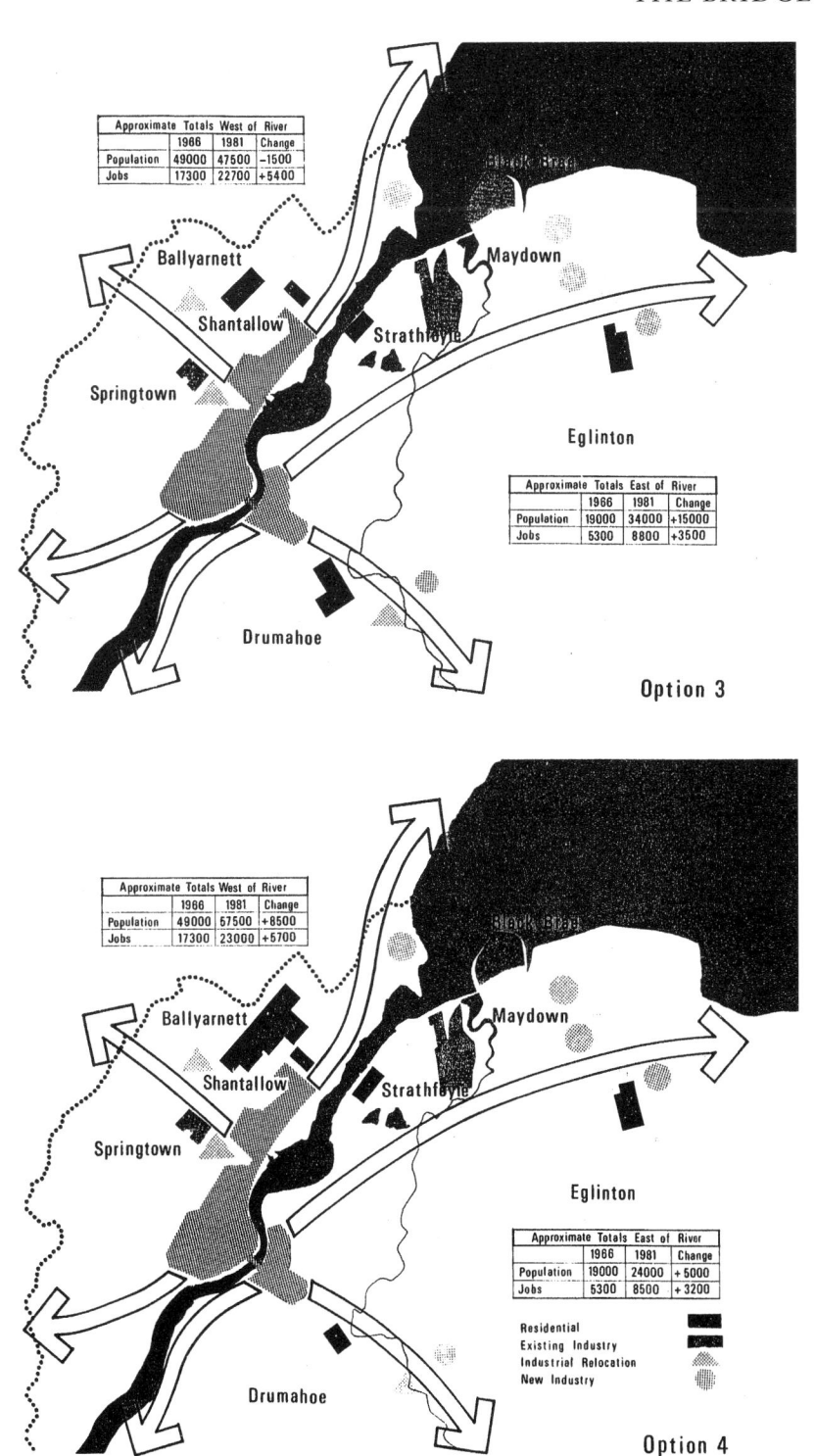

THE BRIDGE 71

25. Options for development 3 & 4

ment could now be clearly shown. Following the allocation of land for industrial use we were able to identify three major areas for large-scale residential development: one at Eglinton, one at Drumahoe, and the other at Ballyarnett/Shantallow. We explained to the committee how we had examined each of the areas against four criteria comprising amenity, accessibility, flexibility, and effect on city and region. Amenity, we defined as the overall attractiveness of an area; for example, such areas would already be attracting residential development. Accessibility took account of the proximity of the area to places of work, public transport, city centre shopping, education, recreation, and social/religious activities. Flexibility referred to the degree of adaptation possible in implementation depending upon faster or slower capital investment over an extended time frame. Finally we asked ourselves whether the expansion would add to or detract from the established regional pattern and city centre development.[5]

Based on our evidence it was obvious that only Ballyarnett/Shantallow on the west bank, which could accommodate a population of 15,000 or more, satisfied all four criteria, but in order to provide choice we also suggested some expansion at Drumahoe and existing villages on the east bank. This was one of four plans we had evaluated with great care, knowing we would be scrutinised for political bias and knowing that our integrity was at stake. To convince the committee, and others if necessary, we recorded our findings on a chart using primary colours to indicate the weight we gave to each option. Peter also wrote me a lengthy memorandum further confirming his belief in the propriety of our decision given additional criteria against which it could be examined. These were all significant, but two are worth quoting here:

26. Ballyarnett/Shantallow looking south with the Springfield industrial estate and city in background

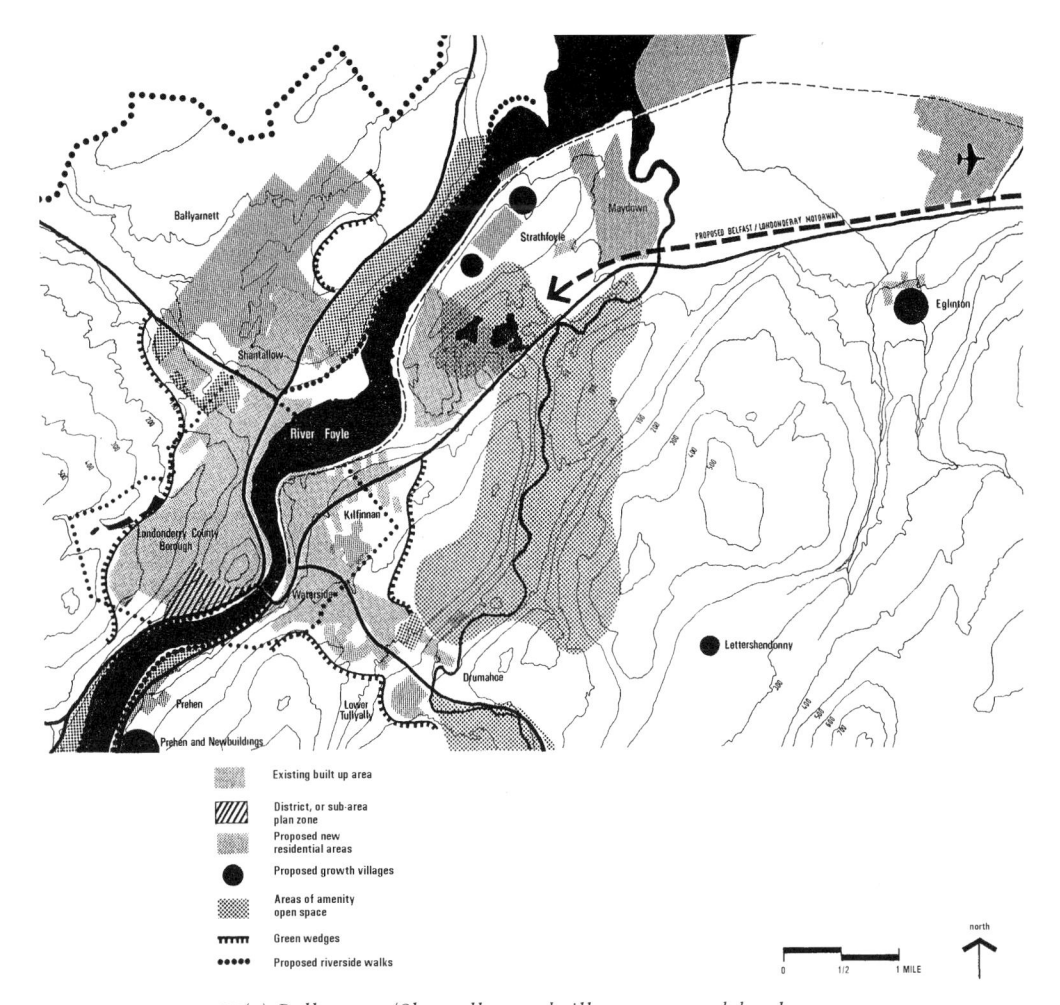

27(a). Ballyarnett/Shantallow and villages: proposed development

'That the grafting on of new development to the old centre is done in such a way that the old city structure is not catastrophically interfered with, and that to some extent the old city can find its own new level *naturally* (in terms of property values, etc.)' and, 'That the final plan proposed has distinct qualities of landscape and three dimensional integration with the *seaboard* form of the present city'.[6] We were careful to present this report as an information report without requesting any endorsement from the committee. We were now confident that we could produce a final plan within a matter of months and did not want at this stage to focus their attention yet again on the controversial housing issue. Besides, we had not yet produced our Communications report and needed approval on several other matters before we could place a comprehensive plan before the committee, and we knew that Colonel MacKinder was still fighting a rearguard action.

A key to the urban structure we had envisaged for the future development of the city was the question of whether or not the existing city centre was sustainable without a major expansion elsewhere. Our economic consultant, Fred Boal and Gerald Eve & Co. had already confirmed that the Covell Matthews proposal for the Waterside would have weakened the city centre. Any

27(b). Ballyarnett/Shantallow actual development

additional space required could be provided by infill and improvement of existing shopping facilities in the central area. We had known this instinctively, but this sophisticated quantitative analysis by shopping experts, based on our surveys, was sufficient to convince the committee that the existing centre had to remain the hub for future expansion. It also proved useful in finally dispensing with the objections of city officials. At the same time we were aware from our Consultants' Report that the strengthening of the existing central area would be a gradual process and that further substantial expansion might not take place until near the end of the plan period. The original hill site rising from the Foyle with its walls and historic buildings gave the city its sense of place, and we were anxious to maintain its character. Again we were well aware of the negative impact that large-scale urban renewal could impose on a historic city and the perils of introducing what Jane Jacobs in a then recent book had referred to as 'cataclysmic money'.[7] So although our proposals might have appeared modest and less glamorous in attracting local

THE BRIDGE

28. Derry—a sense of 'place'

76   PLANNING DERRY

attention, we were convinced that investment in infrastructure, housing, industrial development, and upgrading amenities was sufficient to provide the necessary impetus for expansion of commercial development in the city centre.

Gradual renewal, although not requiring large short-term capital expenditure, requires more care and ingenuity than the Platonic clean canvas approach. Fortunately here again there would be enough land currently occupied by obsolete buildings, many of which were in an advanced state of disrepair, and abutted the two major core areas of shopping: The Diamond and Ferryquay Street at a higher level within the walls, and Waterloo Place and Strand Road at a lower level just outside the walls at Shipquay Gate. Improvements could be made immediately by eliminating unnecessary traffic from major shopping streets and providing parking spaces convenient to the central area. The creation of pedestrian areas, some with bus-only access, would also allow for civic improvements and encourage shop and business owners to maintain and improve their properties.

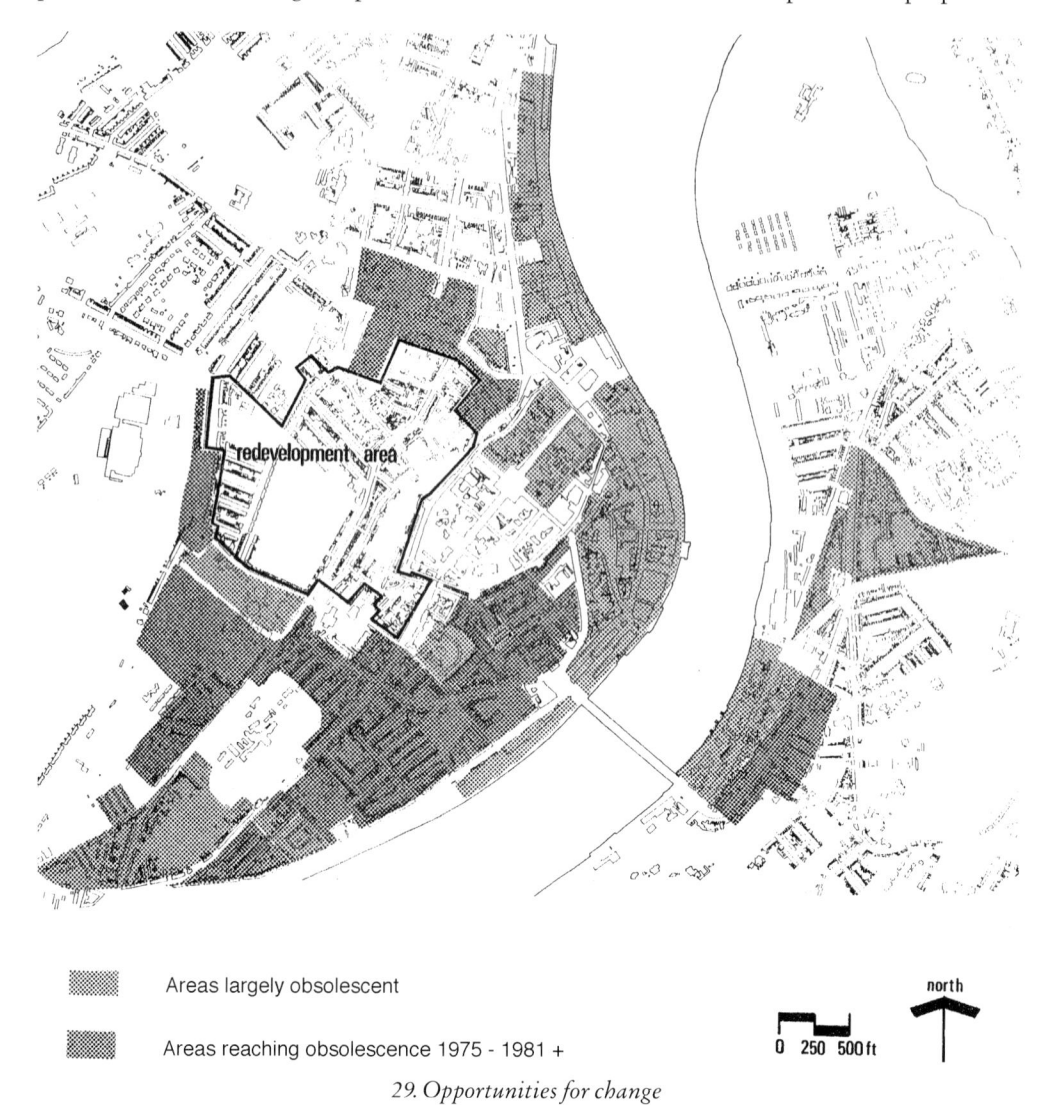

▓▓ Areas largely obsolescent

▓▓ Areas reaching obsolescence 1975 - 1981 +

0 250 500 ft

north

29. Opportunities for change

As we would later explain in our Communications Report, traffic generated by central area uses and major parking locations would be served by a new quayside route that would also serve as a bypass. This would assist in the early clearance of obsolete and unsightly buildings and open up the river to the city. In the long term we envisaged the road having two levels linked to the upper and lower decks of the Craigavon Bridge thereby making it easier to plan for grade-separated pedestrian access to the river's edge. Access to the river for recreation and as a scenic attraction was an important goal in Peter Daniel's Landscape and Tourism Report (No 9). As Peter later remarked it was 'a pity to cut off the River from direct pedestrian access, but what else could we do?' Practically speaking, funds for the development of landscaping urban areas and the removal of obsolete industrial buildings were not available and even with Colonel MacKinder's Lecky Road proposal a substantial riverside route would have been necessary to handle the traffic. With the future of the city centre now secured as an essential part of the plan and our policy for the expansion of rural settlements accepted, by November 1967 we were ready to submit to the Steering Committee our final reports on Communications and Landscape. The pieces of the plan seemed to be falling into place, but the problem of the second crossing remained unresolved.

While we now knew that a new bridge would not be an immediate concern, we were worried about MacKinder's insensitivity to the importance of the existing city fabric. Like Baron Haussmann, 'the most famous exponent of massive urban surgery'[8] in the nineteenth century, who destroyed the medieval areas of Paris to create his splendid boulevards, I saw his approach as essentially military.[9] With the exception of Stan and Jack, the planning team had already decided that a long-span high-level bridge at the Narrows north of Rosses Bay linking the proposed M2 with Buncrana Road was the ideal location, but Stan and Jack, on the other hand, were trying to take a more cautious comprehensive view and subject the imaginative ideas of the team to rational examination. Both felt that it was difficult to justify a high-level bridge on planning

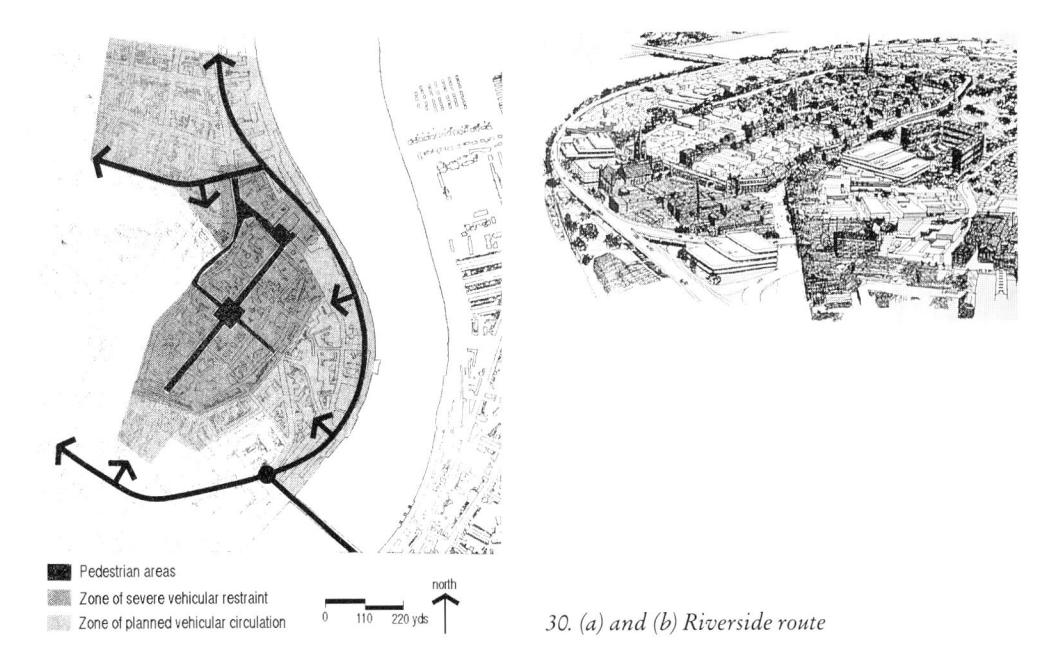

30. (a) and (b) Riverside route

grounds alone, but that it might be justifiable on the basis of future large-scale industrial growth at Pennyburn. As Stan was later to explain 'Given the unknowns, we couldn't go wholeheartedly looking at it from a five to ten years point of view'.

Even though it might not be relevant until the eighties, our focus on the bridge issue was similar to the concern that we had about building a new centre on the Waterside. Instinctively we felt that no plan should create a situation where the city would inevitably be permanently divided by the river into two communities. A plan for a high-level bridge at the Narrows near Madams Bank would be symbolic of intent not to divide the city, and of the government's willingness to invest in the future of Derry. However, circumstances were to delay any firm recommendation on our part. Our next meeting, the thirteenth with the Steering Committee took place at the Rural District Council offices on 11 January 1968, to seek approval of the Communications and Landscape Reports. Attending the meeting, in addition to the regular members, was Mr T.M. Megaw, representing Mott, Hay and Anderson, a firm of engineers who were specialists in bridge construction. This firm had been appointed in November 1967 to report to the city and the Ministry of Development on possible sites for a second crossing. Stanley Cochrane, after summarising our traffic proposals in the report and noting the alternative options that we found acceptable, invited Mr Megaw to address the committee on his findings. He emphasised the preliminary nature of his investigations, mentioned four sites that

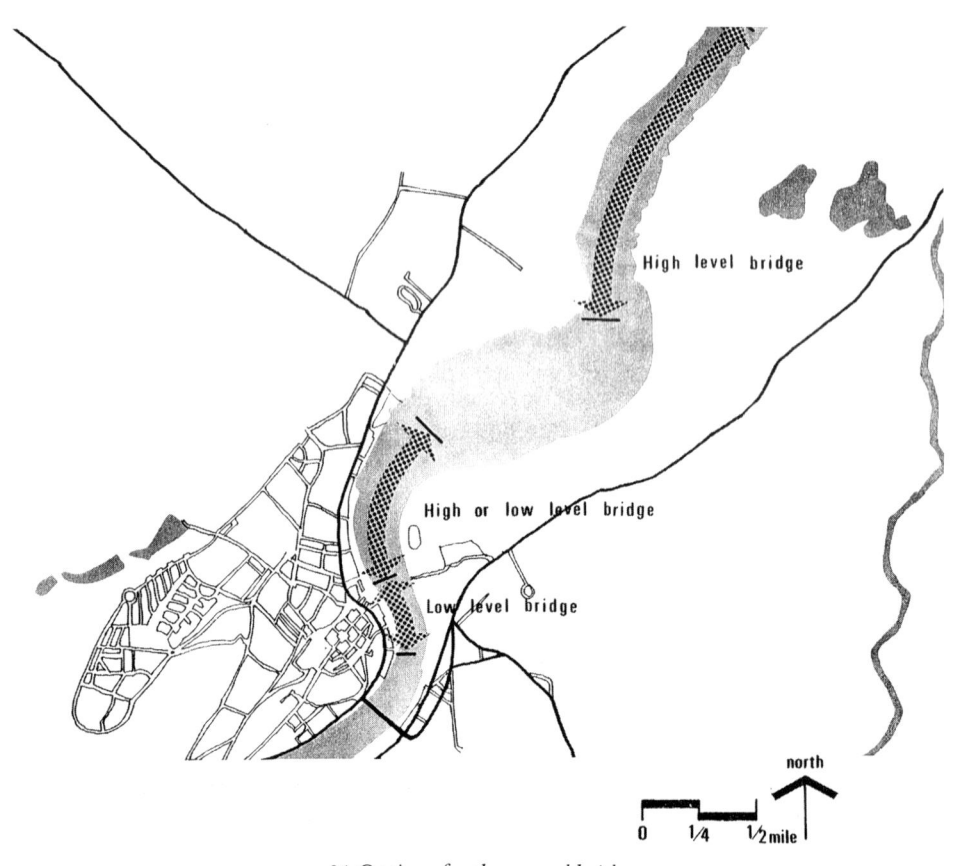

31. Options for the second bridge

his firm was investigating including our favoured options; a low-level bridge just a little south of the Railway Station and the high-level bridge at the Narrows. The other two options, which both he and Colonel MacKinder favoured, would have eliminated St Columb's Park as a recreational area and impinged on the Great James's Street area. The amount of space required for bridge approach roads in both these cases would have torn through the existing fabric ignoring all but the need for the free flow of traffic.

As this put Stan in an awkward position professionally with his engineering colleagues, it was left to me to state the environmental objections we had to these schemes. I also pointed out the relevant passages that Stan and Jack had included in their report on the bridge issue. The important idea put forward was that 'all options should be left open and that "balance sheets" should be drawn up listing the various advantages and disadvantages of all positions so that the right solution could be arrived at'.[10] In addition to considerations related solely to traffic engineering and cost, we emphasised planning and environmental considerations, the effect on harbour activities, acquisition of property and other compensation costs, and the possible effect on property values. These were the considerations that had led the majority of the team to conclude that a high-level bridge at the Narrows was the best option. While we would adopt the strategy of showing only a range of possible locations in the plan, we felt that in the long run the majority choice would be vindicated.

Apart from the issue of the second crossing—heightened in controversy by MacKinder's interventions—the main proposals in the Communications Report were accepted by the committee. Most important of these proposals was the establishment of the idea of Buchanan's environmental areas for the existing and proposed major residential areas, both inside and peripheral to the city boundary. Equally important was the strategy for handling traffic in the

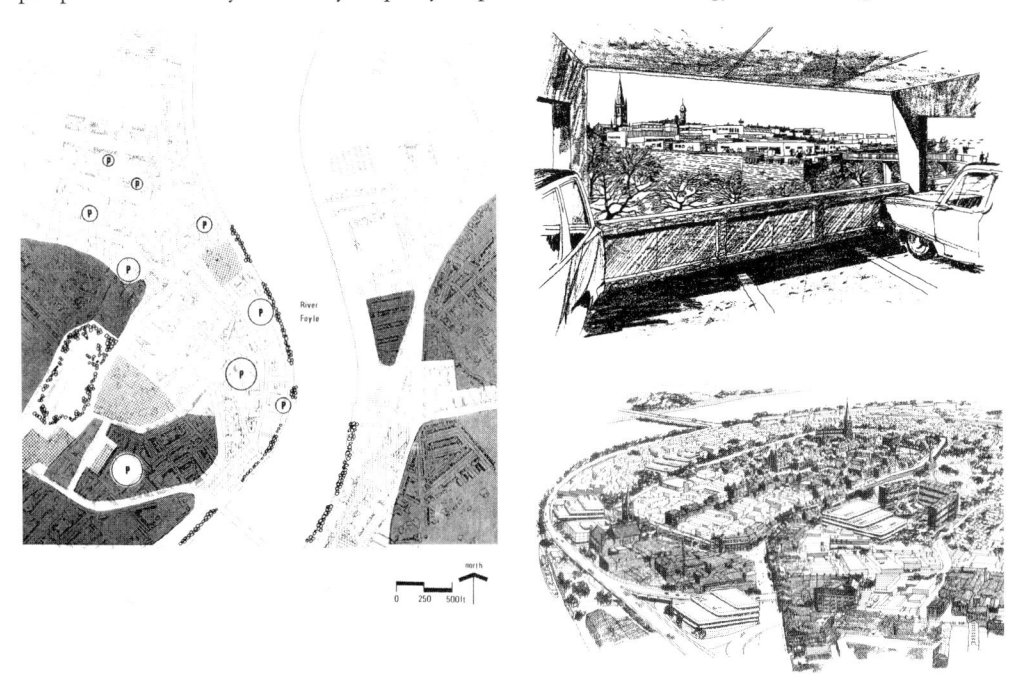

32. (a) Parking locations. (b) Car parking as an integral part of redevelopment. (c) Central area redeveloped

80   PLANNING DERRY

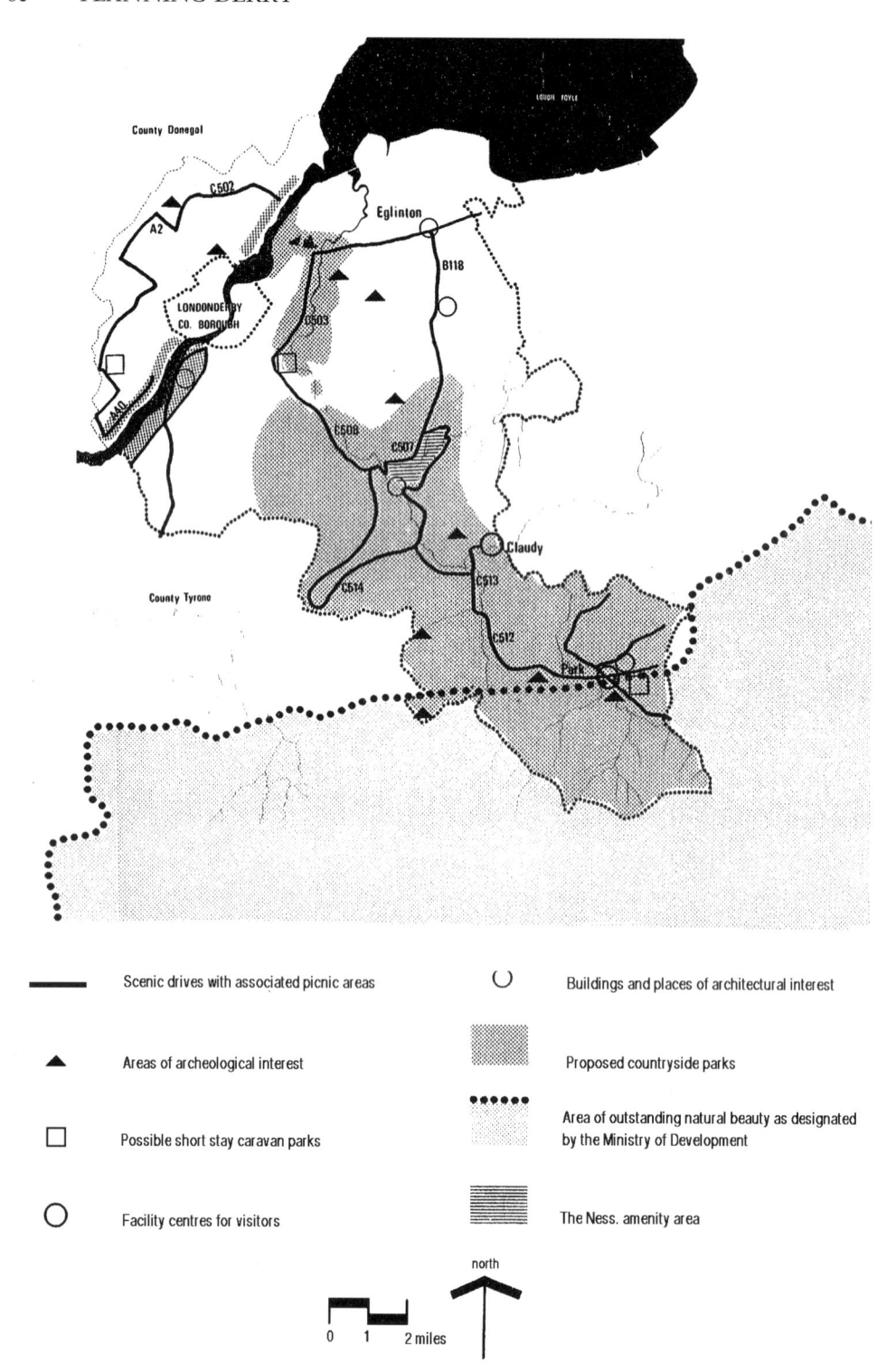

33. *Landscape recreational opportunities*

34. City walls, a tourist attraction

city centre, including the provision for car parks; this also based on the idea of the centre being a major environmental area devoted to commerce.[11] Jimmy Munce was not present at the meeting and missed the acclaim of the committee for the idea of a regional airport. Both the Eglinton and Ballykelly locations were discussed, with the Rural District councillors supporting the Ballykelly site nearer Limavady. Again this was a long-term proposal, and Stan and Jack, despite their reservations, had included both locations as possibilities. The report also dealt with the future of public transportation by rail and bus, and it was recommended that the rail link between Belfast and Londonderry be maintained at least until the M2 motorway was completed. Yet another important recommendation was to consider moving the harbour facilities downstream with expanded container service links.

35. St Columb's Park   *36. City Park*

Following the discussions on the Communications Report, some minor corrections to the Villages Report were drawn to the attention of the committee and it was time to introduce the last report on Landscape, Recreation, and Tourism (No 9). This was introduced by Peter Daniel who, using slides, patiently drew the committee's attention to a number of important landscape features of the area. He described how the 'definition between town and country had become blurred for nearly a century, because the growing city had gradually impinged on its surrounding rural fringe' and how we had then classified the existing landscape of the region into four districts.[12] These were: the human-made landscape of the city or townscape, riverside landscape related to and focused on the River Foyle, seaboard landscape related to Lough Foyle, and the inland landscape of the valleys and lower mountain slopes comprising the farmland of the area. Like the previous reports this was presented in draft form so that the committee could contribute to the process. Now that the more controversial reports had been accepted, the mood of the

37. Farmland

committee seemed to become less obviously negative as the end of the process drew near. Peter's presentation probably evoked some of the best discussion we had experienced, with many members of the committee taking part. The value of tourism as an industry and its impact on the local economy is widely recognised throughout the length and breadth of Ireland. Peter's arguments for the preservation of the historic buildings, places, and parks of the city were readily accepted. Using examples from the area, Peter explained with great clarity that an environment unacceptable to its inhabitants was unlikely to be attractive to visitors, and that growth and its impact on the existing landscape were not necessarily incompatible and could be managed. Some of the criticisms in the report about the state of approach roads to the city and other 'negative comments' would have to be 'softened' to meet the objections of Roy Henderson, the town clerk, and the mayor, but on the whole the report was enthusiastically received. The minutes record that: 'Councillor Doherty and other members spoke of the need to ensure that landscaping was included in all major planning proposals … and the Chairman (Mayor Anderson) asked that the Consultants would write in an additional paragraph on the planting of more trees, and urging legislation to strengthen planning enforcement and make better provision for the preservation of existing trees'.[13]

With the Committee's acceptance of this last report we were now in a position to prepare the draft of the Final Plan. We had come a long way since those early days when it was uncertain whether or not it was possible to produce a plan, given the difficult political situation in the area. The perseverance of the planning team had won through and the last piece of the jigsaw was now in place. With perhaps the exception of Alan Bradshaw, who had accompanied them in their forays into 'enemy territory', most of us remained unaware of the strenuous efforts Jimmy Munce and Bob Simpson made to placate those on the Steering Committee who were against us, and we were never privy to what they put up with as part of the job. Now, residential and industrial location, the development of the central city, an expanded infrastructure of roads and services, the provision of schools and community services to serve a young and growing population, and the preservation and enhancing of the area's natural beauty and landscape had all been encompassed in great detail. Space standards had also been laid down for all these activities and flexibility had been built in with regard to phasing and demand. We believed that there could now be no turning back by the committee on the substantive issues agreed in the nine reports presented to them. At long last we could prepare ourselves for the final thrust.

NOTES

1] Memo from Cochrane to the author dated 27 June 1966. The Munce files on the Londonderry Plan were unfortunately destroyed or lost in an office move by the new firm, Consarc, during the eighties. This memorandum and other material came from Peter Daniel's file.
2] Curl, *Londonderry Plantation,* p. 412. Fig. 336.
3] Memorandum from the City Surveyor to the General Purposes Committee, 14 December 1966.
4] Ibid., p. 3.
5] *Londonderry Area Plan, Report No 5,* pp. 1–5.
6] Memorandum from Peter Daniel to Planning Team, 3 March 1967.
7] Jane Jacobs, *Death and Life of Great American Cities* (New York, The Modern Library, 1961), pp. 291–317.
8] Spiro Kostov, *The City Assembled: The Elements of Urban Form Through History* (London, Thames and Hudson Ltd, 1992).

9] Hausmann certainly succeeded in ridding nineteenth-century Paris of its slums by slicing straight boulevards through older residential areas leaving nothing in his path. One of the motives in constructing these wide streets was to deter the Paris Communes from building barricades and to assist the military in using artillery to quell riots.
10] *Londonderry Area Plan, Report No 8,* pp. 44–5.
11] Buchanan, *Traffic in Towns,* pp. 41–52. The idea within an environmental area [that] the traffic ... should be subordinated to the environment carries with it the important implication that any environmental area must have a maximum acceptable level of traffic. It must, in other words, have a maximum capacity (p. 45).
12] *Londonderry Area Plan, Report No 9,* pp. 3–11.
13] Minutes of the Thirteenth Meeting, Londonderry Area Steering Committee, 11 January 1968, paragraph 14.

8 Selling the Plan

Putting the final plan together would be achieved in a matter of weeks because of the enormous amount of graphics produced by Mike Murray and his team and the availability of both this material and text from the reports. The team had worked day and night for over a year, sacrificing many weekends in the process as had all the team. Because of the nature of their work Mike's group were inevitably at the end of the production line. This usually meant spending anything from two to four days with little or no sleep printing reports to ensure that the Steering Committee's efforts remained focused. Mike told me later that he was never nearer a divorce from his wife Lynn than during this period even though she worked in the office and understood that architects and planners often worked *en charrette* through the night. Alan Bradshaw and Jim Foster were also near the limits of their endurance, but no one complained and the excitement of finally producing a plan and the opportunity to make it public at last kept the momentum going over these final weeks.

I worked with Jim Foster and Mike Murray's team to organise a draft of the final plan, which was to be presented to the Steering Committee at their meeting on 25 January 1968. Taking the text and illustrations from the nine reports, Jim and I proceeded to organise it so that the plan could be read in its entirety by the general public, reducing sometimes lengthy reports into a chapter of twelve pages or so. It was often a struggle to capture the essence of a report using as few technical terms as possible and eliminating any planning jargon that might have inadvertently crept in. With dictionary and thesaurus nearby we would ponder each word and phrase until we were both satisfied, but we had to be careful to keep as near as possible the original text so that the committee would recognise it as something they had already approved. If questioned we would need to be able to refer to the reports and make clear that where changes had occurred they had been made solely in the interests of clarity and continuity. We also had to write a new section to explain the implementation and phasing of the plan and a summary describing the advantages and consequences of implementation.

As all of the text and illustrations had to be rearranged in new format for printing we worked alongside Mike's group to keep the production line moving. During this time Mike had to meet with Sandy Bell in Edinburgh who was to provide additional sketches for the final plan. His sketches in the study reports and John McCrory's photographs had played no small part in muting criticism and winning the Committee's acceptance of our reports. Mike was also making arrangements with Sandy and Peter Daniel to have the large colour fold-out maps prepared. It was no mean feat to produce the draft plan within just two weeks of the previous meeting, and as usual the documents were bound and ready only minutes before we left Belfast for the meeting in Derry.

Since this was the final draft we were hoping that the Steering Committee would not suggest any major changes, as I was worried that they had not even seen the new section on phasing or the summary, which Jim and I had completed two nights earlier. I also knew they would ask for time to consider the draft. In discussing the implementation of the plan, we had been careful to leave

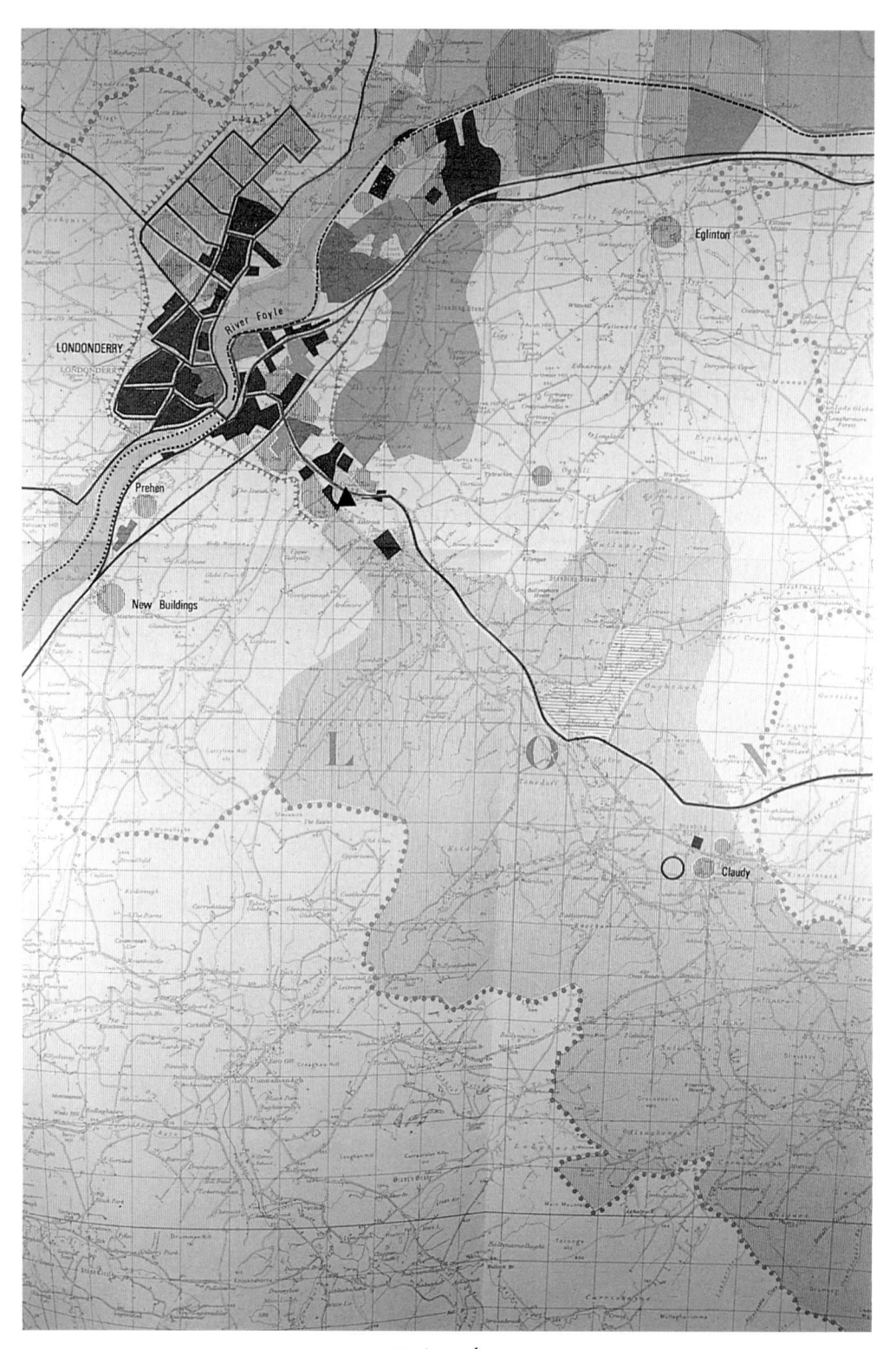

38. Area plan

open the matter suggesting a number of options to the committee. An extension of the city boundary was probably the most controversial political issue, possibly breaking centuries old Protestant domination of the population. We also knew that implementation of the plan by co-operation of the local authorities was equally difficult. Our determination was that the plan would not end up as an academic exercise on someone's shelf, and this pushed us to examine other possibilities however remote.

Jim and I wrote and brainstormed, seeking for a way out of any likely impasse. We favoured the new town option, but this would take power away from the local authorities and place it in the hands of a government-appointed commission. By now New Town legislation in Northern Ireland had caught up with the rest of the UK. Legislation had been put in place under the New Towns Act to select existing towns for expansion as an alternative to building new towns on greenfield sites. We did not know how the committee would react to this, but we carefully buried it in the text with other options seemingly even less feasible. Finally we noted in the plan that:

> Various solutions deserve consideration, such as: implementation by co-operation of all three authorities with arrangements for equity on capital expenditure and return; implementation by means of a boundary extension of the County Borough with the agreement of the Rural District; implementation under the New Towns Act by a New Town Commission; implementation through direct control of the Ministry of Development in association with local authorities; implementation under the aegis of a North-West Sub-Regional Authority, perhaps including the area extending from Strabane through Londonderry to Limavady. Whichever solution is chosen it is imperative that local authorities in the area should co-operate so that the foundations may be laid for future growth to the benefit of all.[1]

By now the committee also appeared anxious to complete the task and a strangely positive working atmosphere persisted. Jimmy Munce had lobbied Commander Anderson long and hard, and although he had seemed reluctant at first, over the last few months he became an almost ebullient enthusiast for the plan. He opened the meeting to talk about how we might now give the efforts of the committee some publicity and announced that he had been in touch with the governor of the Honourable the Irish Society to explore the possibility of a display in the Guildhall in London to mark the launching of the plan. I glanced across at James Doherty to see whether he had noted the colonial gesture, but having endured, I'm sure, many similar proposals inconsiderate of minority feelings, he retained his composure. The Chairman continued noting that the launching 'would probably call for a reception for members of the Society and an invited list of businessmen and others. The theme of the display might be: Londonderry of olden times; Londonderry of the rebuilding in the seventeenth century; Londonderry of Today; and Londonderry of the Future. He had discussed the idea with the Ministers of Commerce and Development who thought it was an excellent suggestion'.[2] Jimmy Munce enthusiastically accepted the task of preparing the exhibition. We had already planned an exhibition as part of our final presentation for the people of Derry. Now it would have to be designed to fit both purposes. The committee members supported the chairman's proposal, which would obviously provide an opportunity to promote the city and also serve as a trade mission. The rest of the meeting was uneventful. Some minor amendments were suggested, including a request for us to find another term to explain urban morphology. The committee also pleasantly surprised us by deciding to release our first five reports to the local councils for consideration and use for planning purposes. Much to my relief no one commented on the various options we had proposed for implementing the plan.

Following the meeting we gathered to discuss the next steps. I would continue to work with Jim, Mike, and Jack to produce the final document, while Alan volunteered to start work immediately on the exhibition. All of this had now to be accomplished in a matter of weeks. Alan must have been anticipating the task, for in a very short time frame he had designed an exhibition which could also be speedily disassembled and packed neatly in a container for transport. It had the added advantage of an integrated lighting system which Alan had also carefully devised. Large-scale reproductions of the diagrams, sketches, photographs, plans, and key text from the reports and final plan were mounted on panels. When assembled, a viewer walking around the exhibition could gain as great an understanding of the plan as anyone reading the final report. Unfortunately yet another obstacle confronted us. The Londonderry Guildhall would be only open to the public for two days instead of the two weeks we had requested. It turned out the main hall would be needed for a badminton tournament and we were unable to find suitable space elsewhere for the whole exhibition.

The exhibition in the Derry Guildhall on 4 March was to be the exciting climax to all our efforts and the opportunity to sell the plan to a waiting sceptical public. It was decided to complement the exhibition, with a public meeting to be held on the evening of the opening, and that I should give a talk and make a slide presentation explaining the plan. Looking back, the evening turned out to be one of my worst nightmares. I had not been on stage in front of a large audience since my brief and unfulfilled acting career in the Drama Society of Methodist College Belfast in the late forties. True I had recently been involved in teaching, but I had enthusiastic receptive audiences of twenty or so students compelled to attend or forfeit the opportunity of timely graduation. I had prepared for the event carefully, albeit hastily, with slides from the various reports. And I was particularly anxious to explain the whole process so that people of all persuasions and political bias would understand the integrity and professional quality of the plan we had produced. In short I was seeking to establish its rational irrefutability. But I did not realise then, as I do now, that it is difficult for audiences to tolerate more than thirty minutes of technical explanations. Although I should have remembered how slide lectures on architectural and planning history, though generally more entertaining than most others, had often the effect of transforming an audience of alert attentive students into a state of languid somnolescence.

The first fifteen minutes or so of my talk went well. I knew there were many in the audience, including local architects as well as those involved in politics, who had their own ideas about how Derry should grow. But as I went through the plan piece by piece, interjecting with the obligatory touch of humour wherever I could, I noticed the audience beginning to reach the point of impatience about the same time as I was about to reach the climax of my discourse. Rather I first noticed Jimmy seated between Commander Anderson and Gilbert Camblin shifting in his seat looking either petulant or distraught, or even both. Then, quickly looked at my watch, I realised I had been speaking for nearly an hour and flipping quickly through the final slides, managed to conclude with as little ignominy as possible giving over the stage to Jimmy and the Commander. There followed some questions from the audience. By and large the evening ended on a positive note, although some reservations were expressed about our proposal for the riverside route and disappointment that we had not been specific about the bridge location. The Derry edition of the *Belfast Telegraph* ran the headline 'Bold Plan for Derry—Putting new life into an old city'. The article was mostly about the Minister of Development's announcement of the 'unveiling of the plan' and Councillor Anderson's proposal to exhibit it in London on 26 March with the help of the Irish Society.[3]

An editorial from *The Derry Chronicle* by Onlooker was much more thorough and informed and began 'Not even the most cynical of our citizens, I think, can escape a flutter of excitement at the prospects of a new, brighter and better Derry opened up by the area plan'. The article went on to welcome even the 'exotic' aspects of the plan and continued:

> Surely the most challenging and utterly realistic objective lies in the field of housing. The planners have set a target of close on 10,000 houses—a rate of nearly 800 a year for the next thirteen years.... Eight hundred houses a year is not an out of the way target for all the agencies involved but it will call for a big step up in the city's post war record of around 100 houses per annum.... Housing is a problem that has been with us for a long time now. Even removed from the all-important context of the area plan it calls for an all-out remedial drive. I'm sure that there are many people in the city who share my view that what they do in this field, will be the test of the sincerity with which the local authorities regard the overall plan for the Derry of 1981.[4]

This was a reassuring editorial for a planning team who could only hope that the plan would prove acceptable to the people of Derry, and who now had to concentrate on the Steering Committee's public relations exercise in London.

Following the opening of the exhibition in London on 26 March a splendid dinner was hosted by the Irish Society, attended by the Lord Mayor of the city of London, a sprinkling of other dignitaries including Edward (Ted) Heath, then leader of the Conservative Party and Field Marshall Alexander, the famous Second World War Ulster General. He was the son of the Earl of Caledon born into the ascendancy in County Tyrone and spent his early years in England attending Harrow and the military academy at Sandhurst. His relationship to his birthplace or with the people of Northern Ireland was no closer than Ted Heath's. This was a publicity exercise, and even if only one or two industrialists became interested in Derry as a result, it would be judged a success. From a professional viewpoint it served to draw some national attention to the plan, and was later reviewed in the *Journal of the Town Planning Institute*:

> The fascination of Londonderry, western outpost of the United Kingdom, comes out vividly in this report on London's first new town ... Recent experience in Northern Ireland seems to indicate the desirability of concentrating new industry in areas where adequate facilities and external economies can develop. It is to be hoped that the necessary public investment will be made to establish the Londonderry area as an effective growth centre, and demonstrate that twentieth-century planners can do as good a job as those of the seventeenth.[5]

It was a good review from a highly regarded planner and while he thought 'the consultants are on safe, if slightly optimistic grounds, in recommending large areas of land to form an industrial land bank', he fully understood the need for public investment in such a situation. Alan Bradshaw and Jim Foster continued with their efforts to increase public awareness of the plan. Unable to get a large enough space to house the whole exhibition, they would show a part of it whenever they could obtain enough space for even a few panels.

For a few months following publication of the plan I continued working on a large housing scheme at Craigavon New Town, which had come into the office and was being designed by two relatively new architects in the office, Graham Spence and Harry Deaney. Jimmy and Bob were trying to garner more work in the Derry area, and Alan and Jim Foster remained in the office there. Our final task with the Steering Committee was to prepare a report outlining the capital costs involved in implementing the plan.

But, in general, things had begun to go awry as the practice became overextended financially with its overseas projects and a growing list of partners and associate partners made the firm 'top heavy'. With the team split up and members engaged in other projects the prospects for additional planning work looked dim. Jimmy fortunately had an incredible capacity for changing focus as circumstances dictated. He was both a committed modernist and futurist with an interest and belief in the benefits of industrial development and atomic energy and had published two books on the subjects. For those of us with interests in planning and urban design, however, the future was less assured. It became clear that any planning work the firm did get could easily be sustained by the use of consultants. As the pace of work slowed, I worried about the security of my young family and began looking out for other prospects. I applied for a position as Principal Planning Officer (Urban Design) with Belfast City Planning Department and took up my new duties in the beginning of June 1968. There I had the task of assisting in the implementation of the city plan prepared by Building Design Partnership (BDP). But again the ramifications of planning and building in a divided society began to impact my life as I became involved in the process of slum clearance and redevelopment. Many of the problems affecting people in the Bogside in Derry were to be found in the Catholic Falls and Protestant Shankill ghettos of Belfast.

NOTES

1] *Londonderry Area Plan,* p. 146.
2] Minutes of the Fourteenth Meeting, Londonderry Area Steering Committee, 25 January 1968, paragraph 1.
3] 'Putting new life into an old city', *Belfast Telegraph,* Derry edition, 4 March 1968, cover.
4] 'A Dream that must come true', *The Derry Journal,* 12 March 1968; chronicle and comment by Onlooker.
5] *Journal of the Town Planning Institute*, 54, no vi (June 1968), p. 295.

9 Interlude

I have often reflected on my decision to leave the Munce Partnership, and while in the long run I had no reason to regret my decision, I realised that my people-participation model did not fit very well with the aggressive entrepreneurial goals of private practice. My planning qualifications had not been acquired without great cost to myself and my young family and I cherished the title of chartered planner. While my ethical standards might have been described as overly conservative at the time, Jimmy's Nietzschean approach to practice sometimes left me unnerved. When we had finished the Derry plan Jimmy had anticipated that we might somehow become involved in its implementation. To his credit he had been prepared to gamble on this and must have sustained considerable losses in producing the plan. While his time commitment and role in Derry had made him a background figure as far as the team was concerned, his advocacy at meetings and his work behind the scenes were critical in dealing with the Steering Committee and getting the plan accepted.

Nevertheless even today I find the necessary marketing aspects of private practice uncomfortable and look back with some nostalgia to what seemed to have been a time when work was earned solely on the basis of reputation. I realise, however, that this pre-fifties model is probably a chimera of my own making, and in this too I have not yet wholly succeeded in discarding my Candide-like persona. But working for the Belfast city planning department, in public service, and being placed in charge of a small office of a dozen or so staff responsible for urban design and design review for a city of approximately 700,000 seemed to be a good alternative to even the imagined vicissitudes of private practice. Also, notwithstanding the spectre of the ring road at that stage in my career it offered a more secure if less exciting livelihood. But my ability to successfully persuade private architects to take more cognizance of the context of their buildings and their social responsibilities, met with more success in contrast to the downright opposition I encountered in my dealings with the city architect's department.

Part of the problem was that the city architect had the responsibility for implementing BDP's plan for inner-city housing, which included proposals for siting medium-rise housing (6 to 8 storeys) along the line of the proposed high-level ring road. One theory behind this strategy was that the higher buildings properly orientated would protect other parts of the neighbourhood from motorway traffic noise. That the idea of putting a large number of people nearest the source of the noise to protect others might seem incongruous, never occurred to anyone. Our role was to comment on but not to delay proposals that would rehouse residents from residential areas earmarked for slum clearance and urban renewal. My negative experiences of this type of housing in Liverpool and my personal antipathy to high-rise and mid-rise development was shared by my staff, who were also familiar with and supportive of Jane Jacobs' views on cities. Our responsibility was to prepare action plans that indicated zoning and allowed for commercial, schools, play space, and other neighbourhood developments. But decisions about housing density and heights along the ring road had already been made, and we could do little to change things especially when the city architect's office was committed to package deals with various contractors. The worst example of this was what became known as the Weetabix housing on the Lower Shankill area—a Protestant district. This name was a local invention to describe ironically the wheat-cereal-like fibreboard permanent form-work for the concrete structure. Medium-rise deck access housing of a different type had already been built in the Catholic Lower Falls and in the Bogside in Derry by the Housing Trust as already described. But there was no tradition in the North of apartment living and these inappropriate mid-rise buildings, like many of their high-rise counterparts in the United States, would be ignominiously demolished by the eighties.[1]

As if these social problems were not enough in themselves, historical Catholic and Protestant civil strife began to emerge as a factor. This had actually started with protests against the liberal policies of O'Neill from followers of the extremist Reverend Ian Paisley. His bigoted clichés concerning a Protestant State were uttered frequently. In June 1966 a young Catholic barman was murdered and two other Catholics wounded by a group calling themselves the Ulster Volunteer Force (UVF), an organisation that had been dormant since the founding of Northern Ireland. The perpetrators were tried and convicted some months later, and O'Neill declared the UVF an illegal organisation under the Special Powers Act. A similar Special Powers Act was in force in the Republic. Under special circumstances the Act allowed that suspected members of the IRA could be interned for belonging to an illegal organisation. O'Neill records in his autobiography that it was now being used for the first time against Protestant paramilitaries.[2] In 1966, as a planner, I took little note of what I considered to be a lunatic fringe as meetings between O'Neill and Lynch continued and evidence of new industrial growth and other developments continued to point to a brighter future. The future had seemed assured when, in 1967, both the Republic and the UK applied for entry to the European Common Market.

That the housing situation in the province would become the tinderbox for civil unrest and violence, on the other hand, should have surprised no-one. By the mid-sixties the power of the conservative Nationalist party in Northern Ireland had begun to wane and was being replaced by more liberal and socialist movements particularly among the urban Catholic populations. The most prominent of these movements to emerge was the Northern Ireland Civil Rights Association (NICRA) based on the civil rights movement in the United States. Another more leftist group, named the People's Democracy, was formed by students from Queen's University Belfast with a young student by the name of Bernadette Devlin prominent among its leaders. The aim of both groups was to demand reform of the franchise in local government elections and in particular to press for not just one man one vote but the establishment of proportional representation as it existed in the Republic. This would, in addition, have made the Unionist propensity for gerrymandering difficult if not impossible. But it would be Nationalist MP Austin Currie who in 1968 would make the move that initially brought publicity and worldwide media attention to discrimination against Catholics in Northern Ireland. In *The Divided Province* Robin Corbett describes how Currie had raised the matter of discrimination in the allocation of housing in his district at the Stormont Parliament. He had completed a housing survey with the help of NICRA and found 'that although the district had a 53 per cent catholic majority, from 1945 to 1968, 71 per cent of all publicly-built homes had been allocated to Protestants'.[3] Finding no recompense for these wrongs in Parliamentary procedure, Currie squatted in a house that had been allocated to an unmarried Protestant woman in preference to a Catholic family. Of course he and other squatters were ejected by the police and prosecuted. But the point had been made and NICRA began a series of marches and demonstrations. The right-wing Protestant reaction from the followers of Reverend Paisley, the Paisleyites, and others was to stage counter-marches.

On 5 October 1986, a march was planned for Londonderry by NICRA but was banned by William Craig (who had become Minister of Home Affairs) because of threats of a countermarch by the Apprentice Boys.[4] I had spoken to James Doherty by phone the day before the march and, knowing the situation in Derry now intimately, wanted to drive up and show my support as I knew he would be participating. Since I was now a public servant and my third child was expected that month I reasoned against going. It was a decision I regret to this day. The marchers were met with water cannons and police batons and later that day rioting broke out in the Bogside area. While I would not necessarily have enjoyed these experiences as related to me by James Doherty after the event, I had failed to follow my conscience. But NICRA was having its impact. In addition to making the case for reform it was exposing the intransigence and bigotry of right-wing Protestants. Finally on 22 November, O'Neill, acting under pressure from Harold Wilson, proposed a list of local government reforms to meet the demands of NICRA. O'Neill relates how he met Brian Faulkner and William Craig in London and went to the meeting in the Cabinet Room without the notes he had prepared. He later wrote, 'In the end, of course, they (Faulkner and Craig) were forced to agree to a package of reforms. It would have been more dignified if we had been able to make our own proposals'.[5] The five-point reform plan included the establishment of the office of Ombudsman to deal with grievances, a promise of electoral reform, fair allocation for local authority housing by means of a points system, and as stated by Corbett 'a review of the Special Powers Act; and the creation of a Londonderry Development Corporation ... to replace the Unionist-controlled Londonderry County Borough Council'.[6]

The latter proposal of course was great news for those that had been involved in the planning of Derry. When Jim Foster and I had suggested the idea of a New Towns Commission we saw it as the only real hope that would prevent the inevitable foot-dragging on the housing issue by the existing councils. But under the circumstances we thought of it only as a remote possibility and one that Stormont might be forced to take if they were serious about having the plan implemented. Now circumstances had forced the Government's hand. But these concessions did not bring an end to the sectarian conflict. In fact the backlash of Protestant extremism and the revival of IRA militancy and terrorism had barely begun. While NICRA had accepted the Unionist five-point plan, for the time being other organisations like the People's Democracy (PD) remained unconvinced. The PD was 'heavily influenced by the wave of left-wing student protest which was sweeping the world during 1968'.[7] They planned a march from Belfast to Derry on 1 January 1969. In her book *The Price of My Soul* Bernadette Devlin notes: 'The respectable people in the Civil Rights Association didn't want to look militant and were on the wane.... Our function in marching from Belfast to Derry was to break the truce, to relaunch the civil rights movement as a mass movement, and to show people that O'Neill was, in fact, offering them nothing. We knew we wouldn't finish the march without getting molested and we were accused of going out looking for trouble'.[8] Her ironic description of the march itself, including running the gauntlet from Paisleyites as they were escorted through towns by an unprotective police force, borders on being hilarious. Yet the small group was in obvious danger and was finally beaten unmercifully by a Protestant mob at Burntollet Bridge near Claudy in County Londonderry, just ten miles from Derry itself. Stones and clubs were used by the assailants as police stood by either unable or unwilling to protect the mainly student marchers. The march was followed yet again by riots in the Bogside. By April 1969, O'Neill had resigned the Premiership leaving an increasingly hardline Unionist majority in Stormont while Bernadette Devlin had become the youngest member of the British House of Commons, representing Mid-Ulster. Her more liberal colleagues in NICRA, John Hume and Austin Currie, had also been considered as candidates, but both were now members of the opposition in Stormont and proved unacceptable in this majority republican stronghold.[9] Devlin, on the other hand, pictured with Eamon McCann at the forefront of every Bogside riot, had become a television personality and her overtly Marxist rhetoric endeared her to the Official IRA movement of the time.

Derry had become the focus of international attention in an opposite sense to what we had hoped for as planners. It has even been suggested that we could have spoken out about the obstacles we encountered in Derry and put the spotlight on the situation. But the attitude of Unionist councillors in the city and rural district was already well known and as consultants we were striving to project a positive image to attract jobs and promote new housing. Ken Bloomfield notes that even Prime Minister Terence O'Neill 'had sought to educate some of the leading Unionist magnificos of the city to the implications for the wider Northern Ireland state if they turned an obdurate face to all suggestion of reform. To many people, it was painfully clear in these exchanges that they did not give a damn what might happen in Northern Ireland at large; they would fight tooth and nail to hold on to what they had locally'.[10] But while the current events seemed negative from the point of view of attracting investment, the positive side was that it had now become possible to deal with the housing situation through the New Town Commission. With encouragement from James Doherty I interviewed for the position of Chief Architect-Planner for the Commission, and I recall that both Gilbert Camblin and the new chairman, former realtor Sir Brian Morton, were present at my interview. James Watson, a planner from Glasgow, was chosen in preference to me. I concluded that either he must have had more experience or more likely that those responsible continued to prefer real expertise from the more intelligent English or Scottish natives. Hardly surprising, I thought, since most chief architects or planners were recruited from outside the province. On the other hand, maybe I had burnt my bridges to some extent when I left Jimmy's office. My failure to gain a similar chief architect/planner position later with the Antrim-Ballymena New Towns Commission, when an English planner was appointed, convinced me that my ability to contribute to the future of the province in any significant role was limited by my ethnicity. But both Jim Foster and Alan Bradshaw were appointed to Watson's staff and brought with them all the enthusiasm and vigour they had shown while making the plan. They would continue as guardians of the plan and key players in its implementation and future development.

Meanwhile throughout the Province the pattern of peaceful civil rights demonstrations were being replaced by traditional violent confrontations between working-class Catholics and Protestants. I was to experience this first hand when Michael Sherry, another planner in the city planning office, asked me to accompany him to Bombay Street in the Catholic Clonard district of Belfast. Rioting had occurred some months previously and Catholic homes had been attacked by a Protestant mob and set alight. The Planning Department had been helpful in waiving some of the planning procedures to allow for speedy reconstruction of the dwellings. But they had proceeded without the approval of the Building Inspector's office. Now that work was complete we were to meet Sean Mackel, a young architect in private practice who was active in working with community groups on housing rehabilitation problems, an interest I and others in the department shared with him. The burnt-out red-bricked three-storey homes, once a depressing site, had been restored. Most of the speeches at the opening were in Irish, which Michael understood but which Sean had to translate for me. The violence experienced in Bombay Street, however, continued to escalate with the focus of attention shifting between Derry and Belfast. In Belfast, Catholics were in the minority, and many were already leaving, fearing the wrath of militant Protestants, themselves fearful of losing their specious privileged position as a result of a civil rights movement supported by the sympathetic Labour government in London.

In early August 1969 the Bogside area in Derry was again the focus of violent confrontations between Catholics and police who received the unsolicited assistance of Protestant extremists. In Belfast Catholic homes were also being attacked and many had begun fleeing to the Republic for safety. With the police unable to handle the situation, British troops were ordered in to separate the warring factions. At first the troops were welcomed by the Catholic population, but as 1969 drew to a close violence lurked around every corner, and the atmosphere was tense. The IRA had not been able to defend the Catholic areas as they wished, although many had participated in the civil rights marches and in the riots that followed. The traditional (Official) IRA had abandoned its militancy in favour of a more political left-wing role. Some members of the IRA in Belfast, frustrated at their inability to defend Catholic areas against attacks by Protestant mobs, had formed a militant breakaway organisation known as the Provisional IRA. This organisation was to become the leading perpetrator of violence in the coming decades. Writing in 1988 Paul Arthur and Keith Jeffery note that:

> Over the past eighteen years the Provisionals have become perhaps the most sophisticated and experienced terrorist group in western Europe.... their role as protectors of the Catholic community soon developed into one of mobilising the community into mass demonstrations both violent and peaceful.... The second main strand in the Provisionals' campaign of violence consists principally of attacks on government security and economic targets with the intention of so destabilising the community that law and order, as enforced by the existing (British) authorities, completely breaks down, the British government gives up the struggle and a demoralised loyalist community acquiesces in the establishment of a United Ireland.[11]

From 1970 on, violence was now no longer confined to the Catholic and Protestant ghettos. Police and military became targets and public buildings and pubs frequented by off-duty police and the army were bombed. The main weapons were bombs indiscriminately placed in cars, left in brief cases, or carried in purses and placed surreptitiously in store display areas. Warnings often came too late and many innocent people would be killed in the years that followed. Protestant paramilitary groups also armed in response to IRA violence and a new organisation, the Ulster Defence Association, was formed. The UVF (Ulster Volunteer Force), working within the same areas, upscaled their murder campaign, killing innocent Catholics in their often fruitless pursuit of IRA members. Death and destruction became commonplace events on the evening television news. The British army established 'peace' lines of walls and barbed wire to separate fractious communities. Yet somehow the majority of people in Northern Ireland endeavoured to go on with their daily tasks stoically and even humorously tolerating the searches and the inconvenience associated with the troubles. But hundreds of innocent men, women, and children would die in addition to police, members of the armed forces, and paramilitary groups. It is sad to reflect that it takes only a handful of fanatics to create mayhem and violence even though the majority of people, whatever their political leanings, may want to go peacefully about their day-to-day affairs. But once factions in the population begin to acquiesce with the action and reaction that violence brings, the level of terrorism begins to escalate and even becomes politicised. In the end acquiescence of violence becomes part of the violence itself, and then all of society must share in the guilt of unscrupulous criminal perpetrators.

In the spring of 1971, I was invited to London to meet my friend Jack Morley, a professor at the University of Kansas, and Charlie Kahn, the new dean of the School of Architecture. Jack, a veteran Second World War navy pilot, had attended Edinburgh University with me and he had been instrumental in arranging my visiting assistant professorship to the University of Kansas in 1965. We discussed the possibility of me returning to Kansas on a permanent basis, and several weeks later I received an offer of a tenured position on the faculty. With my three boys ranging in age from 11 to 3 years old I had no difficulty in making the decision, although I had barely lived in my new home for two years. Besides, my ego was still badly bruised following my rejection for the positions in Derry and Antrim-Ballymena. Barely one month after we left, in August 1971, all hell broke loose as Brian Faulkner introduced internment under the Special Powers Act, and hundreds of IRA and UVF suspects were rounded up and imprisoned without trial. We watched television with the rest of the world as the violence increased in tempo. Shaking the dust off my feet as I left Belfast had seemed easy at the time, but living away from the troubles was almost as bad as living in them. In time other things occupied my mind, but my wife Norma loved Belfast and regretted leaving family and friends. (We would return again in 1973 in an attempt to reestablish roots and, in my case, to make a contribution to the public housing programme. But with the failure of the Northern Ireland Assembly[12] and the unabated campaign of violence by the IRA, I returned to Kansas with my family in 1976, sad and disillusioned but this time determined to start a new life.)

Then in 1972 the British Government prorogued the Stormont Parliament and introduced direct rule from Westminster.[13] The Stormont Government had lasted just fifty years. As a separate state with its own government it had been given responsibility for the welfare of all the inhabitants of Northern Ireland and had been found wanting. John Oliver points out that when it was founded in 1922: 'No one had been campaigning for a separate state. To the protestants and unionists the new settlement represented a second best.... To the Roman Catholics and nationalists it represented such a bitter disappointment ... that they could not find it in their hearts to give their loyalty to it'.[14] Robert Kee in the penultimate chapter of his excellent book on Irish history quotes Eddie McAteer's words concerning the people of Northern Ireland when he said: 'We're all prisoners of history here'.[15] Yet within that prison with all its turbulence, dedicated and determined people would continue planning and building. New public housing, much of it excellent quality, would empty most of the slums of Derry and Belfast. New industries and revitalised town centres would emerge, and while problems both social and political would still exist, the work of reconstruction would go forward. It would remain for Alan Bradshaw, James Doherty, Paddy Doherty, Jim Foster, John Hume, and many others to tell the story of Derry after 1976.

NOTES

1] Note the dynamiting of Pruitt Igoe Public Housing project in St Louis, Missouri, in Oscar Newman, *Community of Interest* (New York, Anchor Press/Doubleday, 1980), p. 88. See also Newman, *Defensible Space* (New York, Macmillan, 1972).
2] O'Neill, *Autobiography,* p. 82.
3] Robin Corbett, 'The Civil Rights Crisis', in Jeffrey, *The Divided Province,* p. 39.
4] Ibid., p. 41.
5] O'Neill, *Autobiography,* p. 105.
6] Corbett, 'Civil Rights', p. 40.
7] Ibid., p. 40.
8] Bernadette Devlin, *The Price of My Soul* (New York, Alfred A. Knopf, 1969), p. 134.
9] Ibid., pp. 183–5.
10] Ken Bloomfield, *Stormont in Crisis A Memoir* (Belfast, The Blackstaff Press: 1994), pp. 99–100.
11] Paul Arthur and Keith Jeffery, *Northern Ireland since 1968* (Oxford, Basil Blackwell, 1988), pp. 64–9.
12] Following the Sunningdale Agreement in 1973 the Northern Ireland Assembly was established on the basis of proportional representation with a power sharing Catholic and Protestant Assembly elected. I had for a brief period the privilege of working indirectly for Austin Currie, the minister responsible for housing. Had Gerry Fitt, John Hume, Austin Currie, and Paddy Devlin of the SDLP and the more reasonable Protestant politicians been able to withstand the assaults of the extreme Protestants and Provisional IRA I would have probably stayed in Northern Ireland. Unfortunately the Assembly was brought down barely one year after its existence by a Protestant workers strike. It marked yet another tragic event in Ireland's history.
13] Northern Ireland was now the responsibility of Westminster with a Northern Ireland office headed by a secretary of state who was a member of the British Prime Minister's Cabinet. The secretary of state assumed all the powers of the former governor and prime minister of Northern Ireland. British MPs were appointed to take over important ministerial posts.
14] John Andrew Oliver, *Working at Stormont Memoirs* (Dublin, Institute of Public Administration, 1978), p. 22.
15] Kee, *Ireland,* p. 248.

10 The Development Commission

The Londonderry Development Commission was established in 1969 by the O'Neill Government as it tried to stave off the impending crisis brought about by years of discrimination against Catholics in employment and housing. Under New Town Legislation adapted from the British model, an existing town could be designated for expansion. As in the case of a new town, a government commission would be appointed to subsume the powers of existing local authorities and implement the plan. The commission would be kept in place until such time as the plan was implemented and the normal process of governance by a town council would thereupon resume.

So Derry, for the second time in its history, became a 'new town'. Neither Jim Foster nor I could have suggested that our speculative suggestion for implementation of the plan, excluding the involvement of the Unionist-dominated local authorities, would be realised so soon. That it did occur was not so much based on the rational objectivity of our recommendation but rather the mounting violence that left a weakened Stormont Government little alternative.[1] It now seemed that some modicum of justice had been achieved as the gerrymandering Derry mayor and his Unionist councillors were despatched with one stroke of the pen. Brian Morton (later Sir Brian), a prominent Northern Ireland realtor, was appointed chairman of the Commission and Stephen McGonagle, a former President of the Irish Congress of Trade Unions, was appointed vice-chairman. Gerald Bryan, formerly Chief Executive and head of the Civil Service on the Isle of Man, turned out to be a highly effective general manager. There was equal representation of both Catholic and Protestant members forming the rest of the Commission, but its establishment would prove to be no panacea for the rising tide of violence. As Stephen McGonagle remembers: 'We met in the Guildhall on 2nd April 1969 only to be met by Luddite squatters led by Eamonn McCann and Bernadette Devlin who were protesting everything.'[2] Thereafter the Commission was forced to hold its meetings in the Rural District offices whose powers it had also subsumed.

The commission now moved swiftly to remove political roadblocks to housing development and to promote industrial development, successfully moving ahead with the development at Springtown, where the first two advance factories were built. Land was also acquired for small industrial estates including the provision of electrical and water services; estates at Springtown, Pennyburn and Campsie were developed, and at the urging of Stephen McGonagle, the first industrial training centre was set up. The Commission had inherited many of the professional and technical staff from the County Borough and the Rural District, among them Colonel MacKinder, William McKee, and David White. The latter two helped the new commission move forward with its housing and industrial programme. The Colonel, on the other hand, was still trying to get his bridge built from St Columbs Park to Northland Road. As Stephen McGonagle recounts: 'I told the Chairman to point out to MacKinder that the purpose of the new bridge was to relieve the city centre of traffic—not to bring more into it!'

It must be remembered that the 1968 plan was a broad brush plan that defined a number of action areas where more detailed plans were needed. The James Munce Partnership, with Peter

Daniel as consultant, had subsequently been commissioned to produce plans for the city centre and other areas, but, the action plans for new housing that were developed to a stage capable of being implemented immediately by the commission were those produced by the Housing Trust and the County Borough Council, which had been delayed for political reasons. Despite some reservations about the quality of new building voiced by the Commission's architects, the production of large numbers of new homes took priority. Given the backlog of housing and the desperate housing need, there was little alternative, and James Watson, the chief architect, proved himself suited to the task. In the circumstances of an accelerated building programme and in the prevailing conditions of social unrest, it was inevitable that mistakes were made. New housing at Gobnascale, a scheme approved by the former Londonderry City Council, went counter to the recommendations in the plan about protecting the skyline. A scheme for redevelopment of the Fountain area near the city walls was designed hurriedly and insensitively. In the disruptive circumstances in which the Commission had to carry out its work, the understanding that public participation would be sought in the development of new schemes became more an exercise in public relations.

However, the Commission made great progress in implementing the 1968 plan and, together with the Housing Trust, developed speedily new areas designated for housing. I personally came to appreciate the difficulties in resisting pressure to produce housing in large numbers. In 1974, the Chairman of the Northern Ireland Housing Executive, Desmond Lorimer (later Sir Desmond), asked me to find ways to accelerate housing production when the Executive was fighting for its political life.[3] C.E.B. Brett, chairman of the Housing Executive from 1978 to 1984, referring to the work of the Londonderry Development Commission in 1986, noted that 'Despite all obstacles, it set in hand a large programme, and by January 1973 a total of nearly 4,000 new houses had been provided',[4] Stephen McGonagle, during the first two years of the Commission's existence, spearheaded the house-building effort by encouraging both architects and contractors to 'fast track' building programmes. But as the commission pressed forward with its programme through 1970 and 1971, the violence escalated, particularly in the city centre and Bogside area. In early August, Internment (imprisonment without trial on suspicion of being a member of 'an illegal organisation') was introduced by the Stormont government. Barely a week later, John Hume and Ivan Cooper, both representing the SDLP (Social Democratic Labour Party) in the Stormont government, were manhandled by British armed forces while leading a peaceful demonstration. In protest to these events, all Catholic members of the Commission, including Stephen McGonagle withdrew their services from the Commission. Catholic members of other area boards took similar action. Early in 1972 an event that became known as 'Bloody Sunday' occurred when British paratroopers fired on a banned civil rights march killing thirteen people after IRA gunmen allegedly opened fire on them.[5] So chaotic had the situation become, the British could no longer support the actions of the Unionist government under Faulkner, and in March 1972, the Ulster Parliament was dissolved. By then a train of events was in progress that would presage the end of Derry's short period as a second new town.

However, the Commission would not be disbanded before a draft of the Londonderry Area Plan 1972 Review was published. Jim Foster and a small group of planners under the direction of James Watson worked on the Plan which did not introduce any major new proposals, but fleshed out details necessary for the 1968 Plan to be implemented. In 1975 it also replaced the 1968 Plan as a statutory document making provision for growth based on a population of 98,800 instead of the original 94,500 forecast in the Munce Plan. Proposals were also made to acquire land in the city centre and prepare the ground for reconstruction as soon as circumstances allowed. The city centre had been badly damaged as a result of riots and vandalism and the constant presence of troops and police in the area surrounding the Bogside. Further recommendations for the expansion of education and recreation facilities and the creation of new jobs in both service and manufacturing sectors were highlights of the revised plan. Finally the plan included a detailed road network for the city and expanded areas with a proposed new high-level bridge at the Narrows just north of Madams Bank. The option for a new airport at Eglinton was left open.

The authors of a government report published in 1970 had noted that:

> Probably no town in Britain has suffered so much from bad publicity as Londonderry has done in recent months.... If peace can be preserved, Londonderry may still be well placed to attract new industry, and to allow existing industry to develop. In addition to the establishment of a large training centre and a new industrial estate, the infrastructure of the area, never nearly as bad as press and television implied, is now being substantially improved, on the lines set out in the Development Plan prepared by James Munce Partnership. Responsibility for implementing the plan was transferred from Londonderry Corporation and Rural District Council to the new Development Commission in 1969. This is one example of the value of administrative change. We have subsequently been much impressed by the vigour of the new body and the progress being made. If a comprehensive plan can now be devised for the harbour area, we shall be reasonably satisfied as far as the development of the town's infrastructure is concerned.[6]

The 1972 Plan Review had noted the deterioration of some of the Harbour facilities without making recommendations beyond those already embodied in the 1968 Plan. The Harbour Commissioners were already considering moving the harbour facilities downstream to the vicinity of Black Brae as recommended in the 1968 Industrial Report (No 4) published as an appendix to the 1968 Plan. This was eventually carried out under the chairmanship of James Eaton with aid from the European Regional Development Fund, which John Hume, who had always supported the move, had helped obtain. Downstream there was more opportunity to expand the port facilities and in particular container services, as recommended in the Report. Reflecting on the move, which was only realised in 1993, James Doherty, who was also deputy chairman of the Commissioners during six critical years of its history, noted that the relocation allowed for 15,000-ton vessels to enter the port, and industries associated with the harbour added value through the expansion and development of grain imports, coal processing, and cement. Not only is the port thriving, but the problems of dredging the channel and maintaining the decaying wharfside buildings near the city centre have been resolved. This allows for the removal of remaining obsolete buildings to accommodate new growth, and the development of the quayside route and riverside walk.

While many developments were taking place between 1969 and 1973, major political changes were occurring as a result of the civil disturbances. The reorganisation of local government had been under review since 1969. In December 1970, the Northern Ireland government accepted the recommendations of the Macrory report for reorganising the functions of the two county borough councils (Belfast and Londonderry), six county councils, and 65 borough, urban district and rural district councils by reducing the number of administrative bodies to five area boards and twenty-six new district councils.[7] In 1971 the Northern Ireland Housing Executive, a large centralised body, was established by James Callaghan, the British Prime Minister, at the urging of SDLP leadership and in particular John Hume. This was to be modelled on the Northern Ireland Housing Trust, and took over housing functions originally the responsibility of the sixty-five councils.[8] According to Charles Brett, and put on record by Housing Trust Chairman Herbert Bryson, James Callaghan stated 'the Trust was the only organisation in Northern Ireland of which there was absolutely no criticism in Whitehall'.[9] Brett also records that the three New Town Development Commissions (Antrim/Ballymena, Craigavon, and Londonderry) were dissolved in 1973 when the Housing Executive took over their housing functions. As already noted, a more dramatic but no less significant change had occurred in 1972 when the British government suspended the Northern Ireland government and introduced direct rule from Westminster.

The early demise of the Londonderry Development Commission fortunately did not halt the impetus of new development, particularly in the case of housing. Gerry Ashton, an experienced senior architect with the Housing Trust, was appointed regional architect by Rae Evans, the first director of development of the new Housing Executive. With Alan Bradshaw, Michael McCafferty, and a number of other architects, landscape architects, quantity surveyors, and engineers formerly with the Commission and Trust, his team was soon leading the Executive in the production of new housing and redevelopment. The major housing development of Ballyarnett/Shantallow recommended in the Munce plan was well under way. Other planning functions affecting the city were taken up by the Department of the Environment (DOE)—Roads Service, Planning Service, and Water Service. The DOE for Northern Ireland was managed by the Civil Service reporting to a permanent secretary who in turn reported to the secretary of state for Northern Ireland. David White became the development officer for Londonderry, with James Watson and Jim Foster both on the planning staff, and William McKee responsible for Water Services. The Northern Ireland Electricity Authority co-ordinated electricity services, and there was a Board for Education and Libraries. The city council was re-established, this time with a majority of Catholic supported political parties. However, its role, like the other new area councils, was no longer multi-functional but restricted to functions such as recreation, public health, and cemeteries, and its relationship to the new administrative bodies was advisory.

David White had been aggressively pursuing land acquisition on the large scale necessary for the implementation of the plan. He successfully acquired large areas of land in and around the city centre, along the quayside and in the rural district to provide access for new roads, and in the city and urban/rural fringe to accommodate potential new industries. It was his foresight and hard work at this stage that ensured that the strategies outlined in the plan would be achieved. Now, as chief administrative officer, his importunity knew no bounds as he pressed the Stormont regime for funds to implement the 1972 Plan. There was a public inquiry in 1974 to review the Plan, and the participation of interested citizens demonstrated that it now had more widespread public support. Success with the provision of new housing and the establishment of new industries against all odds were persuasive cards that White did not hesitate to play as he pleaded the case for development of the city centre and a new roads programme that would include the new bridge. Most of the Commission's successes had been in the development of new areas away from the central area, as the seventies was a period of sporadic disturbances and confrontations between rioters and security forces. Businesses were leaving the city centre, which at this time had the appearance of a war zone—which of course is more or less what it had become.

The situation was later described in the *Guardian* newspaper under the banner headline 'Tumbledown Derry'.[10] Peter Hetherington's description and Robert Smithies' photographs painted a bleak and depressing picture of the situation. Between IRA bombings and DOE road clearances, the city centre looked rather like cities that had been heavily bombed and shelled during the Second World War. Hetherington noted that: 'In the last three years more than 5,200 houses have either been destroyed or badly damaged, 124 business premises, mainly offices and shops, have also been destroyed and 1,809 damaged. The city has been so devastated that the entire centre will have to be rebuilt.' He went on to describe his visit to David White's office with plans for Derry's future pinned on the walls around him. He was surprised by the positive attitude in the midst of the chaos when White told him, 'What appals me is the negative nature of all of this. If somebody came along with over 7 millions and said "here, make Derry a better place to live in", think of what we could do.' Hetherington went on to point out that, 'the total cost of redevelopment up to 1981 was originally put at £110 million but it is likely to be more than £140 million by now.'

Paradoxically, the turbulence and destruction in the city also served to emphasise the need to improve the situation by the injection of more government funds. In February 1973, a photograph of William Whitelaw, the first secretary of state under direct rule, standing behind a scale model of the new bridge had appeared in the *Derry Sentinel*. Below the photograph was the announcement that he had guaranteed government support for the project. White, who had been lobbying Stormont officials for months on the need for a second bridge, had actually stage-managed the occasion. John Hume, also active in promoting the needs of his constituency and native city, was a spokesman for the project. In 1972 the UK and the Republic of Ireland joined the European Economic Community (EEC), and Hume now represented the Derry area in both the European and UK parliaments. Money for the implementation of the plan could now be sought from both sources, but most funding over the next two decades would come by way of direct subsidies from the British government.

David White persisted in his efforts to get funding for the new bridge and to encourage investment in the city centre, but even as the violence began to subside, his task seemed impossible. The 1968 Munce Plan had placed a great deal of emphasis on the redevelopment and expansion of commercial activities in the city centre. In doing so, we had assumed that living patterns would continue as they had in the past and that the expansion of residential development to the north would enhance the economic viability of the central area. In discussing our strategy, Peter Daniel had used the analogy of the development of Edinburgh's nineteenth-century new town expansion in relation to its medieval town. During the turmoil of the seventies a change of population took place that none of us could have envisaged. About 15,000 of the west bank population (mostly Protestants) moved to the east bank thereby increasing demand for commercial facilities in the Waterside.[11] Undoubtedly some families moved because of IRA intimidation, but the exodus was mostly driven by fear (one should note that Catholics in Belfast, intimidated by Protestant mobs, were moving out of mixed areas for similar reasons). Figures from the 1991 census in Derry indicated that 95 per cent of the population on the west bank was Catholic, while on the east bank 40 per cent of the population was Catholic and 60 per cent Protestant.

Notwithstanding the population trends that had begun to develop in the late seventies, David White remained convinced of the need to redevelop the central area and continued to pursue the original goals of the Munce plan. He continued to enter into negotiations with several potential developers despite his concern that the successful new district shopping centres at Shantallow on the west bank and Lisnagelvin on the east bank might eventually erode the commercial viability of the city centre. These negotiations were frequently interrupted by nearby explosions in or around the city centre. By 1976, now almost desperate, he succeeded in persuading a developer to submit a proposal. A scheme was drawn up by Keppie Henderson, a large Glasgow firm of architects who had designed major shopping malls elsewhere in the UK. But at the last minute, the developer withdrew. Undeterred, White continued lobbying the secretary of state's officials for funds to build the new bridge and to kick-start development of the central area. He now had the outline scheme for the Richmond Shopping Centre and he argued that the speedy implementation of both the bridge and the Centre were essential to the future of the city. While Ken Bloomfield, the permanent secretary, was supportive, Minister Philip Goodheart was not. He suggested waiting for another twelve months. But White was adamant that no developer viewing the devastation of the central area would be willing to invest in the project when the government itself was fearful of taking the same risk. Eventually his argument prevailed and by 1981 both the new bridge and the Richmond Centre were under construction. Nearly twelve million pounds was invested by the government in the shopping centre, which was officially opened in 1984 by Chris Patten, MP, later Governor of Hong Kong. According to Jim Foster 'this investment and the subsequent leases taken up by large national stores saved the commercial life of the centre. Traders who had stayed during the worst of the violence began to experience an increase in trade.'[12] By the 1980s, the violence had begun to tail off but the market was still depressed by the continued security threat. But also by this time, the government had introduced the Urban Development Grant Programme (UDG) to encourage the repair and development of city centre property. The UDG was intended to make up the difference between the cost of carrying out the development and the value of the development on completion.

Again according to Jim Foster, government investment has provided real muscle while powerfully supporting the enterprise of those in private sector behind the recovery of the city centre. Up to the present, by means of Urban Development Grants, the government has invested almost twenty-five million pounds in about five hundred projects now valued at one hundred and sixty million. These projects range from small improvement schemes in the thousands to the recently built multi-level Foyle-Side Centre costing in the range of sixty-five million pounds to build. In addition to the efforts made by existing traders to improve the centre, in 1981 Paddy Doherty (known affectionately by the local population as 'Paddy Bogside') took upon himself the enormous task of trying to restore and improve historic buildings within the walls. He attacked the problem head-on by buying a derelict building in London Street and restoring it with money he had raised from community donations. Thereafter, in 1983, he established the Inner City Trust and set about the task of renewing and developing the area within the walls. The first chairman of the Inner City Trust was Michael McCafferty, an architect from the Housing Executive, and Paddy Doherty was its chief executive officer. Between 1983 and 1996 the Inner City Trust saved and refurbished a number of properties in Pump Street. Doherty also began work on a

39. Richmond Centre under construction, and section of high level bridge being floated downstream behind Guildhall

40. Chris Patten and David White at the opening of the Richmond Centre

100-bedroom hotel on Butcher's Street, a youth hostel on Magazine Street, and a replica of the sixteenth-century O'Doherty's Fort on its historic site to house a museum and craft village. Apart from being major tourist attractions, these latter developments are all sensitively carried out and both respect and enhance the existing context of walls and historic streets.

House completions continued to rise during the seventies and eighties through the efforts of the Housing Executive. Though producing smaller numbers than the Executive, the Derry Housing Association continued to build family homes, and made a considerable contribution under the leadership of Father Anthony Mulvey. By the eighties the Association had begun to provide small attractive sheltered housing schemes for special needs populations not being accommodated by the larger developments of the Executive. Industrial development was

THE DEVELOPMENT COMMISSION

41. (a) Richmond Centre, entry from Shipquay Street. (b) Shipquay Street looking east towards Guildhall

42. Housing—Derry Housing Association, Father Mulvey Park

43. High level bridge at the Narrows

also picking up momentum. Here, David White was again involved in pressing the government for resources to meet the special needs of Derry. Courtaulds had abandoned its large petrochemical operation at Campsie, and the Department of Commerce had offered no incentives to persuade them to stay. He argued that Enterprise Zone legislation should be utilised to assist new industries, small businesses, and manufacturing distribution. When White retired, the cause was taken up by Joe Cowan who became development officer for Derry from 1986 on. Cowan modestly puts the enormous progress made in implementing the plan during the next decade down to being in the right place at a fortunate time when violence was waning. Clearly, without his exceptionally focused energy and creative enterprise and the groundwork of his predecessor, Derry would not be the place it is today. He was quick to realise that Urban Development Grants could leverage three to four times value in private sector development and he looked at ways to make legislation work for the development of the city. Cowan was also working in the department led by Richard Needham who was minister at the time, had a good working relationship with John

Hume. Moreover, Hume had stirred Needham's interest in utilising funding mechanisms to improve the situation in Derry.

Elsewhere in the UK, Enterprise Zone legislation was used to assist retailers. Within enterprise zones the government guaranteed a tax-free exemption for a period of ten years and also made available urban development grants. The government accepted White and Cowan's special needs argument in the case of Derry. John Hume had also been successful in pressing the case for Derry with the European Union and, as mentioned, had obtained a regional grant to help in the construction of the new bridge.

Today, Pennyburn, Springtown, and Maydown industrial estates are full while Courtaulds' original huge plant has been converted into small rental units. The establishment of plants in Derry by Fruit of the Loom and Seagate, a computer industry, has given the economy a boost. Existing industries such as Du Pont (petrochemical) and Hunters (shirt manufacturing) continue to provide a stable industrial base. Of the new indigenous industries, Perfecseal, producing packaging for medical equipment, stands out as one of the most creative and productive enterprises. The 1981–6 Area Plan carried out under the direction of Jim Foster was a reappraisal of the 1968 Munce Plan and the 1972 Review Plan, adopted with amendments in 1975.[13] It established growth proposals for a new target population of 102,000 by 1996. The formation of new households and replacement of older dwellings was estimated to require the construction of

44. Fruit of the Loom

45. Seagate

46. (a) and (b) Guildhall Square looking east in 1968 (left) and 1996 (right)

47. Guildhall Square looking south   *48. Guildhall Square looking north*

7,500 new dwellings. An additional 773 acres would be required for industry mostly from the area designated as an industrial land bank in the 1968 plan.

From 1981 on, the worst of the violence would subside, and through the efforts and industry of the Derry people the city would become one of the most attractive and liveable cities in Ireland. Cowan with his planning officers, Arnold Bloomfield and Jim Cavalleros, had managed to implement many of the pedestrian areas designated in the Munce Plan and set the stage for future development. This achievement was followed by the establishment of the giant shopping centre at Foyle Street after a four-day public inquiry in March 1990. It attracted the interests of large stores such as Marks & Spencer, Boots, and Dunnes, who are today the anchor stores in the £62 million development.

It was the good fortune of the city to have citizens of the fortitude and calibre of Stephen McGonagle on the Development Commission during its turbulent second period as a new town, and to have entrepreneurial public servants of the calibre of David White and his successor Joe Cowan to carry on the work. One must pay tribute to their staff and to those in the Housing Executive who carried out their tasks with determinism, even optimism, in the midst of chaos and mayhem. Had David White not pressed on with the acquisition of land and property for development during those bleak times, none of the Munce or subsequent planning proposals could have been implemented.

NOTES

1] Oliver, *Stormont Memoirs*, p. 98. Seemingly unaware of the recommendation in the plan states that: 'it became clear during the autumn of 1968…We struck upon the idea of using our new town legislation.'
2] Stephen McGonagle, conversation with the author, Derry, 1996.
3] C.E.B. Brett, *Housing A Divided Community* (Dublin, Ireland: The Institute of Public Administration, 1986), pp. 48–9.
4] Ibid., p. 35.
5] An earlier event in Dublin in 1920 involving IRA murders and later Black and Tan retaliations was also known as 'Bloody Sunday'.
6] Professor Sir Robert Matthew, Professor Thomas Wilson and Professor Jack Parkinson, *Northern Ireland Development Programme 1970–75* (Belfast, HMSO, 1970), p. 22.
7] Government of Northern Ireland, *The Re-Shaping of Local Government—Further Proposals* (Belfast, HMSO, Cmd 530, July 1969); frequently referred to as 'The Macrory Report'.

8] John Hume, *John Hume, Personal Views, Politics, Peace and Reconciliation in Ireland* (Dublin, Tower House, 1996).
9] Brett, *Housing A Divided Community*, p. 31.
10] Peter Hetherington and Robert Smithies, 'Tumbledown Derry', *Guardian,* 24 May 1974.
11] See Martin Kettle 'A tale of two cities: the people of divided Derry', *New Society* (12 July 1979), pp. 67–70.
12] Jim Foster, conversation with author, Derry, 6 August 1996.
13] Department of the Environment for Northern Ireland, *Londonderry Area Plan 1981–96 Written Statement*, November 1981.

11 Community Resolve

'Derry is a city in the hands of inspired leaders.'[1] The talent and energy of the many civic leaders of Derry is indeed incomparable and explains how this city, which has suffered so much, can reach beyond mere survival to embrace the future. Spanning just one generation John Hume, the consummate politician, and Phil Coulter, the composer and entertainer, have gained recognition far beyond their national and cultural boundaries. Their attachment to their native city is expressed by one in practical terms, while the other is inspired to express it in music. But there have been many others, perhaps not so well known, who have been instrumental in the development of their city. As A.E.J. Morris points out, 'Theoretical planning expertise is of little significance in the absence of community resolution'.[2] Eamonn Deane, James Doherty, Paddy Doherty, and John Hume are but a few of Derry's many leaders.

Although no longer as prominent an activist as he was in the fifties and sixties, James Doherty continues to serve the needs of the people of the area. He remembers his service as chairman of the Education and Library Board as one of the most rewarding and fruitful periods of his many years of public service, but what I remember most are his contributions to promoting the housing needs of Derry in the making of the Munce Plan and his consistent and unswerving belief in the benefits of planning for the future. John Hume's career and his continuing contributions to the development of the city and its population, from the sixties on, are unparalleled, and the scope of his career is different in that locally, nationally, and internationally it could be considered an example for aspiring politicians everywhere. In a recent book, he describes growing up in the Bogside and how he was drawn into the civil rights movement and a career in politics.[3] Since 1972, he expanded his work to promote industrial development and secure investment in Derry by establishing ties with politicians in Europe and the United States. Much of the progress seen in Derry today is a direct result of these contacts.

After studying at the *Institut Catholique* in Paris, John Hume returned to Derry in 1960 to take up a teaching position and founded the first credit union in Northern Ireland in the Bogside, and took the role of treasurer collecting the deposits. In conversation[4] he recalled how he had studied the growth of credit unions in the US, and how he had always been committed to the idea of self-help and the self-esteem that accompanied it. The Bogside Credit Union grew from a membership of four and assets of £7 in 1960 to today's membership of 14,000 and assets of £21 million. When only twenty-seven years old, Hume was elected president of the Credit Union League of Ireland representing all credit unions in the country, north and south. He stresses that although he played a prominent role, the founding of the Credit Union was a community effort, and he is generous in his tributes to Paddy Doherty, Michael Canavan, Father Andrew Mulvey, and others on the founding board. He also believes that the credit union, 'kept money in the community that helped in the regeneration of the community—money that would have gone elsewhere in higher interest rates. The average interest rates on loans over the thirty-seven years of operation was around 6 per cent compared to the enormous rates elsewhere during that period.'

Hume's efforts were not confined to just the credit union movement. During the early sixties, he was a leading figure in the Derry Housing Association, a community group established to address housing need, and his interests in housing and community development were accompanied by his strong belief in the wide-ranging benefits of education. In 1965, recognising that educational facilities were a major factor in attracting new industry, he organised the University for Derry Committee. His committee brought the city to a standstill for a day, when 2,000 cars were driven by city residents to Stormont to support the demand that Northern Ireland's new university be located in Derry.[5] His obvious leadership qualities, and his important and responsible role in the Civil Rights movement, led his peers to persuade him to enter politics in 1969. As a leader of the SDLP in 1971, he was largely instrumental in persuading James Callaghan, the British Prime Minister, to transfer housing powers from local authority jurisdiction to the new Housing Executive.

Before the publication of the Munce Plan, Hume had advocated the need for a second bridge, and later, as a Member of the European parliament, he was able to secure backing for the necessary funding from Europe to see the dream realised. He talks about attacking the problem of peripherality as he describes his vision of Derry's role in the European community. Unlike many politicians, he espouses not only the theory but becomes actively involved at grassroots level in making the vision happen. In addition to securing funds for the bridge, he persuaded the European Commissioner, Bruce Millen, to meet with the harbour commissioners and helped secure the funds to support the move downstream.

Jimmy Munce's recommendation for a new airport at Eglinton was also realised largely due to Hume's efforts. The new City of Derry Airport at Eglinton began operations in 1989 with 75 per cent of its approximate cost of sixteen million having been provided through the European Regional Development Fund. Not content with his success in securing funding for economic development from Europe, Hume also looked westward to the United States in his efforts to bring even more international attention to the attractiveness of his native city and its location. He sought and gained support from Richard Needham, the Northern Ireland minister, for a delegation from Derry to accompany a delegation from Galway to the first Boston Trade Fair in 1988. Mindful of Derry's historic links with Boston and together with the mayor of Boston and Derry city council, he established Derry-Boston Ventures to publicise the advantages of the Derry area for industrial location and tourism.

At the Boston Trade Fair the following year, he persuaded an American development company to become involved in the proposal for the central area development of Foyle Street. In the end they withdrew, but without this initial interest from an American investor it is doubtful whether the present 250,000 sq. ft. Foyle Shopping Centre, with its multi-level parking for 1,300 cars, and which created 1,200 service sector jobs, could have been completed by 1994. Another spin-off was the establishment of the American clothing company Fruit of the Loom and a computer company, Seagate. John Hume's face lit up with a broad grin as he

49. New City of Derry Airport

described to me how he met the head of the Seagate firm in the Duke of Edinburgh bar in Santa Clara, California. He was considering locating a factory in Europe, and Hume persuaded him to build his new factory in Derry. At the ground-breaking ceremony for the factory, the president of Seagate, recalling their chance meeting in the Duke of Edinburgh, announced to those assembled that 'the Royal family insisted on us coming here'. Seagate has been an enormous success and now employs 1,150 people. Hume sees this as a first step in fulfilling his dream of establishing a silicon valley around Derry.

Hume's vision, energy, and integrity have contributed much to the social and physical regeneration of the city, and it is difficult to imagine where Derry would be today without his efforts. He has been consistent throughout his career in extolling the virtues of a society that would respect tradition and diversity in a Northern Ireland, and eventually in a new Ireland, where Catholic, Protestant, and Dissenter could live side by side.

Paddy Doherty, though not so well known, is one of the most charismatic of the community leaders in Derry.[6] He exudes both energy and charm as he proudly describes the work of his brainchild, the Inner City Trust and the optimism in his voice cannot fail to inspire even the most disinterested listener. A clerk of works[7] by trade there is very little he doesn't know about the art and science of construction. He recalls that the apathy that prevailed in Derry before 1968, 'Was a kind of frozen violence'. At the time he was unconvinced about the effectiveness of the Munce Plan, prepared under the direction of a Unionist dominated Steering Committee. His major concern was in working with others to try and attract new industries to the city. He was also involved with John Hume in the Credit Union, 'a most potent force for change in Derry. It gave people a sense of pride in their own achievements.' When the Development Commission was formed he immediately saw an opportunity to put his professional skills to bear on the housing crisis. Although he was offered a high-level position it was not confirmed by Stormont (allegedly for political reasons) and in the end he accepted a job supervising a major construction project in the West Indies. He returned to Derry in 1972 after the events of Bloody Sunday to find the Bogside in a state of siege under the banner of 'Free Derry', with residents surrounded by the British army and police.

While pondering the future—he thought of establishing a building business with his sons, one of whom was a quantity surveyor[8] and another an accountant—he met Professor Ivor Browne of University College Dublin at a meeting of the Ballyfermont Community Association, which was concerned with establishing community organisations, dealing with results of conflict and involving people in decision making. When he told Professor Browne that he was a builder, Browne said, 'Then build people. Anyone can build buildings!' Inspired by this encounter Paddy began to think of ways to help the Bogside community. He had already been involved in trying to restrain the youth of the area from involvement in the escalating violence often forced upon the community by the actions of the security forces and the Provisional IRA. These young people were, as Browne had explained to him, 'the children of war and of violence'.

As he contemplated ways of channelling the energies of young people in a positive direction, he knew that he could teach them how to build. It was then that he hit upon the idea of renovating buildings damaged in the confrontations between Bogsiders and the security forces. With the help of Michael McCafferty and Charlie Hegarty, another local architect, he began to make plans for restoring some of the damaged historic buildings. In an interview published in the journal *Perspective,* he recalls, 'The city was in such a state the heart had been taken out of it by

50. Museum and Craft Village

51. Craft Village dancers

the bombing campaign and people had fled from it. Our aim was to reinstate the inner city—in so doing we could carry out the dual purpose of giving people jobs and bringing back the city to what it was.'[9] Paddy and Hegarty set out to restore a living city and not create a museum. The O'Doherty Fort Museum, opened by the President of Ireland, Mary Robinson, was built on waste ground within the city walls, close to Magazine Gate on the ancient site of the fifteenth-century castle of the O'Dochartaighs. Integral with the Fort Tower and Museum is the Craft Village. Pedestrian areas in Guildhall Square and Waterloo Place completed by the Department of Environment's environmental programme as proposed in the Munce Plan allow citizens and tourists easy access to the village and other commercial uses within the walls.

Through the efforts of the Inner City Trust, formerly unemployed people became skilled in restoration techniques including the installation of stained glass. In training young people for this work, Paddy Doherty wanted them to understand the nature of both responsibility and authority. Time was taken off from construction work for educational discussions and computer training. Most of what has been achieved in the restoration and adaptive reuse of city centre buildings is a result of Doherty's entrepreneurial skills. As each building was successfully restored, he would mortgage it to provide funding for more buildings. While securing charitable donations from many sources he also took advantage of government training grants available from both Westminster and the European Union. He keeps in touch with Glenn Barr a Protestant activist from the Waterside, who is also attempting to keep young people out of trouble through training programmes. Although rightly proud of his building achievements in the historic centre, Paddy's focus remains on building people and working for peace between the two communities with their different cultures. His efforts over almost two decades have contributed much to peace in the city and have greatly increased its attractiveness as a tourist centre.

In a city where so many have committed their talents to building the Derry of the future it is perhaps invidious to single out individuals for mention. But the Catholic population, suppressed for so many years, even centuries, seems to have spawned the most active and far-sighted civic leaders. As one of those who try to reach outside the narrow confines of religious divisions and take a synoptic view of Derry's place in the global village, Eamonn Deane's contributions must also be acknowledged.

Deane is director of the Holywell Trust, an organisation committed to breaking down the animosity between the Catholic and Protestant communities that has been exacerbated by a quarter century of violence. Although acknowledging the importance of the improved appearance of the city and its economic progress over the past decade, Deane poses the Platonic question, 'What constitutes the *just* city?'[10] He also ponders what an ecological city would look like. Involved in community work for over twenty years, he realises that his vision of the future has to be worked for step by step: 'All of us together can build a new Derry resulting from a celebration of the human spirit, a vision not confined to that of the politician, the fixer, or even the architect.'[11] His energies are directed toward working for the establishment of a pluralistic society freed from its historic prejudices. He edits a lively monthly magazine entitled, *Fingerpost*, which encourages contributions from the Derry community and elsewhere. Deane's membership in innovative social organisations is reflected in the magazine's many interesting articles dealing with diverse cultural and societal issues. Referring to the city's divisions, often exploited by extreme Protestant organisations and the Provisional IRA, he says, 'Awful though it seems at times there is a reason for being here in the constructive and creative sense—even the joyous sense. True it is a small place full of extended families and lack of anonymity, but beyond that there is a great sense of liberation.'

Deane agrees with Vaclav Havel when he says, 'We must live in truth'. He continues, 'One has to accept that the worst kind of conservatism and reactionary forces exist in both communities. Socially the hierarchical conservative aspects of society are difficult to cast off.' He admits to being influenced by American philosopher John Rawls' *Theory of Justice* and the writings of Murray Bookchin, the ecologist. Together with a group of other leaders, he arranged an international conference in Derry in 1992 entitled *Beyond Hate: Living with our Deepest Differences*, the proceedings of which were published.[12]

Dr Carol Rittner of the Elie Wiesel Foundation for Humanity in New York came to Derry at the invitation of Deane and the others in 1990 to organise the conference. This landmark event in the history of Derry was held in the Guildhall and was attended by participants from twenty-five countries from four continents.

Among the many well-known participants were Mary Robinson, the president of Ireland, and the four Beirut hostages, Terry Anderson, Lawrence Jenco, Brian Keenan, and Terry Waite, and messages were received from former President Jimmy Carter, Nelson Mandela and Archbishop Desmond Tutu. The conference visitors saw a Derry largely recovered from the physical scars of its recent violent past and now regarded as one of the most architecturally and historically interesting cities in the UK and Ireland. The major task confronting its citizens and the citizens of Northern Ireland then and now was to heal the scars resulting from years of ethnic conflict. The Inner City Trust, the Holywell Trust, the North-West Centre for Learning and Development, and the Healthy Cities Movement are all organisations concerned with healing divisions in the community. Typical of the work they engage in is the promotion of the city as an international meeting place for people of diverse political views. The city council also held a year-long celebration called IMPACT (International Meeting Place for Alternative Cultural Traditions).

The people of Derry are proud of today's city and its historic past, but it is not a pride born of parochialism. They have shown their desire to reach out to other parts of the world to share their gift and their hope, and their links with the United States and particularly Boston have been revived. Today Derry is a place with a sense of purpose and a belief in her future place in Ireland and the world. Eamonn Deane sums up the situation well when he writes, 'To those who view "Londonderry" as a microcosm of Northern Ireland, there is a sense that the present troubles began in "Derry", a sense that Derry might also point the way to resolution, which was why the Centre for Creative Communications wanted to organise a conference on the theme, *Beyond Hate: Living With Our Deepest Differences*.'[13]

This is an idea that Deane shares with Hume who has articulated for many years the idea that Derry can become the paradigm for community relations in the whole of Ireland. Hume is quick to point out that the cultural and ethnic composition of Derry with its majority Catholic population approximates that of Ireland as a whole. There is less local animosity between these populations on a daily basis than exists elsewhere in the province and in particular the Belfast area where Catholics are in the minority. But Hume is also emphatic that unity cannot and should not be achieved through force or coercion: 'Nothing has changed the undeniable reality that force, from whatever quarter, can only perpetuate, not resolve, the conflict.'[14] He believes in the broader view that current Protestant intransigence (exacerbated by the violence of the Provisional IRA and the violent actions and reactions of Protestant paramilitaries) can be replaced by a gradual acceptance of the benefits that can accrue from national unity within the European Union.

NOTES
1] Alan Bradshaw, conversation with the author, Derry, 6 August 1996.
2] Morris, *History of Urban Form,* p. 224.
3] Hume, *Personal Views.*
4] Except where otherwise noted the description of John Hume's role in the regeneration of Derry is taken from a conversation between him and the author in Belfast, 11 January 1997.
5] See Bloomfield, pp. 78–9 for an account regarding the controversial issue of the decision of the Lockwood Committee to recommend the Coleraine area instead of Derry for the new university. 'Monocular vision rather than deliberate discrimination was often the problem.'
6] Except where otherwise noted, the paragraphs about Paddy Doherty's work are taken from a conversation between him and the author, Derry, 12 August 1996.
7] There is no equivalent in the US to the position of Clerk of Works, the nearest being 'construction supervisor'.
8] The equivalent of a quantity surveyor in the US would be an estimator or construction manager.
9] *Perspective: The Journal of The Royal Society of Ulster Architects:* Special Edition (September 1993): p. 47.
10] Plato, *Republic Book II*: 'I propose therefore that we inquire into the nature of justice and injustice, first as they appear in the State and secondly in the individual ...'
11] Eamon Deane, conversation with author, Derry, 6 August 1996.
12] Eamonn Deane and Carol Rittner, eds, *Beyond Hate: Living with our Differences* (Derry, YES! Publications, 1994).
13] Ibid., Preface, p. x.
14] Hume, *Personal Views*, p. 148.

12 Retrospect and Prospect

Edmund Tinney looked out of the window of a house near St Columb's College and surveyed the acres of new housing that had engulfed the Ballyarnett/Shantallow area. He turned to his friend James Doherty. 'James,' he said, nodding towards the area, 'do you remember when they told you that it would never happen and that this was all pie in the sky?' By the mid 1970s, most housing anticipated in the Munce Plan for new greenfield sites was in various stages of completion. The Northern Ireland Housing Executive had quickly taken up the task from the Development Commission, and Derry's housing problem was already becoming a bad memory—a memory of when waiting time for a house had increased from two years in 1954 to six years in 1970.[1] Development of the Pennyburn Industrial Estate was also proceeding apace and only the central area, subjected to rioting and continuing violence, awaited the renewal process. Twenty years later the city centre had become a magnet for citizens and tourists alike. Under its new leaders Derry was taking its rightful place in Ireland and making its impression in the new Europe.

This regeneration of Derry had been the optimistic goal when, just over thirty years ago, our small enthusiastic team met for the first time to plan the Londonderry area as it was then called.

52. Ballyarnett/Shantallow showing bridge (far right)

Since religion has unfortunately for so long been a criteria in determining the actions of people in Ireland, I must place on record that, although the issue was never discussed, the majority of the team were at least nominally 'Protestants'. But even now I see no need to apologise for this contingence of social history. Had the team in any way departed from the professional and ethical standards to which we were all as individuals committed, I would have felt compelled to record it in the story of making the plan. Even in the case of the principals involved peripherally in the process, Jimmy Munce and Bob Simpson, I can attest personally to their 'hands off' attitude as far as the team was concerned when decisions had to be made that threatened the political control extremist Protestant Unionists held over the area. Once the team became aware of the gravity of the political situation, we were all the more determined to ignore political pressure from any side and frame our recommendations in an impartial and objective manner. To some people the plan might have been viewed as a naïve academic study; some of the members of the Steering Committee may have viewed it merely as an exercise in public relations while enabling them to maintain the *status quo*. Other rural district representatives on the committee may have been overwhelmed by the idea of urban sprawl and city dwellers invading their tranquil rural preserve,[2] but we were determined, from the beginning, to make a plan that could not be lightly set aside and that would accommodate the needs of the people of the area until 1981. In the Derry area, the vacuum that occurred in the period after 1968 and the troubles that followed was filled by a plan that allowed for steady progress in developing new neighbourhoods on the city's urban fringe, even while the worst of the violence was at its height. David White's perspicacity and propitious timing in assembling all the land needed for implementing the plan when everything seemed lost, has enabled development to continue. Had it not been for his efforts, development could only have proceeded piecemeal with the existing city centre abandoned in favour of centres on the urban fringe and across the river. In retrospect it was not so much a case of an enlightened population enthusiastically embracing the plan but rather that the plan was there and available when most needed.

'Subsequent plans were,' Jim Foster explained, 'children of the '68 plan.'[3] A new team of planners at the DOE, under the direction of Jim Cavalleros published preliminary proposals for the Derry Area Plan 2011.[4] Like previous plans, the policy is to encourage commercial, industrial, and residential growth while maintaining the attractiveness of the area for recreation and tourism. Had the 1968 Plan been a typical masterplan of the immediate post-war period, with every aspect clearly defined, it might well have been set aside during the traumatic events that engulfed the city during the late sixties and seventies. Its broad brush strategic nature allowed for a freedom and interpretation by others that ensured steady progress in its implementation and further development. While development of some kind was inevitable, even in the absence of a plan, it is doubtful whether much needed large-scale housing developments on the west bank would have taken place or that the existing city centre would have remained the focus for future commercial development.

How does one measure the success of the 1968 Plan and its influence on successive plans and development? In a *Guardian* article written in 1994 the author of *Tumbledown Derry*, Peter Hetherington, sees a new Derry emerging:

> You sweep towards the old walled city across the new Foyle bridge, with the gentle Donegal hills beckoning in the distance over the border three miles away. Past modern industrial and housing estates, plush executive homes and a growing university campus, you soon reach the splendid Georgian terraces of Derry running down to the river. And,

RETROSPECT AND PROSPECT

beside the construction cranes preparing a £65 million riverside redevelopment, you ask a simple question: whatever happened to the city where the Troubles began 26 years ago? … Realistically, few would dare suggest that the city where the Troubles began is back to normal. But it has begun the long slow march to recovery.[5]

While the Civil Rights movement of 1968 had its roots in housing inequities and voting rights, the troubles had never been far from the surface since the establishment of Northern Ireland. In Belfast there was an equal and perhaps greater amount of devastation at the outbreak of the troubles, but the larger, more widespread urban area of Belfast made the situation appear to be less troublesome than in Derry; moreover, relationships between Catholics and Protestants in Derry never reached the same pitch of open warfare witnessed at the boundaries of Catholic and Protestant ghettos in Belfast. Apart from the Provisional IRA bombings, not much of the violence in Derry was between communities, it was more often the result of confrontations with security forces. One of the disappointing outcomes of our 1968 Plan, and despite our hopes for the future of Derry, is that the west bank of the river has now an overwhelmingly Catholic population while Waterside on the east bank is dominated by Protestants. Underlying the whole physical strategy of our plan was the hope that by retaining and expanding the role of the existing central area, we would avoid the development of twin cities with twin centres based on ethnic choice. In the sixties most planners at least hoped, if they did not believe, that social goals could be achieved by sensitive planning of the built environment. Planners since have been aware, at least from the early seventies, that social goals can seldom be achieved by physical means. It is still the hope of many that the beauty of the river, from bridge to bridge, will become the focus of the whole city rather than the physical divide it now appears to have become.

Better housing conditions, the attraction of new industries, expansion of port facilities, a second bridge, an improved and increasingly viable commercial centre, a new regional airport, and the establishment of a branch campus are just some of the physical and economic developments that have already paid dividends in alleviating Derry's problems. While the problem of unemployment has been halved from that prevailing in the sixties, at more than 10 per cent, it is still almost twice the UK average. As Hetherington, writing in 1994, pointed out, 'almost one in four men are jobless in a city where 55 per cent of the population is under the age of 30.'[6] Although at first sight this is a depressing number, with increased educational opportunities and training programmes, it is reasonable to argue, that this burgeoning young population represents a valuable resource for any incoming industrialist and is just one of the numerous attractive assets that the area holds for industry. Certainly the size and population of the area is attractive for industrial expansion. A recent report by the Derry City Council estimated that a total of 85,000 people lived within the urban area and a total of 100,500 in the area now under Council juris-

53. Beauty of the River from bridge to bridge

54. Houses, William Street   *55. Houses, Caw, Derry*

diction.[7] Despite all the difficulties it has experienced over the last three decades, Derry has been able to retain its position as Northern Ireland's second largest city and the centre for the north-west of Ireland. Its area of influence includes large areas of Donegal, and its total catchment area population is more than 250,000.

Derry's excellent housing stock is now one of the most appealing aspects of the area. It is a far cry from the situation in the late sixties, described earlier, when there were long waiting lists for

56. Riverside housing, west bank

57. Creggan Street redevelopment

58. Clooney hostel for homeless

59. Housing, Brigade, Derry

new council housing and executive-type housing was also in short supply. The area now boasts some of the best housing in Europe situated within one of the most attractive and picturesque areas of Ireland. Adding to the efforts begun by the Londonderry Commission, the Housing Executive has added 7,000 new homes and improved 8,500 existing dwellings in the past 25 years.[8] In addition to this, public housing achievement, housing associations such as the Derry Housing Association and private developers have provided a similar number of new dwellings. While there is now an ample supply of housing, it is estimated that about 9,900 new dwellings may be required by the year 2011 to accommodate population growth.[9]

At times it seems as if the whole population is involved in promoting the area as a location for new industries. This is the kind of welcoming atmosphere that has succeeded in attracting international firms to the area. The Chamber of Commerce and Derry City Council are at the forefront in extolling the obvious assets of the area as a base for both industry and tourism. Gerry Henry is the director of City Marketing, which over the last decade has marketed the city under the theme 'Something special in the air'. Using the number of enquiries at the various tourist centres as an indicator, Henry concludes that there has been an increase in tourism from just 7 per cent in 1992, to 55 per cent in 1994, and to 75 per cent after the announcement of the current peace talks. He enthusiastically informs me that the new descriptive motto for Derry is 'A *Special* Place', and in keeping with the new drive to attract investment, the Derry Visitor and Convention Bureau has been established. This will be operated by a board, chaired by the mayor, and comprised of four city councillors and four members from the private sector. While, according to Henry, there are six similar convention bureaux in Britain and about 300 in other parts of the world, this is the only organisation of its kind in Ireland. A new building to house the bureau is planned just south of the new Council Offices overlooking the Foyle.

The Boston-Derry Venture has now been superseded by Northwest International, another board promoting the north-west including Donegal, and yet another promoter of the city is the University of Ulster. At first a bone of contention with its first campus established in the Coleraine-Portrush-Portstewart triangle, it now has a growing second campus around the former Magee University College as suggested in the 1968 Plan. Today it is involved with the City Council and Chamber of Commerce in the promotion of tourism and economic development. Active involvement by Derry groups in trade conferences such as the Pittsburgh Investment Conference organised by the White House and a conference in Miami to promote ports of call for cruise ships are just two examples of initiatives being taken to promote Derry. In the latter effort Derry co-operated with Dublin, Waterford, and Cork in promoting Ireland as a cruise line destination. This co-operation has raised the number of cruise ships visiting Ireland from an annual average of 66 to 118 in 1996. Derry hosted its first cruise ship in 1995, and four more cruise ships visited in 1996. While these short-term visitors are welcome and substantial contributors to the economy, Henry estimates 'the city with just 351 hotel rooms will need a further 1,000 rooms in the next five years to cope with current demand'.[10]

A recent City Marketing Department publication notes that since 1990 a total of around £440 million has been invested in the city's industrial infrastructure, while between 1980 and 1995, net retail space in the city more than trebled. These figures are encouraging in themselves, but without doubt the greatest symbols of Derry's bold grasp of the twenty-first century are its new bridge, harbour, industries, and airport. The new Foyle bridge provides easy access to Donegal and the west of Ireland from the new port at Lisahally. Over £22 million was spent in establishing the new port, which is now a gateway to Europe and the rest of the world for north-west Ireland. The port can handle ships of 30,000 tons, and the new facilities provide a quay almost 400 yards long with a minimum depth of over 30 feet at berth.[11] Only minutes away is the new airport at Eglinton which has won a Royal Institute of British Architects design award for its modern terminal building. The expected passenger annual throughput is around 70,000, and currently the airport provides service to thirteen destinations in Britain and the Channel Islands. Belfast Airport is just over an hour from Derry, but as the city grows, it is reasonable to expect a demand for direct flights to all parts of Europe.

The crowds of shoppers and the obvious success of the pedestrian areas, reflecting the economic achievements of the city centre, is everywhere in evidence. Unfortunately, this is not always matched by the design quality of new buildings. The new red brick multi-storey car park location overlooking the river between the Guildhall and new city council offices is a disappointingly mundane addition to the city image. The new shopping centres, Richmond and Foyle Street, are both successful in integrating the interior malls with street levels within and without the city walls. The Foyle Street centre interior mall is as attractive as the best malls in the US and UK, but despite their success functionally, the exteriors are neutral and inconspicuous at best and ersatz at worst. They do little to add to their architectural surroundings. Certainly the giant store sign proclaiming the importance of Marks & Spencer, seen from across the river, is a detriment to the historic skyline of the city, but one must remember that there is little a city can do to

RETROSPECT AND PROSPECT

60. New bridge and access to Donegal from new port at Lisahally

61. New Foyle Street shopping centre from Waterside

control the often barbarian aesthetics of developers when economic necessity prevails. Most people in Derry are grateful that these businesses decided to come here when others would not, and there can be little doubt that measured against the eighteenth- and nineteenth-century buildings of the city, any architect would find it a challenge to establish a neighbourly relationship. Ironically the recently built O'Doherty Tower Interpretive Centre, considered to be kitsch by planners because of its medieval pretensions, fits quite well into its historic surroundings. Paddy Doherty's other development in historic renovation and renewal within the walls is successful in recognising historical context. The attractive promenade offered by the city walls, and mentioned as a special feature for tourists in the Munce Plan, is somewhat diminished by barricades of various kinds established by the security forces. These provide unfortunate eyesores for all but the most ghoulish tourist. In the late seventies, Alastair Rowan, writing from the perspective of a preservationist, commented:

> Throughout the 1970s plans have been prepared and in part implemented, to modernise the city. This initiative, from a historical point of view, has not been good for Derry. In terms of urban conservation the proposals are poor, limited by a doctrinaire and unimaginative approach to the problems of old buildings, and seemingly discounting the value of the Victorian contribution to the appearance of the city. Wholesale clearances have been carried out, and the sense of place as a built environment, which has developed through the centuries has been sacrificed to two notions, both equally misconceived: of stripping the seventeenth-century walls bare to reveal their original appearance (and remove thereby all the picturesque organic city growth that had occurred around them in a century-and-a-half of life); and of ringing the central city with a belt of roadway which both cuts an alien swathe through Bishop Street Without and the hillside to the East, and—for the length of the quays—sets a barrier of a motorway between the city and the river that has always been its lifeline.[12]

Rowan does not take into account that the Victorian commercial and residential buildings fronting the walls were in an advanced state of disrepair and many on the verge of collapse. Today where the walls have been exposed and the talus landscaped, they form attractive glimpses of how the walls might have appeared when first built in the seventeenth century. Overall, this policy must be judged a success notwithstanding Rowan's comments. The Munce Landscape Report and Plan had recommended this strategy in support of the policy of the city council at the time. Unfortunately, the riverside route, which he also deprecates, although successful in diverting traffic without a destination in the city centre, departs from a basic premise in the Munce Plan. We believed that the riverside could accommodate a peripheral route for the central area and still permit pedestrian access to the river at the

62. Walls exposed and talus landscaped

RETROSPECT AND PROSPECT

same time. Indeed as discussed earlier, there had been only two possibilities to accommodate traffic, one that would have cut through the Bogside (the Lecky Road Flyover) or the quayside route. Neither of course was entirely satisfactory, but in choosing the lesser of two evils, we had demonstrated that a two-level route connected to the two-level Craigavon bridge could accommodate pedestrian access to the river. Moreover we had recommended the establishment of a maritime museum in conjunction with a riverside walk as part of the scheme.

It is unfortunate to record that the riverside route today does make pedestrian access to the river difficult, and it is made worse by large areas of parking at ground level between the road and the river. Certainly, for the tourist and motorist, it provides both a convenient and picturesque route through the city, and has not closed off the river completely from the population, one is always aware of its presence. For the next century it should be a goal of the city and its planners to devise a scheme, similar to that proposed in the Munce Plan, which accommodates vehicular

63. Presence of the river

traffic, allows for pedestrian access to the river, and utilises the riverfront with historic vessels symbolising the city's long maritime history. However expensive this may prove to be, it should be given high priority if the attractiveness of the city for tourists is to be preserved. With regard to new development in the central area, the difficulties that building within a historic context presents are regarded as opportunities by the best architects and developers. At very least, a useful start would be preserving the best of what exists and devising design guidelines for developers that ensure that appropriate building materials are selected to take account of the texture and colour of older buildings. Aspects of proportion and scale must also be considered. Competitions, both open and invited, should be used and a design review board appointed to select the best architects and developers for the city's most important buildings.

These comments like Rowan's earlier criticisms should be taken in a positive vein. After all, the detailed aspects of the physical environment are but a backdrop to the social, cultural, and economic aspects of city life. Derry today is a vibrant community in all three aspects, and the general physical ambience of the city with its spectacular location is a pleasant surprise to visitors. Once the peace process is firmly established and the withdrawal of security forces from the city is assured, the walls can be cleared of impediments and further expansion of shopping, offices, civic buildings, and hotels. Currently, there is some public discussion of building a pedestrian bridge from the central area to the Waterside. This could become part of a broader action plan for developing the riverfront. It is encouraging to see that the *Derry Area Plan 2011* includes recommendations addressing many of these issues including a strategy for riverside development.

The DOE has been very successful in preserving valuable open space and park land both within and on the fringes of the urban area. Peter Daniel's recommendations in the Munce Plan have generally been followed. Without doubt, the beauty and attractiveness of the area very much depend on the retention of this delicate synthesis of town and country. Again the plan for 2011 introduces measures to protect scenic areas along the Foyle and restrict proposals leading to urban sprawl and ribbon development. There is still plenty of land available to accommodate industrial and housing needs without detriment to the landscape. Although 70 per cent of all employment is currently in the service sector, efforts continue to attract high-calibre manufacturing industries. Overseas companies wishing to expand their operations to Europe would do well to look at the advantages offered in the Derry area.

There may still be some reticence to invest in the area because of the seemingly insurmountable difficulties surrounding the peace process, but it should be noted that throughout Northern Ireland there were fewer people murdered and injured on an annual basis, even at the height of the Troubles, than is the case in major American cities taken as a whole. While political problems persist, crime has never been a serious problem and the vast majority of people in Northern Ireland, whatever their affiliation, want peace. According to an early supporter of the Munce Plan and currently Director of the Chamber of Commerce, Frank Guckian, 'Derry is a wonderful example of how people have become confident in the future of their city and where the despair of the seventies has been replaced by hope.' During the preparation of the 1968 plan, we were constantly aware of the need for public involvement in implementing the plan. Because of the strictures imposed by the Steering Committee at the time we were unable to involve the public as directly as we would have wished in making the plan, yet the many people we did consult saw in the plan a hope that Derry would no longer be neglected in favour of the Belfast region. We had pointed out that, 'It is quite wrong to think that other people will find anything attractive in an area which is not wholly satisfactory to its own inhabitants.'[13] Given the attractiveness of the area, the people of Derry can be proud of what they have already achieved in adding to the quality of life of the area.

Today, Ronnie Spence, permanent secretary of the DOE, is emphatic about the need for widespread public participation in establishing a vision for the future of the city. A new 1996–9 Urban Regeneration policy has been initiated which acknowledges that, 'the city of Derry has the potential of becoming one of the most dynamic and successful cities in these islands'. The emphasis is on social and economic issues and a City Partnership Board involving all political parties, and the business community has been established whose remit is to go beyond land use and physical planning issues. A large number of community leaders have been sponsored by the department for training by the Seattle-based Pacific Institute run by Lou Tice, which emphasises self-help, self-esteem, and investment in excellence. Education and training, combined with community development and involvement, are being given high priority. In addition economic development at both the regional and local level is to be encouraged, and the most disadvantaged communities will be identified and given priority.

In 1967 Ian Nairn asked that London's moneybags should be opened to help her first new town. Some efforts to establish industry in the city were certainly made during the late sixties, but the Northern Ireland government's priorities had been in the east around Belfast. Amends were made in the eighties and nineties which, in combination with funding from the European Union, enabled Derry's citizens to show their spirit in accepting the challenge of building a new Derry. Derry's citizens had learned the value of planning for the future, but most of all, their leaders had taught them the value of self-help.

Despite all the positive aspects contributing to the rejuvenation of Derry in the Munce Plan, its failure to draw together the communities of the west bank and the Waterside is one that prevails. This only highlights what has been known for some time—that physical planning has its limitations no matter how flexible planners try to make it as an instrument for future development. Paradoxically the same chaos and civil disturbances that unpredictably ensured the adoption of the plan were the same set of circumstances that ensured the divide between the two communities would be perpetuated and entrenched. That the whole community recognises the seriousness of the divide and is working to repair it, is a lesson for Ireland as a whole. One important idea behind the late modern masterplan was that with public participation it could provide a vision of the future—a not too far distant utopian image of what the city might become.

Today that vision is being formulated by the City Partnership Board with its emphasis on social, economic, and cultural goals. Another physical goal is emerging and being promoted by the Third Millennium Community Footbridge Company, who hope to build a footbridge combined with a tramline and performing arts venue. An article in the *Belfast Telegraph* noted that the bridge is estimated to cost £10 million and quotes, Colm Cavanaugh, chairman of the company as stating: 'The footbridge will create a link between the two [the West Bank and the Waterside] that is currently missing, it will help unlock development in the Waterside and also help change the mindset of people.'[14] In addition to dramatic proposals to strengthen the magnetism of the centre there is also the desire to rebuild and develop new inner city housing areas. The enthusiasm for growth and for new jobs, combined with the efforts of so many to heal the wounds of the past thirty years, is a feature already touched on. Yet Derry's main attraction as a place to live, besides its people, is that wonderful sense of place to be found in both the natural and human-made landscapes. It is an asset to be protected from indiscriminate growth as well as one to be beneficially exploited. Derry could best be described as a place that is almost just right.

Throughout Northern Ireland the majority of people, Catholic and Protestant alike, hold on to their dreams of a peaceful future in better times. But Northern Ireland's political climate has changed little since the introduction of Direct Rule in 1972. Former US Senator George Mitchell, with the help of both British and Irish governments, has fought to keep the peace process alive, but there is always the danger that both the Provisional IRA and Protestant paramilitaries will continue with the diplomacy of the gun as a means of threat and persuasion. Random acts of violence, including so-called 'punishment attacks', are still taking place.

The peace process must eventually succeed. There is simply nowhere else to go. Intransigent Unionists and reckless Republicans can never wipe away the stain left on their consciences by murders and destruction brought upon the innocents of Northern Ireland, Manchester, London and elsewhere. Beginning in the late sixties, the friendly and optimistic handshakes of O'Neill and Lemass were replaced by the clenched fists of brutality. Civilisation stepped back centuries as the best of Ireland handed over their future to the worst. Among the belligerents in Northern Ireland no one is innocent. Bigotry is a two-way street. Since 1922 there have been many genuine grievances with the Protestant/Unionist state and the exclusivity of its Catholic/Gaelic neighbour to the south. Thirty years of violence from both the PIRA and Protestant paramilitaries is more than enough. Sadly, the violence has brought only pain and suffering, and has solved nothing. The kind of state envisaged by the PIRA would have little in common with the free democratic society enjoyed by its hyphenated American supporters. In our global society the goal of Nationalism itself has become a paradox. But the establishment of the rights of individuals to live peacefully in a just democratic society of their own choosing is now a stronger goal than ever.

Today no one in Northern Ireland wants the continuation of violence save the demoniac coterie of minds on both sides of the divide who prefer to live in the past. Derry's citizens live in the same beautiful city and surroundings that inspired poetry and song and ask those with courage and initiative to help them as they build the Derry of the next millennium. Under inspired leadership they show the way forward to a better future. Plans and the planners who make them will play an important role as they continue to overcome political difficulties and thirty years of civil strife, but it will be the citizens who make the city.

NOTES
1] *From Oakgrove to City—Twenty-Five Years of Housing*, A short history of the Northern Ireland Housing Executive in Londonderry 1971–96, p. 21.
2] Bloomfield, *Stormont in Crisis*, pp. 99–100. Bloomfield records O'Neill's concern over the 'Protestant oligarchy's' manipulation of the housing situation to control power. Some councillors may have been feeling pressure from Unionist followers of O'Neill to change their ways, although in the end O'Neill knew the situation was intractable.
3] Jim Foster, conversation with the author, Derry, 7 July 1996.
4] Department of the Environment, *Northern Ireland Derry Area Plan 2011* (Northern Ireland, HMSO, 11/94 C 15).
5] Peter Hetherington, 'Breaking down the barriers that spell trouble', *Guardian*, 2 Feb. 1994.
6] Ibid.
7] *The Re-making of Derry: A Strategy for Local Economic Development*, Derry City Council Area, 1995–9.

8] *From Oakgrove to City—Twenty Five Years of Housing.*
9] *Derry Area Plan 2011,* p. 21.
10] Gerry Henry, conversation with the author, Derry, 14 January 1997.
11] Londonderry Port and Harbour Commissioners, *Londonderry Port—A Landmark for Prosperity,* p. 6.
12] Alistair Rowan, *North West Ulster* (London, Penguin Books, 1979), p. 372.
13] *Londonderry Area Plan,* p. 131.
14] Maeve Quigley, 'Derry-second to none', *Belfast Telegraph,* 7 January 1997.

Appendix: Northern Ireland Regional Plans

PRELIMINARY TERMS OF REFERENCE FOR CONSULTANTS ON A FIFTEEN-YEAR PLAN FOR THE LONDONDERRY AREA

Professor Sir Robert Matthew placed Londonderry at the head of a list of key centres for industry outside of the Belfast Region. The recommendations of Professor Wilson and subsequent studies by the Ministries of Development and of Commerce suggest that by 1981 the population of the Urban area of Londonderry (60,000 in 1961) is likely to be 80,000 rising possibly to 100,000 at the end of the century.

The advent of large-scale industrial development could, however, have a considerable effect on the growth and distribution of population and plans for the area should be sufficiently flexible to meet such contingencies. The Consultant will be required to take into account Londonderry as a port, an industrial, commercial, cultural and tourist centre, and to suggest means of stimulating development for the benefit of its citizens and Northern Ireland.

The area of study is to be the County Borough and Rural District of Londonderry but the area should be looked at in its total context of adjoining areas and the Province as a whole. The work will involve examination of the existing structure, resources, population, employment, communications and services and the making of proposals for physical renewal of the area in terms of land use, transportation, environmental standards and general character. Particular attention is to be paid to the possibilities of expanding existing and creating new villages within the general area, to the promotion of local and regional recreational facilities and the conservation of agricultural land and areas of high amenity value.

The Consultants will be paid by the Ministry but will report in the first instance at agreed regular intervals to the Steering Committee composed of representatives of the County, the County Borough and the Rural District. They will also work in close consultation with the officers of these Authorities and of the Ministry of Development and of appropriate Statutory Undertakers. During the period of work the Consultants will be required to advise on important applications for Interim Development.

Plans are required to cover:
(a) the whole area to show the population distribution, communications, services, recreational proposals, etc., and broad zonings indicative of the planning policy proposed to be adopted (possibly $2\frac{1}{2}''$ scale);
(b) the Urban area to show land uses, road proposals, environmental areas, and be a key to any special proposals (possibly 12" scale); and
(c) outline proposals for central commercial or other special areas giving an indication of the architectural character desired.

It is expected there will be supplementary survey, etc., maps including, e.g., a record of buildings worthy of preservation.

The timetable from commencement of commission is as follows:-

1. Clearance of current Local Authority proposals as quickly as possible in order of urgency.
2. Interim reports on new housing sites and associated matters as soon as possible.
3. Draft Report and Plan submitted to and approved by the Steering Committee: 18 months.*

The Consultants will thereafter collaborate with the Ministry's officers and HM Stationary Office to arrange for the publication of the Report and Plans.

During the course of the study the Consultants are encouraged to stimulate public interest by press releases or conferences in agreement with the Steering Committee. The fee to be agreed should cover any specialists the Consultants may think it necessary to employ, e.g., sociologists, shopping research experts, etc. The Consultants will not, however, be expected to pay out of their fee for any material required for the study from Government Departments, e.g., O.S. maps.

February, 1966.

Note
* If possible a preliminary Draft Plan should be submitted to the Steering Committee in 12 months.

Bibliography

PRIMARY SOURCES

Books

Arthur, Paul and Keith Jeffery. *Northern Ireland since 1968*. Oxford: Basil Blackwell, 1988.
Bloomfield, Ken. *Stormont in Crisis: A Memoir*. Belfast: The Blackstaff Press, 1994.
Brett, C.E.B. *Housing a Divided Community*. Dublin: The Institute of Public Administration, 1986.
Buchanan, Colin. *Traffic in Towns*. London: Her Majesty's Stationery Office, 1963.
Camblin, Gilbert. *The Town in Ulster*. Belfast: Wm. Mullan & Son, 1951.
Churchill, Winston S. *The World Crisis: The Aftermath*. London: Thornton Butterworth, 1929.
Curl, James Stevens. *The Londonderry Plantation 1609–1914*. Chichester, Sussex: Phillimore & Co. Ltd., 1986.
Devlin, Bernadette. *The Price of My Soul*. New York: Alfred A. Knopf, 1969.
Evans, E. Estyn. *Irish Heritage: The Landscape, The People and Their Work*. Dundalk: W. Tempest Dundalgan Press, 1942.
Hume, John. *John Hume: Personal Views, Politics, Peace and Reconciliation in Northern Ireland*. Dublin: Town House, 1996.
Jacobs, Jane. *Death and Life of Great American Cities*. New York: The Modern Library, 1961.
Jeffery, Keith. 'Orange and Green.' In *The Divided Province: The Troubles in Northern Ireland, 1969–1985*. London: Orbis, 1985, 12–33.
Johnson-Marshall, Percy. *Rebuilding Cities*. Edinburgh: Edinburgh University Press, 1966.
Kostov, Spiro. *The City Assembled: The Elements of Urban Form Through History*. London: Thames and Hudson Ltd, 1992.
Lacy, Brian. *Historic Derry*. Irish Heritage Series, vol. 61. Dublin: Eason & Son Ltd, 1988.
Mitchell, Brian. *Derry: A City Invincible*. Eglinton: Grocers' Hall Press, 1994.
Morris, A. E. J. *History of Urban Form*. Harlow: Longman Scientific & Technical, 1994.
Mumford, Lewis. *The City in History*. London: Secker and Warburg, 1961.
Nairn, Ian. *Britain's Changing Towns*. London: British Broadcasting Corporation, 1967.
Newman, Oscar. *Community of Interest*. New York: Anchor Press/Doubleday, 1980.
——. *Defensible Space*. New York: Macmillan, 1972.
Oliver, John Andrew. *Working at Stormont: Memoirs*. Dublin: Institute of Public Administration, 1986.
O'Neill, Terence. *The Autobiography of Terence O'Neil*. London: Rupert Hart-Davis Ltd, 1972.
Plato. *The Republic*. Translated and edited by Francis M. Cornford. Oxford: Oxford University Press, 1941.

Reps, John W. *Town Planning In Frontier America*. Princeton: Princeton University Press, 1965.

———. *The Making of Urban America*. Princeton: Princeton University Press, 1965.

Rowan, Alistair. *North West Ulster*. London: Penguin Books, 1979.

Tyrwhitt, Jaqueline, ed. *Patrick Geddes In India*. London: Lund Humphries, 1947.

Young, Michael and Peter Wilmott. *Family and Kinship in East London*. Rev. edn Baltimore: Pelican Books, 1962.

Plans, reports and articles

Aitken, J. M. 'Regional Planning in Northern Ireland.' Report of the Town and Country Planning Summer School, Queen's University Belfast, 1967.

Black, W. and J. V. Simpson. 'Growth Centres in Ireland.' *The Irish Banking Review* September (1968): 19–29.

Department of the Environment for Northern Ireland. *Londonderry Area Plan 1981–1986: Written Statement*. Londonderry, November 1981.

———. *Derry Area Plan 2011*. C15. HMSO, November 1994.

'A Dream That Must Come True.' *The Derry Journal*, Chronicle and comment by 'Onlooker,' 12 March 1968.

'From Oakgrove to City: Twenty-five Years of Housing.' In *A Short History of the Northern Ireland Housing Executive in Londonderry 1971–1996*. NIHE Report, Belfast.

Hetherington, Peter. 'Breaking Down The Barriers That Spell Trouble.' *Guardian*, 2 Feb. 1994.

Hetherington, Peter and Robert Smithies. 'Tumbledown Derry.' *Guardian*, 24 May 1974.

James Munce Partnership. *Londonderry Area Plan*. Belfast, 1968.

'Londonderry Area Plan Review.' *Journal of the Town Planning Institute* 54 (June 1968): 295.

Kettle, Martin. 'A Tale of Two Cities: The People of Divided Derry.' *New Society*, 12 July 1979, 67–70.

Londonderry Port and Harbour Commissioners. *Londonderry Port: A Landmark for Prosperity*. Londonderry, 1993.

Matthew, Sir Robert. *Belfast Regional Survey and Plan*. Cmd. 451. Belfast: HMSO, 1963.

Matthew, Sir Robert, Thomas Wilson and Jack Parkinson. *Northern Ireland Development Programme 1970–1975*. Belfast: HMSO, 1970.

Northern Ireland Economic Council. *Londonderry as a Location for New Industry*. Belfast: HMSO, 1966.

Northern Ireland Housing Executive. *House Condition Survey 1974*. Belfast, 1974.

Northern Ireland Housing Trust. *Annual Report. 1966*. Belfast, 1974.

Perspective: The Journal of the Royal Society of Ulster Architects. Special Edition. September 1993: 47.

Planning Advisory Group. *The Future of Development Plans*. Belfast: HMSO, 1965.

'Putting New Life Into an Old City.' *Belfast Telegraph*, Derry Edition. 4 March 1968.

Quigley, Maeve. 'Derry: Second To None.' *Belfast Telegraph*, 7 January 1997.

The Re-making of Derry: A Strategy for Local Economic Development. Derry City Council Area 1995–1999. Derry, 1995.

Wilson, Thomas. *Economic Development in Northern Ireland*. Cmd 479. Belfast: HMSO, 1965.

HISTORY SOURCES

I am not a historian but included the chapter on history at the request of colleagues who felt it would be helpful to many of my US readers. In this regard I have deliberately chosen some history books that would appeal to the general reader. I have referred to these in the text and indicated them below with an asterisk. A bibliography of books on Irish history would fill many pages and the selected list that follows, like my summary chapter, is barely adequate.

Beckett, J. C. *A Short History of Ireland*. London and New York: Hutchinson University Library, 1952.
Clarke, Randall. *A Short History of Ireland*. London: University Tutorial Press Ltd, 1941.
Coogan, Tim Pat. *Eamon De Valera: The Man Who Was Ireland*. New York: HarperCollins, 1995.*
Curl, James Stevens. *The Londonderry Plantation 1609–1914*. Chichester, Sussex: Phillimore & Co. Ltd, 1986.
Foster, R. F. *Modern Ireland 1600–1972*. London: Allen Lane/Penguin Press, 1998.
———. *The Oxford Illustrated History of Ireland*. 1989. Reprint, New York: Oxford University Press, 1991.*
Kee, Robert. *Ireland: A History*. Boston: Little, Brown and Co., 1980.*
McDowell, R. B., ed. *Ireland in 1800*. In *A New History of Ireland* eds. T. W. Moody, F. X. Martin and F. J. Byrne. Oxford: Clarendon Press, 1986.
Moody, T. W., J. G. Simms and C. J. Woods, eds. *Ireland 1921–76*. Vol. 7 of *A New History of Ireland*, eds T. W. Moody, F. X. Martin and F. J. Byrne. Oxford: Clarendon Press, 1986.
Moody, T. W., F. X. Martin and F. J. Byrne, eds. *A Chronology of Irish History to 1976*. Vol. 8 of *A New History of Ireland*, eds T. W. Moody, F. X. Martin and F. J. Byrne. Oxford: Clarendon Press, 1986.
Somerset Fry, Peter Fry and Fiona Somerset Fry. *A History of Ireland*. New York: Barnes & Noble Inc. (by arrangement with Routledge), 1993.*
Vaughan, W. E., ed. *Ireland Under the Union 1801–1921*. Vol. 6 of *A New History of Ireland*, eds T. W. Moody, F. X. Martin and F. J. Byrne. Oxford: Clarendon Press, 1986.

Index

Adams, Gerry, 5–6
Airport (at Eglinton), 110
Aitken, James, 54
Americans, 1–2
Anderson, A. W., 20, 42, 87,
Antrim-Ballymena, 20
Apprentice Boys, The, 93
Armstrong, John, 56
Arthur, Paul, 95
Ashton, Gerry, 101

Bacon, Francis, 32
Belfast: compared to Derry, 30–1; dominance of, 30–1; growth centres, 59; housing, 7–8
Belfast Telegraph, The, 89
Bell, Sandy, 85
Beyond Hate: Living with our Deepest Differences (1992 conference), 113
Black Brae area, 60, 62 fig.22
"Bloody Sunday", 99
Boal, Fred, 26, 46
Bogside community, 111
Bogside Credit Union, 109
Boston Trade Fair, 110
Brackney, Patsy, 2
Bradshaw, Alan, 4, 22, 25, 49
Brett, C. E. B., 99
Brooke, Sir Basil, 9
Browne, Ivor, 111
Bryan, Gerald, 98
Buchanan, Colin, 27

Callaghan, James, 101
Camblin, Gilbert, 21
Car parks, 79
Carter, Jimmy, 113
Catholics: discrimination against, 3–4; early organisations, 9–10; and grammar schools, 3; living in ghettos, 48–9; tensions with Unionists, 63–70

Catholic Defenders, The, 9
Centre for Creative Communications, 113, 114
Churchill, Winston, 11, 13
City centre, 63, 69, 79–81, 77, 102
City walls, 36, 36 fig.6, 84 fig.34, 122 fig.22
Civil unrest, 92, 94–5, 99
Clarke, George, 21
Cochrane, Stanley, 18, 26, 47, 66–7, 72–9
Collins, Michael, 11
Congrès Internationeaux de l'Architecture Moderne (CIAM), 25
Connolly, James, 10
Coulter, Phil, 109
Covell Matthews and Partners, 45–6, 64, 73–4
Cowan, Joe, 5, 105
Craig, William, 18, 47, 49–50, 93
Craigavon, 19–20
Craigavon Bridge, 37 fig.7
Cromwell, Oliver, 3
Currie, Austin, 92

Daire Calgach, 32
Daniel, Peter: 27–8, 102; and housing plan, 45; landscape and tourism report, 77, 82–3; final plan, 85
DeValera, Eamon, 10–13
Deane, Eamonn, 113–4
Deanery, The, 36, 36 fig.6
Derry: affected by 1921 Treaty, 37; and American colonies, 34–5; British settlers of, 35; commerce, 36; compared to Belfast, 30–1; compared to Boston, 35; compared to Savannah, Georgia (U.S.), 34; during World War II, 37; early industry of, 37; eighteenth century, 35; as a fortress town, 33–5; founded 545 A.D., 32; geography of, 30–1; growth of, 38–9; hinterlands, 57 fig.17; investment in, 119–20, 124; named Londonderry, 32; and Matthew Plan, 19–20; nineteenth century, 36–

37; political divisions, 4, 19; as a port city, 35; seventeenth century, 32–5; 1689 siege, 35; as a symbol of liberation, 5; violence in, 117
Derry Area Plan 2011, 116–7, 124
Derry-Boston Ventures, 110
Derry Chronicle, The, 89
Derry Housing Association, 63–5, 119
Derry Sentinel, 102
Derry Visitor and Convention Bureau, 119
Development Commission, 20
Devlin, Bernadette, 93–4
Diamond Street, 76
Divided Province, The, 92
Doherty, James: 4, 109, 115; description of, 20; and NICRA march, 93; support of Munce team, 48–9, 63; support of the Housing Trust, 44–5
Doherty, Paddy, 5, 103, 111–2
Dower, Michael, 56

Easter Rising 1916, 10–11
Edinburgh University, 25
Elevated roads, 18
Enterprise zone legislation, 105–6
European Regional Development Fund, 190

Faulkner, Brian, 14
Ferryquay Street, 76
Fingerpost, 113
Fitzpatrick, Eamon, 25
Foster, Jim, 4–5, 15, 26, 85–7
Foyle Bridge, 10–23, 120, 121 fig.60
Foyle Shopping Centre, 110
Fruit of the Loom, 110–1

Gallagher, Rev. Eric, 3
Geddes, Patrick, 24, 42–3
Gerald Eve and Company, 26
Gerrymandering, 48, 92
Great James Street, 79
Guardian, The, 102

Harbour facilities, 100
Havel, Vaclav, 113
Hegan, Mervyn, 25
Henderson, Roy, 21, 45, 46, 67, 83
Heriot-Watt University, 26
Hetherington, Peter, 116–7

Home Rule Bill, 10
Housing developments, 72, 89, 91–2, 118 figs.54, 55, 56; 119 figs.57, 58, 59
Housing shortage, 43 fig.12, 44, 117–9,
Howard, Ebenezer, 24
Hume, John, 5–6, 63, 109–11

Industrial development, 39, 54, 59
Industry, 128
Industry for Derry Committee, 60
Inner City Trust, 103, 112,
Interim Housing Report, 45–7
Ireland: economy of, 15; emigration, 12–13, 15; history of, 7–9; political divisions, 7; during World War II, 13
Irish Free State government, 11
Irish Republic, 12,
Irish Repubican Army (IRA/PIRA), 11, 13–14, 64, 95, 126
Irish Volunteers, 10
Irish Society, 37, 87–9

Jackson, James, 21
Jacobs, Jane, 74, 91
Jeffrey, Keith, 95
Journal of the Town Planning Institute, 89

Keppie Henderson (firm), 103
Kropotkin, Peter, 24

Landscape, 77, 82–3
Landscape Report, 80 fig.33
Le Corbusier, 42.
Lecky Road flyover, 27
Londonderry Area Plan Steering Committee: and final plan, 85–8; first interview with Munce team, 18–23; and housing, 42, 45; make-up, 20; objections to housing report, 47; relations with Munce team, 49–50, 68
Londonderry Development Commission, 98–100
Lorimer, Desmond, 99
Lurgan, 19–20

MacDonagh, Thomas, 10
MacKinder, James, 21, 27, 46, 66–8, 77, 98
MacKinnon, Gordon, 28

INDEX

Macrory Report, 101
Manchester Martyrs, 15 n.6
Mandela, Nelson, 113
Methodist College Belfast (MCB), 3
Matthew, Sir Robert, 25, 29
McAfferty, Michael, 111
McAteer, Eddie, 14
McCahon, Arthur, 21
McCormick, Jackson, 27
McCrory, John, 25, 85
McDowell, R. B., 9
McFarlane, Sir Basil, 19
McGonagle, Stephen, 5, 98, 99
McKee, William, 21, 27
Megaw, T. M., 78–9
Millen, Bruce, 110
Ministry of Development, 29
Morris, A. E. J., 109
Morton, Brian, 98
Mot, Hay, and Anderson, 78–9
Mulvey, Father Anthony, 63
Mumford, Lewis, 24
Munce and Kennedy (later Munce Partnership), 17, 18
Munce, James Frederick, 17, 59–60, 81, 87, 90–1
Munce Partnership, 25, 90–1, 98–9
Munce Plan: bridge sites, 78–9; communications report, 79–82; construction of final document, 25; engineering aspects, 27; exhibition, 87; failures of, 125; geographic surveys of area, 26; housing report, 51–2; implemented, 101, 115; and industrial estates, 59–60; industrial report, 56–63, 62 fig.21; infrastructure, 26; interim report, 51–2; land use proposals, 68–72; maps of historical growth, 34 fig.5; obstacles to completion, 47–8, 66–8; and political issues, 45, 51, population projections, 29, 52–6, 55 fig.16; preservation, 27–8, 74, 76–77; surveys, 26–7; timetable for, 29; traffic engineering, 27, 77; transportation, 67–8
Munce team: approach to political issues, 51 56, 72–3; awarded project, 23; community relations, 25–6, 88–9; "crescent of development", 59, 60 fig.19; ethical standards of, 116; make-up, 22–3; philosophy of, 24–5, 27–8, 29 n.4, 72–6; relations with Derry Housing Association, 63–4; relations with Steering Committee, 49–50, 68
Murray, Mike, 22, 24–5, 85

Nairn, Ian, 125
Nationalist Party, The, 4, 12, 14
Needham, Richard, 103, 105
New Town Development Commissions, 101
New Towns Act, 87, 93, 98, 125
1963 Matthew Plan, 19
1924 Boundary Commission, 12
1921 Anglo-Irish Treaty, 11
Northern Ireland: boundaries determined by Treaty, 11–2; economy of, 13, 14; financial dependence on Britain, 12; 1973 housing stock, 44; peace initiative, 5–6; social and economic inequities, 7; and violence, 2, 126
Northern Ireland Assembly, 96, 97 n.12
Northern Ireland Civil Rights Association (NICRA), 92, 93
Northern Ireland Housing Executive, 101, 115, 119
Northern Ireland Housing Trust, 30 n.1, 44
Northern Ireland Labor Party, 4
Northwest International, 120

O'Doherty Fort Museum, 112
O'Doherty Tower Interpretive Centre, 122
Oglethorpe, James, 33
O'Neill, Terence, 9, 14, 15
Orange Order, 2–3, 9, 10, 15 n.3

Paisley, Rev. Ian, 91
Parnell, Charles Stewart, 3
Pearse, Patrick, 10
Pennyburn, 63–5
People's Democracy, 92, 93
Perspective, 111–2
Pittsburgh Investment Conference, 120
Plunkett, Joseph, 10
Population, 39, 52–4, 53 fig.15, 102–3
Portadown, 19
Potato Famine of 1845, 36
Price of My Soul, The, 93
Protestants: and architectural firms, 3–4; militant organisations, 14

Public housing, 42
Public transportation, 81

Redevelopment, 42–4
Reps, John, 33
Retail development, 120
Richmond Shopping Centre, 103, 104 figs.39, 41a
Rittner, Carol, 113
Road development, 47
Robinson, Mary, 113
Roche, Louis Adair, 27
Rowan, Alastair, 122–24
Russell, Bailie, 27
Russell, Sean, 13
Ryan, Frank, 13

Saint Columb's Cathedral, 32, 36, 36 fig.6
Saint Columb's Park, 79
Scott, Harold, 21
Seagate, 111
Shipquay Gate, 76
Simpson, Bob, 18, 45
Smyth, Jack, 27
Spence, Ronnie, 125
Steering Committee (see Londonderry Area Plan Steering Committee)
Strand Road, 76

Terrorism, 95–6
Third Millennium Community Footbridge Company, 125

Tinney, Edmund, 115
Tite, William, 67
Tourism, 77, 81 fig.34, 83, 104, 120
Tutu, Archbishop Desmond, 113
Twelfth Night of July, 2–3

Ulster Defence Association, 95
Ulster Volunteer Force (UVF), 92
Unionists: 4, 126; formed, 10; and housing districts, 92–4; political dominance of Derry, 14, 45; tensions with Catholic population, 63–70
United States, 2
University for Derry Committee, 110
University of Ulster, 120
Urban Development Grant Program, 103

Waterloo Place, 76
Waterside district, 45–7, 64, 73–4
Watson, James, 99
Westminster (direct rule), 96, 97 n.13
White, David, 5, 21, 101, 102, 103–5, 116
Whitelaw, William, 102
Willmott, Peter, 43
Wilson, Jack, 25
Wilson, Thomas, 19, 29
Wolfe, Sue, 25
World War II, 13

Yeats, W. B., 11
Young, Michael, 43